Rich
Wolf

There's No Expiration Date on Dreams

JEREMY LIN

by Rich Wolfe

Published by Lone Wolfe Press, a division of Richcraft. Distribution, marketing, publicity, interviews, and book signings handled by Wolfegang Marketing Systems, Ltd.—But Not Very.

Cartoon Credits:
> Cartoonaday.com
> Michael Ricigliano
> *The Baltimore Sun*

BookLayout: The Printed Page, Phoenix, AZ
Cover Design: Dick Fox
Cover Art: Ed Hansen
Poster Design: Dick Fox
Poster Art: Michael Ricigliano
Author's agent: T. Roy Gaul

Rich Wolfe can be reached at 602-738-5889

ISBN: 978-0-9846278-7-5

*PAGE TWO. In 1941, the news director at a small radio station in Kalamazoo, Michigan hired Harry Caray who had been employed at a station in Joliet, Illinois. The news director's name was Paul Harvey. Yes, that PAUL HARVEY! "And now, you have the rest of the story . . . .

CHAT ROOMS

PREFACE   **7**

CHAPTER ONE: THE TAIWAN SYNDROME   **11**

Yao Ming: A Towering Figure in Basketball Circles. 12
Tien-Wen Tao Wiedmann: We're Gonna Get to the Bottom
    of this Even If We Have to Go All the Way to the Top! 16
Meng Wang: Harvard: The Stanford of the East 22
Fran Blinebury: Houston Had a Problem. 28
Yang Yi: Are You Now or Have You Ever Been a Columnist? . . 34
Yu-Lung Tsai: Jeremy Lin is Just a Regular Guy Who
    Some Days Wears a Cape. 37
Rick Quan: Hello Again Everybody! 39
Benjamin Chen: Crimson and Clover Over and Over. 43

CHAPTER TWO: THE WRITE GUYS   **45**

Bob Ryan: For the Love of Ivy 46
Phil Mushnick: It Was a Ball. 53
John Horgan: Where the Past Is Present 63
Marc Spears: Hey Now, You're An All Star, Get Your Game On.
    Go Play 70
Dave D'Alessandro: The Write Stuff 77
Frank Isola: Covering Jeremy Lin Is Like Playing
    Hooky From Life. 82
Sam Hitchcock: The Boast Of The Town 88
Andrew Mooney: And When the Scalpers Get All the Way
    Back Up To "Broke", They're Gonna Throw a Party 95

CHAPTER THREE: PUT ME IN COACH   99

Mike D'Antoni: A Coach Is a Teacher...With a Death Wish. . .100

Peter Diepenbrock: Take This Job and Love It 104

Mark Grabow: Experience Is What You Get When
You Don't Get What You Want. 111

Eric Musselman: These Seven Things Are the Ten Reasons
to Love Jeremy Lin 121

Doc Scheppler: They Shoot Baskets, Don't They? 125

Phil Wagner: Jeremy Lin's Million Dollar Secret 138

In Case You're Ever on Sports Jeopardy 148

CHAPTER FOUR: CALIFORNIA HERE WE COME   149

Jim Sutter: A Play-Tonic Relationship 150

Kirk Lacob: The Son Also Rises 160

Kevin Trimble: Gym Dandy. 173

Mike McNulty: If You're Lucky Enough to Have Jeremy Lin
as Your Student, You're Lucky Enough 194

David Kiefer: All It Takes Is All You Got 200

Raymond Ridder: The Dos and Don'ts of Dealin'
with Jeremy Lin: DO! 208

CHAPTER FIVE: JEREMYPALOOZA   217

Jerry West: Zeke from Cabin Creek. 218

Bruce Tinsley: Washington: First In War,
First In Peace, Last In the National League. 220

Joellen Ferrer: Yeah, That's the Ticket 226

Stephen Chen: Sometimes God Just Hands You One. 230

Pastor John Love: Here's What Love's Got to Do With It 234

David Weaver: A Good Lawyer Knows the Law, A Great
Lawyer Knows the Judge 239

DEDICATION

To all the Jeremy Lins of the world
who never had a real shot at the brass ring

ACKNOWLEDGMENTS

Wonderful people helped make this book possible, including Jim Young in Cleveland, Ed Hansen in Chicago and Josh Rosenfeld and Mike Ashmore in New Jersey. Special thanks to Scott Campbell, Mike Tulley, Terry Lyons and Dan Schlossberg.

And a big shout out to John Sutphin, a great guy and a business whiz in the New Jersey area, as well as to Beth Ball in Maryland Heights, MO. A tip of the hat to Fran Blinebury in Houston. Not to be forgotten is my paginator, the wonderful Lisa Liddy in Phoenix, AZ, as well as Nicole Baldocchi in San Francisco.

Thanks also to Sam Hitchcock of newjerseynewsroom.com and Andrew Mooney with Boston.com.

We better remember Cartoonaday.com, Michael Ricigliano, and *The Baltimore Sun*.

How about Tucker Wolfe in Phoenix, Mary Kellenberger in Bettendorf, Iowa and John Lynch in Lake Forest, Illinois.

PREFACE

Just a few months ago, I was more likely to be struck by lightning, while honeymooning with Christie Brinkley than to be writing a book on Jeremy Lin. You would have been more likely to see a left-handed female golfer than you were to read a book on Jeremy Lin. But then, Jeremy Lin went marching into Madison Square Garden with a duffel bag full of determination, a touch of confidence and a ton of intensity. That's when Jeremy Lin hung the moon and scattered the stars over New York City and America's sports landscape.

Growing up on a farm in Iowa, I avidly read all the Horatio Alger-style of books of John R. Tunis, the Frank Merriwell collection, and Clair Bee's Chip Hilton series, all of which preached the values of hard work, perseverance, obedience and sportsmanship, where sooner or later, one way or another, some forlorn, underweight, underdog would succeed beyond his wildest dreams in the arena of life. Frank Merriwell, thy name is Jeremy Lin. Jeremy Lin is better than Frank Merriwell. He's real life...more natural than Roy Hobbs...a Rudy with talent. Lin is manna from heaven for the National Basketball Association and every other beleaguered sports league.

I only write books on people who seem admirable from a distance. The fear, once you start a project, is that the subject will turn out to be a jerk. With Lin's California background and Harvard education, it could easily follow that he could be a self absorbed, arrogant, rude, boor like many people in his business. As you will soon find out, you would want your son, your brother, your husband or your friends to possess his qualities—a joy for living, a passion for playing and the love of basketball.

Even though I can't type, have never turned on a computer, and have never used the internet, I have been very blessed to be able to do almost four dozen books using a format that is rather unique. Of these 40+ books, my favorite book was on Tom Brady, the New England Patriots quarterback...not a favorite in the New York area. There are many similarities between Jeremy Lin and Tom Brady...mainly their manners, their thoughtfulness, their kindness and their incredible work ethic.

From the age of ten, I've been a serious collector of books, mainly sports books. During that time—for the sake of argument let's call it 30 years—my favorite book style is the "eavesdropping" type where the subject talks in his own words...in his own words without the 'then he said' or 'the air is so thick you could cut it with a butter knife' waste of verbiage that makes it hard to get to the meat of the matter. Books like Lawrence Ritter's *The Glory of Their Times* or Donald Honig's *Baseball, When the Grass was Real.* Thus, I adopted that style when I started compiling the oral histories of the Vin Scullys and Bobby Knights of the world. There is a big difference in publishing a book on Bobby Knight or Vin Scully than writing one on Jeremy Lin. Those two, as well as other subjects I've done such as Mike Ditka and Harry Caray, were much older than Jeremy Lin. Thus, they had many more years to create their stories and build on the their legends. Furthermore, several of those have been known to enjoy liquid fortification against the unknown, which leads to more and wilder tales... and multiple **DIVORCES***. So, the bad news is when you have someone as straight as Jeremy Lin, who rarely drinks, who is not a skirt chaser and works so hard at his craft, there is not much time to create off-the-court stories.

* In 1949, Harry Caray's first wife Dorothy **DIVORCED** him. In 1979 Harry wrote her: "Dearest Dorothy, Enclosed is my 360th alimony check. How much longer is this _ _ _ _ going to continue?" Dorothy responded: "Dearest Harry, Til death do us part. Love, Dorothy." Harry paid monthly till he passed away in Palm Springs in 1998.

I don't even pretend to be an author. I'm just an old man who loves sports and books who struck oil with this unusual format. This book is designed solely for other Jeremy Lin fans. I really don't care what the publisher, editors or critics think but I am vitally concerned that my fellow Jeremy Lin fans have an enjoyable read and get their money's worth. Sometimes the person being interviewed will drift off the subject but if the feeling is that the reader would enjoy the digression, it stays in the book. If you have a negative feeling, don't complain to the publisher...just jot your thoughts down on the back of a $20 bill and send it directly to me. In an effort to include more material, the editor decided to merge some of the paragraphs and omit some of the commas which will allow the reader to receive an additional 20,000 words—the equivalent of 50 pages. More bang for your buck...more fodder for English teachers...fewer dead trees.

Among the biggest obstacles of putting this book together was the problem with repetition. It was a very similar problem with the Tom Brady book. Sometimes repetition is good. For instance, in a book on Mike Ditka, seven people described a Ditka catch and run in Pittsburgh—the week of JFK's assassination—as the greatest play they had ever seen. Yet only one of those stories made the book. The editor didn't understand that when the readers finished the book, few would remember the importance or singularity of that catch and run, whereas, if all seven had remained intact, everybody would realize that one play summarized Ditka's persona and his career. So too with the repetition with Jeremy Lin, except many times greater. It was overwhelming. Almost 60 pages were deleted from this book because there were constant, similar or duplicate testimonials. Even so, many remain. It is also interesting—as you will find—how some people will view the same happening in completely different terms.

Now I have a terrible confession to make. I've only been to one NBA game in the last 15 years. Before that, I had been a season ticket holder for the Phoenix Suns for eight years. Eventually, I just got disgusted with the palming of the ball, the traveling violations that were not called, the showboating, the selfishness of the players, the hanging on the rim, the chest thumping, etc. But Jeremy Lin has been a breath of fresh air and has brought me back to the NBA. Because of his background, style of play, and how he conducts his affairs, now I'm watching every New York Knick game that I can. It's been a heck of a ride with Jeremy Lin and for Jeremy Lin fans. Let's hope this fun carousel continues for a long time.

Go now.

An excerpt from the "Mallard Fillmore" syndicated comic strip series (see page 220)

Chapter One

TAIWAN SYNDROME

On the Road Again

A TOWERING FIGURE IN BASKETBALL CIRCLES

YAO MING

Yao was the first overall pick in the 2002 NBA draft by the Houston Rockets, an 8-time NBA All-Star, who retired in 2011 due to chronic foot **INJURIES** **. Yao is now attending Jiaotong University in Shanghai to study history, economics and management. He is the owner of the Shanghai Sharks of the Chinese Basketball Association.*

If he keeps playing like this, Jeremy Lin could be an All-Star, don't you think? Right now, he is handling everything—the game and the attention he is getting—perfectly.

Fans here in China are very excited about Jeremy Lin. He is news all over the place. His story is always on the cover page of the newspaper now. He is not drafted. He signs a minimum contract. In his first year he barely gets minutes to play. Then he gets a chance and in one night he owns New York town.

Since the NBA games are on in the morning because of the time difference in China, you wake up every day and you want to see what he did. What was the score? What were his points and assists? Every day the excitement grows. Where does the story go next?

Almost every good sports team at any level in America is one play away (INJURY**) from being average...Average time lost due to injury in high school football is six days...Healing time due to injury to a high school cheerleader is 29 days...Among the sixteen most popular college sports, spring football has the highest injury rate.*

I know that Jeremy was born in California and we both had very different backgrounds growing up. But I feel that we are both Chinese and I am happy that a guard like him could come out of nowhere and make this big effect on the NBA. I hope it is the next step for us.

Please, don't let anyone think that Yao has given him any secrets about how to play. First, Jeremy doesn't need my help. He is very talented himself. And I am a big man and could not teach him how to be a guard.

I know Jeremy. We have exchanged text messages, just normal stuff, not deep. I congratulated him this week. That is all.

> Since the NBA games are on in the morning because of the time difference in China, you wake up every day and you want to see what he did.

We met in the summer of 2010 when I was hosting a pair of charity all-star games in Beijing and Taipei that also included Steve Nash, Baron Davis and Brandon Jennings, among others. After the first game in Beijing, I read that the Golden State Warriors had signed Lin to a contract.

I had heard of him before. I knew he went to Harvard, a very good school, but not one of the strong basketball teams. I also knew that his family came from Taipei, so I thought it would be great if he could come and help us with the game there. I knew there would be great interest from all of his friends and fans there. There were only three days between games. But I contacted his agent and Jeremy was willing to come right away to join us in Taipei for the game. He made a quick decision to help.

When he played I was impressed. I liked his game. We exchanged contact information and stayed in touch, but not constantly. That's the time I was concentrating on my last rehab for the NBA. He was not my main topic of conversation. And like I said, I don't want anyone to think I was giving him tips about how to play. He is different than me. I am from Shanghai. He is from California.

I am a center and he is a guard. That is the biggest difference between us, especially for all of the basketball fans here in China. Lin is different than most of the Asian players who have been in the NBA. I am 7-6 and Wang Zhizhi was a 7-footer and Yi Jianlian is a 7-footer and Mengke Bateer was 6-11. It has been a steady line of big men of going from China to the America.

> Lin is 6-3, more like a normal-sized person, and I believe that is what makes him even more popular in China. He is the size that the average person can relate to.

Lin is 6-3, more like a normal-sized person, and I believe that is what makes him even more popular in China. He is the size that the average person can relate to. They like watching him play against many taller, bigger players and succeed. That is why Chinese fans always liked Kobe more than Shaq and why they liked guys like Steve Francis and Allen Iverson.

I will tell you, I believe there are young guards in my country that have the raw athletic talent to match Lin. They are quick. They can drive. They can shoot. They can pass. But they are undeveloped. And you must remember that is not just a physical game. It is mental. Jeremy is smart. You can see the way he plays. He has high basketball IQ, but he also has more. He has an IQ about how to get along with people. He communicates.

A player like Jeremy has to reach out and connect and I think we can see he has done that. Look at his teammates. I believe Steve Novak likes him. I believe Jared Jeffries likes him. And Landry Fields and all of the rest. He seems to be natural at making friendships and getting the team to play with him.

Many great players, LeBron (James), Hakeem (Olajuwon), (Michael) **JORDAN*** for that kind of player, the game is not hard for them, everybody and everything on the team is going to them. And they dominate with their body.

What I see from Jeremy and what I hear in his interviews is he appreciates everything. He pursues his dream. His attitude is so peaceful, but there is strength to him. It is not a violent strength like fire or something aggressive. It is like the ocean, very peaceful, very quiet when you look at it. But you can never underestimate the power that is in there.

> He pursues his dream. His attitude is so peaceful, but there is strength to him.

My life is away from basketball as a player, but I don't think the game will ever go away from me. I can be a fan. I can watch Jeremy Lin now and be happy for him.

*Michael **JORDAN** was given his first set of golf clubs by fellow University of North Carolina classmate Davis Love, Davis Love, Davis Love.... In 1994, the Chicago White Sox recalled Michael Jordan from Double-A Birmingham to play against the Chicago Cubs in the Mayor's Trophy Game at Wrigley Field. Jordan singled and doubled against the Cubs.

WE'RE GONNA GET TO THE BOTTOM OF THIS EVEN IF WE HAVE TO GO ALL THE WAY TO THE TOP!

TIEN-WEN TAO WIEDMANN

Dr. Tien-Wen Tao Wiedmann, a former professor at Stanford University School of Medicine, worked in medical research and education in the U.S. for over 45 years. Dr. Wiedmann, who was born in Shanghai, China, and graduated from Harvard Medical School, has a keen interest in educational, cultural and athletic affairs. She is the chair of the organizing committee of Stanford's Chinese Faculty and Family Club, and she is an academic advisor for Stanford's men's and women's squash teams. Dr. Wiedmann, who was also schooled in Hong Kong and Taiwan, finds the Jeremy Lin phenomenon intriguing on many levels. She believes Lin's Harvard education plays a critical role in how Chinese-Americans view his rapid rise.

The Jeremy Lin phenomenon is really making people think. A lot of people are pondering what makes it so special. Two days ago, we had a gathering of law school students at Stanford and the discussion was, 'What is this Linsanity phenomenon? Is it culture? It it race? Is it media?' People are curious. 'What is it? Why do we have this phenomenon?' It's not like Jeremy Lin is the best basketball player ever, right? To me, it's a combination of everything. The Lin situation is a novelty as far as I'm concerned. He breaks the mold of how people think about stereotypes.

Everybody I know feels it's a great thing that Jeremy Lin succeeds not only in basketball but also in education. That breaks the mold because people don't usually think about someone being very good in sports and having a good education at the same time. That Lin went to Harvard is a pretty big factor. Harvard has a magic name with the Chinese because it's your oldest university here.

Most people are pretty proud of Jeremy Lin. Everyone wants to claim him—Taiwan wants to claim him, China wants to claim him and the U.S. wants to claim him. That's normal. When there's something big, everyone wants to connect to that person. I still think a lot of these things are generated by the media. If the media weren't interested, we would not have any of that stuff. Media people picked up on it and maybe some business people picked up on it, so that opens up a lot of opportunities. Media people are interested in people who are different, special. Because Jeremy Lin succeeded, everyone wants to have a piece of him. That's how the world is.

But that still doesn't explain why the Lin phenomenon is such a hot thing. As Chinese, we say if someone can succeed in both sports and education, that's a great thing. It breaks the mold for what people always think about Asian-Americans. Many people associate Asian-Americans with always being in technical professions—they're good in math and areas like that. From that standpoint, I don't think the Lin situation is any different than the mayors of San Francisco and Oakland being Asian-American. If you really think about it, there are not that many mayors who are Asian-American just because politics are not what Asians go into. It's a lot more difficult. Technology is a lot easier. That's why in the old days, it was much easier for Asian-Americans to have a great career by going into technology. But now they're spreading out a little bit more. Looking at the Jeremy Lin phenomenon, basketball is a sport that's dominated mostly by African-Americans. But now for Asians brought up in this country, there's a new perception—you can make it in a sport that's dominated by somebody else. This is probably another factor in why Linsanity has caught everyone's attention.

A lot of Asian-American kids in the Bay Area play sports. It's one way of getting into good schools. But it's their education that's at the center. They want to get into good schools through sports. But as far as many of them wanting to play professional sports, that's not the desire of most families. The kids will play sports, but that's just one of the things they'll do. They'll also play music. Those are both ways of rounding out an education and getting into good schools in this country. In China and Taiwan, it's very different because you have kids that would go into professional sports. That's their only goal—to go into professional sports. But I think for a lot of Asian-American families in the U.S., the goal is still to get a good education. A lot of people are impressed that Jeremy Lin went to Harvard. He went to Harvard and he graduated. I'm not sure what kind of student he was, but it doesn't really matter. Among the Chinese-American families I know, education is always, always No. 1. Playing sports, being an entertainer or being a celebrity, those are kind of looked down upon in Chinese communities. If your kid wants to be a rock star, he's almost looked down upon. So in a way, that's one of the reasons why there aren't that many Chinese-American professionals in fields like entertainment and sports.

We've talked about the Jeremy Lin phenomenon in the Chinese faculty club we have at Stanford. Everybody here feels it's great. But if he were just a basketball player, let's say, and he didn't have a decent education, people may not have thought of him as highly as they do. But since he got a great education and also plays professional sports, they can accept his sports success as a real

> Without the education, he's just one of the basketball players—and there's nothing special about that.

success because he did not fail in the education part. That's the general feeling here. Without the education, he's just one of the basketball players—and there's nothing special about that. People would just say, 'Here's an Asian-American who made it into the professional sports ranks.' But because he got a good education, people have a lot more respect for him than if he hadn't had it. Of course, that view is a little slanted and prejudiced in a way. I don't know what the Chinese community overall thinks, but that's the perspective of the educated Chinese. We think he can almost be forgiven to play professional sports because he did have a good education—so that part is accomplished. Then he becomes a very positive role model, in a way, for young people. But without that education, I don't think a lot of Chinese families, especially educated ones, might get all that excited. Education is a very, very major piece. No matter what our kids end up doing, they should all have a good education in this country. That's what this country can offer—education and opportunities. But I don't know if the American society views his education as a big plus.

If you look at it from another viewpoint, Jeremy Lin is an underdog because he's the minority in the professional basketball world. He has to prove himself just like all minorities in the U.S. Like any minorities, you have to be that much better than the rest in order to be recognized. A lot of the Chinese immigrants are professionals—they're educated—so that's why this whole attitude still perpetuates. In order to succeed in society or even just as a person, you have to have a good education, as good an education as you can get. That's a little bit overdone among the Chinese, I think. They feel that you have to go to specific schools to get a good education. Having taught in universities all my life here, I don't think that's the case. You can go to a lot of different schools and still be very successful. You don't have to go to the top few schools. It's what you make of it, what you make of the opportunities.

But among the Chinese-Americans, it's very important to go to these so-called prestigious schools.

The uniqueness of Jeremy Lin's combination has to be a huge factor in why we have this phenomenon. He's the first Asian-American to make it in the pro basketball world—so that's something new, just like when anybody breaks a barrier. But if you talk about China or Taiwan, they themselves have produced a lot of top athletes. Yao Ming surely makes many more millions than Jeremy Lin does, but he's directly from China. He's big in China. But Yao Ming is their own product because he was brought up in China. Look at the Olympics and how many good athletes there are from China. That's not a phenomenon. But the fact actually is Jeremy Lin was not born there. He was born here. So he's really American. That makes it different—that we would embrace an Asian-American athlete.

> ...the fact actually is Jeremy Lin was not born there. He was born here. So he's really American. That makes it different...

Michael Chang, the tennis star, is an earlier example of that. But basketball is much bigger in this country—it's an American game. Tennis is a much smaller sport, but Michael Chang was also embraced by everything Chinese. He was born here but of Taiwanese parents, just like Jeremy. His early tennis career was actually supported by people in Taiwan before he had endorsements. It's very expensive to have coaches. Chang was very big in China, even though he had nothing to do with China per se. But he actually traveled to Asia and China quite a lot, and he was big then. Whatever it is, if anybody can find a connection with you...that's human nature. If you have something in common, if you speak the language, that's good enough. You don't have to be brought up there. But because of the media, it's a lot bigger now than Michael Chang was. Basketball is big everywhere. China is already immunized with the Yao Ming phenomenon, so it's not new to them. Jeremy Lin has to thank the media for a lot of his hype. It all goes so fast. Everybody jumps on the bandwagon. The thing is, I just wonder how long it will last.

To me, the Jeremy Lin story is really positive. He ends up doing what he really loves to do, which is to play basketball. I'm sure he will have a career that he can fall back to once he finishes his basketball career. A lot of it will open doors for him, with the college degree. He can do pretty much whatever he wants to do. It's great. I don't see anything negative out of this.

JEREMY LIN EXPECTING HUGE NIKE PAYOUTS.

HARVARD: THE STANFORD OF THE EAST

MENG WANG

Wang is a journalist with Titan Sports, *Beijing, China. He has covered the Chinese Basketball Assocation and the NBA for more than a decade. Wang spent seven seasons in Houston documenting the exploits of Yao Ming. He wrote a book entitled* A Shorter Yao in My Eyes, *which was published in Mandarin.*

Before Jeremy Lin finally lost his first game as a starter for the New York Knicks the people in China were calling him Ling Shu Hao, which sounds like his Chinese name of Lin Shu Hao. Literally the translation means: Zero loss Hao.

He is a nice point guard, a qualified NBA point guard, but he is not a modern-type NBA guard. It seems that nowadays, the NBA guards are all of a kind who are quick, strong and they can attack. But Lin is not in that category. He is strong enough to take the physical contact. He is quick enough to penetrate and great asset is an ability to change speeds and change his rhythm on his dribble and his drive. His advantage is his passing ability and his vision on the court. He is kind of like Steve Nash, but he has a long way to go to reach that level of an All-Star and a two-time NBA MVP. He needs to be steady, to learn more on the court and to get more experience.

He could be a starter, but he could not get the starter position on any just any and every NBA team. He needs a certain team, certain coach, certain style of play for system to take full advantage of his individual ability and to show of what he's got. That is the situation he had with the Knicks and playing for a coach like Mike D'Antoni. D'Antoni was using an offense that wants to get up and down the court very fast, puts the ball into the point guard's hands and allows him to make the decisions on when to pass and shoot and who among his teammates to set up for a shot. He could not make all of this happen if he were to put on any other team. It was not good for him when D'Antoni resigned.

Of course, for this story to happen there had to be so many different factors at work here. And one of the most important is that the **KNICKS*** were not a normal team in a normal situation when he was put onto the court and given the job. This all came about because he was in the right place at the right time on the bench of a desperate coach. We must remember that D'Antoni wasn't saving Lin for a special time.

> People in China were calling him Ling Shu Hao, which sounds like his Chinese name of Lin Shu Hao. Literally the translation means: Zero loss Hao.

He did not think this could happen earlier or he would have made him the starting point guard much earlier. This only happened because the Knicks were playing so bad and their season was very close to going away and D'Antoni was close to even losing his job. D'Antoni was at a point where Carmelo Anthony was injured and he had absolutely nothing to lose by turning it over to Lin. I don't believe this kind of story would happened on a normal team, in a normal situation for any coach if he is not desperate, if he got other choice as a point guard who could lead the team for a win. If not for this very big factor, Lin's story just does not happen.

This kid's story did not prove other coaches are wrong or other NBA general managers and scouts are blind. It only goes to show how much of an unusual, so-called "miracle story" this really is. I have never seen anything like this before. I bet there are many old men who have watched and studied basketball

*Former **KNICK** Dick McGuire and his brother Al McGuire are the only brothers in the Basketball Hall of Fame.

for years who have never seen such a thing either. It must come from God's hand.

Lin got the chance that he needed to prove that he can play and compete in the NBA and now he has probably secured himself a job for years in the league, just with what he did in his first seven games, all wins, looking perfect and like the hero as he was undefeated and filled New York with such amazing excitement. There is no question that D'Antoni was going to stick with him as his starter and keep using him as the man to run his offense through. But an All-Star? I don't think so. Maybe the fans—especially all of them in China—will get him there with his popularity and their sheer numbers. But as a player and the things he shows on the court to get there, I don't think so. He's good. He can play. But he's not that good. Nobody can seriously compare him as a point guard with Derrick Rose or John Wall or Rajon Rondo or maybe even the rookie Kyrie Irving in the Eastern Conference. The good thing with Lin and the Knicks is the fun story that has happened already. Maybe it has saved their season. Maybe they can turn things around and try to make a bid for the playoffs. But what is most important is that the whole Jeremy Lin story made people think about the Knicks again and get interested in a positive way. Before this, the Knicks were again becoming a joke. They had got the star players Carmelo and Amar'e Stoudemire and Tyson Chandler that were supposed to make them contenders and instead they were failing. It was all going very, very bad and then this kid comes in and the the Lin miracle happened.

Of course, I never believed it could stay at such a great level and last forever. The Knicks were bound to get off the highway and go back to driving on the regular road. But it has lifted them and lifted Lin. Actually, what Lin got is way more than he dreamed, beyond the imagination of anyone. Now with Amar'e and Carmelo back into the regular lineup, Lin will just play the role he needs to play—a point guard who can dish the passes and get everyone else involved. He is not the franchise player and in truth I think in the long term that will eventually make him more comfortable and make the Knicks a better team.

Though he has done a great thing in an amazing first two weeks, he changed the culture, he showed the team, especially Carmelo, that the team could play like a team, and make the other players enjoy playing. They could feel themselves more involved in the winning or the losing. That culture change might turn Knicks a better team, a winning team.

> ...the thing we used to always say about Yao Ming came to my mind. He is a better person than a player. Lin is the same way.

When I see him, and after I got to know him a little bit, the thing we used to always say about Yao Ming came to my mind. He is a better person than a player. Lin is the same way. I think he has a great personality. I first saw him in the 2010-11 season opening game when he was with the Golden State Warriors against the Houston Rockets. He was not even on the active list for that game. I saw him working hard before the game on the court and he attracted a lot of Asian fans to the arena that night. Many of them arrived early to get a look at him and to support him and they were cheering for him. When I read his face, I saw only humbleness and appreciation. When I and a lot of members of the Asian media tried to talk with him before the game his locker was so crowded overcrowded. He kept apologizing and saying he was sorry to all of his teammates whose lockers were near him and he kept his voice low when talking to us. He was very embarrassed by all the attention that he was drawing on his team. He was obviously very uncomfortable with the fact that he was only Warrior who was getting that kind of attention before the first home game of the season. He was amazed that nobody in the media seemed to want to talk to players like David Lee or Stephen Curry, other proven NBA players. It was very awkward for him.

At that time I did not know what to expect from Lin or from his career. It was just too hard to predict. I just knew that he was eager to get a chance. I had watched a few of his games before. One of my friends from Taiwan showed me video of him before. But I must admit that I did not see any evidence of a guy who could one day average 20 points a game in the NBA and do all of these amazing things. But I know everyone who knew him was wishing him good luck because all of them believed he was a good person.

He came to China this past summer, in 2011, because he wanted to visit his mother's hometown, and also to get a feel of what basketball is like here. I know his family wanted him to get a feel of the Chinese Basketball Association, because no one knew how his career would progress in the NBA and, of course, there was the lockout at the time, too. He with the CBA team called Dong Guan New Century and played in a tournament too, almost immediately after he got off the plane from America. The first thing he asked of the team was where he could practice. He brought two NBA balls with him to play with. He was very humble, even he has NBA experience. He worked pretty well with the teammates. Back then, people including me talked with him and his family, trying to tell him that China would be a good place for him, the most logical place, because after mostly sitting on the bench at Golden State, it seemed that it might be too hard for him to secure his position in NBA. No one knew how long he could stay in the NBA at that point. That's why I tried to tell him that coming to China would be good. His goal is to try to help people as much as possible. I thought to reach that goal, he would need to have more influence and recognition. I thought if he came to play in China his ability here would be at the elite level. His image is good, because he comes from a very good school at Harvard. Parents would want to kids to learn from him, but both he and his parents said his dream is there in the U.S, in the NBA. He wanted to try more.

His story causes many arguments right now in China. Some argue and ask why do so many in the media talk about this American? Many others agree his story is good inspiration no matter Chinese or American. If you like this story, if you feel touched, that is good enough I know, the game against Lakers and the video has been viewed more than 10 million times. On sina.com he is the hottest topic. Many magazines use him in the front pages. He was on the **FRONT PAGE*** of our newspaper for four consecutive issues in the week of Linsanity and in one of them we used nine pages to cover his story.

I don't think he could compare to Yao since they come from different background. Yao is from the Chinese system. They both had different obstacles and both were hard.

He won›t change anything about the Chinese system of developing the players for the national team or for guard play in China. His story is so unique. Also because he was born and educated and trained in the U.S., that won't change anything here. The system in China is political among the teams and the government and nothing is going to change to make it easier for players to exit China and learn to play against better competition around the world.

I don't think we should expect too much. Jeremy Lin is not going to change basketball in China or change the New York Knicks into champions. What he changed is his own life. It is a wonderful story and one that we can all enjoy.

---

*In 2009 Tiger Woods was mentioned on the **COVER** of the *New York Post* 20 consecutive days. The previous record was 19 days for the 9/11 disaster in 2001.

HOUSTON HAD A PROBLEM

FRAN BLINEBURY

A Philadelphia native, who attended La Salle University and was weaned on Big 5 college doubleheaders at the legendary Palestra. Blinebury was marveling at **WILT CHAMBERLAIN**** and trying to shoot jumpers like Hal Greer from the time he could reach the basket. He has covered the NBA since 1977, starting as a beat writer with the Julius Erving-Doug Collins-Darryl Dawkins Sixers, moved to Houston in 1982 to cover the Rockets from Moses Malone to Hakeem Olajuwon to Yao Ming. Blinebury has traveled to six continents (they don't have an outdoor hoop yet in Antarctica) in search of basketball games and players and stories.*

Quite simply, Jeremy Lin is the fundamental reason that most of us watch and love sports: We never know what is going to happen. Here's a modern, 21st-century world that is scouted and analyzed to death by everyone from fans to coaches to general managers to mathematicians and nobody saw this coming. Nobody. You have to love this, if only for the dropped jaws, shaking heads and looks of amazement on the faces of the experts who are supposed to know it all. I love the fact that Daryl Morey, the Houston Rockets general manager and one of the ultimate stat geeks, went on Twitter and essentially said: "We blew it." The Rockets had Lin on their training camp roster and cut him two days before Christmas to make room for the signing of free agent center Samuel

---

* In his autobiography, **WILT** claimed to have been "with" 20,000 women. Most men have not peed that many times.

Dalembert. Of course, the Rockets try to comfort themselves by saying there was simply no room on their team for Lin, because they already Kyle Lowry and Goran Dragic at point guard. They both had guaranteed contracts. In their defense, Lowry has had an almost All-Star worthy season and Dragic has played quite well. But you're trying to tell me that you wouldn't have wanted "Linsanity" in your arena and in your locker room and making your city the buzz-word and the talk of the basketball and non-basketball world?

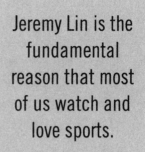

Jeremy Lin is the fundamental reason that most of us watch and love sports.

Lin is one of those once-in-a-generation stories that we'll be talking about years from now like Mark "The Bird" Fidrych of the Detroit Tigers in the 1970s or Roy Hobbs, the fictional character from literature and the movies. Lin is like that thunderbolt and summer storm that arrives all of a sudden and refreshes the air and cleans things out. LeBron, Wade, Bosh, the Heatles? Kobe, Blake Griffin, the Lakers vs. the Clippers? Forget all of them. Night after night for a week or two weeks or two months or however long it lasts, all we want to know is whether the Knicks play tonight and what could Lin possibly do next.

In the space of two weeks he goes from being a 23-year-old who probably has to show his driver's license ID to get through the employees entrance at Madison Square Garden to the guy they're talking about on Letterman and Leno and even with the women of *The View*. His name pops up in the White House briefing room. For crying out loud, **PRESIDENT*** Barack Obama is giving him a shout out.

*In 2008 Tyler Hansbrough played basketball with Barack Obama. Later, after Obama became **PRESIDENT**, Hansbrough was asked if he would treat Obama differently next time. Hansbrough, a standout at the University of North Carolina and recently with the Indiana Pacers said, "Yeah, I'll pass him the ball more."

This has gone way beyond basketball and sports to becoming one of those underdog stories that resonates across borders and across oceans and in seemingly every culture on the planet. Lin has got to feel like one moment he was standing inside a black-and-white house in Kansas and then a giant twister came along to lift him up and drop him down somewhere over the rainbow.

As big as the story has become in the U.S., it might be even bigger in China. Because even though Lin is an American, born in Los Angeles and raised in Palo Alto, and his family is of Taiwanese descent, the citizens and the fans of mainland China regard him as one of their own. Lin comes along at the perfect time in year after China's most famous basketball playing son, Yao Ming, retired from the NBA due to chronic foot injuries.

For nine seasons since he was the No. 1 **DRAFT PICK*** by the Houston Rockets in 2002, Yao was the headline phenom star in China. Almost a decade before "Linsanity" there was "Yao-mania." When Yao was drafted by the Rockets, the world's most populous nation developed an insatiable appetite for the NBA. Basketball had long been a quite popular sport in China, but Yao's entrance as the No. 1 pick in the best basketball league on the planet sent the interest clear through the roof. From his rookie season, when he was still very tentative and unsure, the Chinese fans flooded in the All-Star voting via the Internet and made Yao an All-Star starter. He was the starting center for the Western Conference eight times in his nine season (one year he was sideline entirely with a broken foot), regularly beating out Shaquille O'Neal and every other familiar American name.

It is that fan interest from China that makes me predict that Lin will be a starter for the 2013 NBA All-Star Game to be

*The last few picks in the first round of the NBA **DRAFT** today would be fourth round picks in the 1960s.

played in Houston. Actually, I believe if "Linsanity" had struck three weeks earlier when the voting was still open, he'd have been starting for the East this season in Orlando. The Chinese fans' devotion to those they consider their countrymen—all political debates about Taiwan and China aside—is unrivaled in passion and sheer numbers. He has become one of the most popular topics for millions on the Chinese equivalent of Twitter. He has become the cover boy every day in the newspapers and he is a daily feature on TV. They cannot get enough. His New York Knicks jersey bearing his name sold out immediately in Beijing and Shanghai. That Chinese market alone will be a financial windfall that changes Lin's life.

> It is that fan interest from China that makes me predict that Lin will be a starter for the 2013 NBA All-Star Game.

As a journalist I covered Yao Ming in the U.S. for his entire career and I made several trips to China with him. His level of popularity in his home country is astounding, almost unimaginable for Americans. He's like a cross between Kobe Bryant, Justin Bieber and **THE BEATLES*** during the British Invasion. "Sometimes I wish I could just go out and get ice cream," Yao once told me. "But I cannot walk down the street."

A promotional and marketing bonanza, that will now be Lin's future in China. Promoters want him to play exhibition games in their arenas. Fans just want to reach out and touch him. The added appeal of Lin in China is that he is a guard and stands only 6-3. The line of Asian players who preceded Lin to the NBA were 7-6 Yao, 7-foot Yi Jianlian, 7-foot Wang Zhizhi and 6-11 Mengke Bateer. So Lin is the first who is not a giant

---

* The **BEATLES**' last concert was at Candlestick Park in San Francisco on August 29, 1966. It lasted 33 minutes.

literally and that means the average fan and citizen can relate to him more easily. Most Asian fans in their love for basketball have always preferred smaller players over large ones. During the heyday of the L.A. Lakers NBA championship "three-peat" a decade ago, Kobe Bryant was always far more popular than Shaquille O'Neal in China and throughout Asia. The fans preferred the "small" player who had to use his wits and guile and athleticism to overcome the giants and succeed. So that's another serendipitous angle that works in Lin's favor.

All credit to Lin, a hard worker who was ready when the chance came. But this is about circumstances as much as the player. I predict a future with **DOLLAR SIGNS***. The player cut by two teams this season and unable to get off the bench for a third until recently just clinched a guaranteed contract as a restricted free agent in the summer, and not just for one season. And then there are the marketing opportunities.

> As for his future, I'm not sure I want to look past the next game. I'd rather enjoy the moment.

I see control and patience in running the pick-and-roll, which the Knicks were desperately missing. Most of all, I see an unbelievable amount of confidence from a guy who would be out of a job if Mike D'Antoni didn't give him a shot against the worst defensive team of the last 20 years (that's the Nets). I love that he has no fear of failure or fear of getting sent to the floor by opposing big men, and that his confidence doesn't lead to selfishness. Predicting his future is impossible, because there is no precedent for what he's doing. Obviously, he's going to come back to earth a bit, but I'll guess that he'll be the Knicks' starting point guard for the next few years, especially because they have little financial flexibility going forward.

*The head football coach at Army makes three times as much **MONEY** as the President of the United States.

What I'm seeing is a guy who plays the game with a joy reserved for a select few, a player who has persevered in spite of all of the superficial obstacles that would sack the average man, a player so smart and so skilled that he was able to pick up the Knicks' system in a matter of weeks and flourish as the Knicks' floor leader. I like everything about Lin. He's tough, smart, fearless (as that big shot to beat the Raptors showed) and completely comfortable in the spotlight that has engulfed him. I also like the fact that he doesn't seem to be trying to play above and beyond his capabilities. It looks completely organic, what he's done in this mercurial stretch. As for his future, I'm not sure I want to look past the next game. I'd rather enjoy the moment, the way his teammates, coaches, Knicks fans—and sports fans in general—are these days.

My first memory of Jeremy Lin is from a tryout for the Metro Mirage AAU basketball team back in fifth grade. There were a bunch of people at the tryouts. The coach, Jim Sutter, came out and said there were 11 spots on the team. I thought that was weird because there should have been 12 spots. But then Jim said that Jeremy Lin would not be trying out. Jeremy was sick, but he would be on the team. It was quickly apparent why.

When we were really young, Jeremy was good. And he was good partly because he was smart—basketball smart—but it was really because he could shoot the heck out of the ball. And that's why I think it's been strange during this whole Linsanity thing now when people say, 'We'll see if he can knock down his jumper' or 'Let's see if his shooting percentage stays up.' He could always shoot the ball extremely well. That's never been a problem.

—**ERIC FARRELL**, Millbrae, CA, Lin's teammate for six
years on the Metro Mirage Basketball Club

ARE YOU NOW OR HAVE YOU EVER BEEN A COLUMNIST?

YANG YI

Yang Yi is a journalist, columnist & editor with Titan Sport *in Beijing. Yi covered the Yao Ming years with the Shanghai Sharks in the Chinese Basketball Association and his arrival in America as the No. 1 pick in the NBA draft.*

I believe that Jeremy Lin has the speed and the explosiveness and the ability to handle the ball that will continue to keep him as a starter in the NBA for many years. What has happened with him over the first few weeks of starting for the Knicks is not luck or coincidence or just about being given an opportunity. It is clear that he has the basketball IQ that is missing in many young point guards. He can see the floor. He understands how to run an offense and he can distribute the ball to his teammates so they can score and take the most advantage of their abilities.

> I believe he has the tools to have a 10-year NBA career as a significant player.

Even though Lin is not physically stronger, you can see that he is a fierce competitor from the way he attacks the middle and finishes around the basket. He has also worked hard to improve his outside shot, which was a weakness, and now I believe he has the tools to have a 10-year NBA career as a significant player.

There is no doubt that Lin will become an All-Star, probably next season. The Chinese fans who are watching all of his games and who cannot get enough of him will do that by voting for him in large numbers online. We saw this happen with Yao Ming. Of course, Yao had more of a basketball background when he entered the NBA as the No. 1 pick. But he was still learning in the early years and was voted onto the All-Star team several times just on the strength of China.

> They saw a player with yellow skin, black hair, black eyes, a Chinese name and they thought he was Chinese.

The first time that I saw Lin play was on game videos from his university career at Harvard. At that time, I was like most other people and didn't think his future in the NBA would be very bright. I thought that he would give the NBA a try, but that his best chance for a long professional career would be in the Chinese Basketball Association. With his family ties to Asia and his skill level, I thought that he could definitely help a CBA team and have individual success for a long time.

When Chinese fans got their first real look at Lin when he began to play as a starter for the Knicks they went crazy. They saw a player with yellow skin, black hair, black eyes, a Chinese name and they thought he was Chinese. They immediately embraced him with the same kind of proud feelings they had for Yao Ming. It made many fans who had gone away from the NBA games after Yao's retirement come back to watch the NBA on TV. The numbers of the audiences for games went up big. Before Lin began to have his explosion in NY, most stories on TV and the newspapers didn't even mention his name. He was not a significant player.

When his name first burst out on the websites, the question was immediately asked about whether Lin would play for the

Chinese national team in the **OLYMPICS*** and World Championship. It was natural because of the Chinese name. But, of course, Lin was born in America. He is an American citizen. Why would he play for China? This is something that I believe Chinese fans will understand as they learn more about his story and his background. Then maybe when the fans here understand that he is not Chinese, maybe some of the heat will calm down. There is no way that the story of Jeremy Lin and what he is doing with the Knicks is even close to when Yao Ming went to the NBA. Yao is Chinese. He represents the whole country. He is also the No. 1 pick in the draft.

What Lin's success can do to give a Chinese, yellow-skinned small guy an opportunity to dream. Personally, I believe that is still only a dream that we can never really copy in China. Lin is a product of the American basketball system and American culture. That is not something that can come out of the Chinese sports and education systems, where young kids are identified when they are 12 to 13 years old and then placed in government run programs. These are choices that families have to make when kids are early in life. They have to identify the correct sport and then commit themselves to that. Much of the early process in basketball is based on height. That is why the all of the good players from China who were sent out into the world like Yao and Wang Zhizhi and Mengke Bateer were all big guys. That's what the programs were looking for— height and size. There is no program that seeks out smaller players, point guards and that is not going to change. Unfortunately, that means that there will not be a Chinese Jeremy Lin any time soon.

*Michael Jordan wore number 9 in the '84 OLYMPICS. All player numbers were between 1–10. In the NBA he wore numbers 23, 45 and 12. The latter occurred in Orlando one night after his uniform was stolen.

JEREMY LIN IS JUST A REGULAR GUY WHO SOME DAYS WEARS A CAPE

YU-LUNG TSAI

Yu-Lung (Dennis) Tsai is a reporter with the Daily Apple, *a Taiwanese newspaper. He hastily arranged a trip to New York following the breakout of Linsanity and attended all five games of the Knicks homestand just before the All-Star break.*

When the Knicks beat the Mavericks we put out a special edition, breaking news, and nearly 200,000 copies were printed and distributed. Imagine how crazy it is in Taiwan.

Originally I first covered him last season, I went to San Francisco and covered his pre-season game, training camp and his first regular-season game. This is crazier than last year in San Francisco. In the Bay Area only Asians and Asian-Americans rooted for him. In New York, everybody roots for him.

We in Taiwan love everything related to Taiwan. His parents are from Taiwan so we root for him and even though he's only been in Taiwan several times in his lifetime so far we still root for him. The past two summers he came back to Taiwan so I had time to spend with him. But in New York it's crazy so I don't have time to spend with him because we are not allowed to have an exclusive interview. No more going with him to a restaurant. We have little short chats in the hallway, things like that. He speaks good Chinese, but slowly. He speaks well.

His impact will be very heavy in the Asian community. Now we start to believe that if Jeremy Lin can do this, if we work hard like him maybe we can change the image. Before we didn't think there was any chance an Asian player could do this, never, never. Unless you were as tall as Yao Ming you had no chance to play in the NBA. Now, with Jeremy Lin, we start to believe, kids start to believe.

We noticed his first start. Then we wait, wait, wait until we saw he continued to play well before planning the trip.

HELLO AGAIN EVERYBODY!

RICK QUAN

Rick Quan is a veteran, award-winning sports reporter and a sportscaster for the San Francisco CBS affiliate for twenty years. Currently Quan produces video and is a fill-in sports anchor/reporter at **ABC-7*** *in San Francisco. Quan has won two Emmy awards, various press awards and was named the best Bay Area anchor four times by readers of the* **OAKLAND*** *Tribune and the Alameda Newspaper Group. He likes to focus on Asian athletes as he feels people tend to overlook them. These can be seen at asianamericansports.com.*

The Asian-American community is especially excited to see that an Asian-American young man has been able to break a lot of stereotypes and do so well in the NBA. For a long time Asian-American men have had negative stereotypes about them, i.e. being weak, geeky, not very athletic and lacking in masculinity. So to see a guy like Jeremy who was born here in California, nobody gave him a chance but when given the opportunity he has really proven himself. He is a starter and a

*In 2010, **ABC** celebrated the 50th anniversary of *Wide World of Sports* even though the show had not been on the air for 13 years.

*The **OAKLAND** A's colors are green and gold because their late owner, Charles O. Finley, grew up in La Porte, Indiana and loved Notre Dame... When he bought the **KANSAS CITY** A's, he changed their uniforms to the Notre Dame colors...The Green Bay Packers also adopted Notre Dame colors because Curly Lambeau played at Notre Dame.

> For a long time Asian-American men have had negative stereotypes about them, i.e. being weak, geeky, not very athletic and lacking in masculinity.

star and we are all just so proud of him. That's the basic take I have on him right now.

It is rare to have Asian athletes. There has never been an Asian-American basketball player I can think of. Some people get confused because they think of guys like Yao Ming. He was born in China. We've never had a full-blooded Chinese American. We've had some but they were mixed. We had Rex Walters who was a guard who played for both the Sixers and the Miami Heat. He is now a co-chair at the University of San Francisco, the men's basketball coach. He is Japanese and Caucasian. His mother was from Japan. He doesn't look Asian at all. If you looked at him, you'd think he was white. You'd think he was Caucasian. But he really has a strong allegiance to his Japanese side. Jeremy is the first full-blooded Chinese American to play in the NBA.

The last full-blooded Asian-American to play in the NBA was a Japanese man in 1949. His name was Wat Misaka but of course the game was totally different back then. They had very few teams and just not nearly as popular as it is today.

So that's why everyone is making such a big deal about it. For one, Jeremy is the first full-blooded Chinese American to reach that level. Two, he has a great underdog story where nobody gave him the chance. Nobody drafted him. Nobody gave him a scholarship for college. He had already been cut by two teams. And yet, he, when given the opportunity, ended up making himself stronger. Those two things have really intrigued the country.

I myself was born in Texas. I am Chinese American. When Yao Ming came, we were all very proud of Yao Ming because he is Chinese but he was not born in America so he didn't have that same connection as we do to Jeremy because he was born in America. It is just different cultural upbringings. It just has a different feel to it.

It's a much stronger tie to Jeremy.

It seems everybody is hoping that it will open doors and eyes but it's not like it will open a floodgate of Asian-American athletes in the NBA. Traditionally parents still steer their children more towards education and traditional occupation, like a doctor, engineer, and scientist. And not so much toward athletics. I don't think we will see a big wave of Jeremy Lins coming in to the NBA anytime soon.

What it does though is it opens that possibility. Hey somebody did make it, so we can't write off that possibility like we may have done in the past.

His parents are from Taiwan. There is again a huge surge of pride. Everyone wants to claim Jeremy as theirs right now. Even the mainland Chinese want to say he is part of them. Then the Americans want to claim him because he was born here. It's just a source of pride.

> When Yao Ming came, we were all very proud of Yao Ming because he is Chinese but he was not born in America so he didn't have that same connection as we do to Jeremy...

Everybody wants to grab a piece of him. Because his parents are from Taiwan, the people over there are especially excited about that.

That's just the way it is these days, when somebody achieves a certain status. Some people in the NBA said they have never seen anything like this before the way "Linsanity" has taken over the league. The way social media and the medias these days, it is like times ten the attention people get. Anybody who has a tie to Jeremy, it just goes back to pride. In Taiwan, one of their own is doing it on the big stage, so people want to talk to anybody that is related to him to get that exclusive story.

> There have been more presidents from Harvard than Harvard players in the NBA.

It is rare to have athletes come from the Ivy League. Very rare, especially Harvard. There have been more presidents from Harvard than Harvard players in the NBA. There have been maybe four that came from Harvard to the NBA. In general, there have been very few players from the Ivy League schools. The Ivy League level of competition there is okay but it's not anything like the other conferences where basketball is the strength of their programs.

I sat down for a long interview with him last summer. I asked him about some of the racial things that were said to him, like they called him "sweet and sour." They told him "the band is on the other side of campus." They made fun of his eyes. I asked him if they called him "chink." My feeling is I needed to ask him because I wanted to find out how bad it got out there on the courts. I've had that slur called against me, too, and it has hurt a lot.

It gave him a little bit of a chip on his shoulder. Like "Hey I want to prove you wrong. Perhaps you're underestimating me, kind of thing."

It gave him more fuel to prove himself.

CRIMSON AND CLOVER
OVER AND OVER

BENJAMIN CHEN

Like Jeremy Lin, Benjamin Chen is an alumnus of Palo Alto High School and Harvard University. Chen, who has lived in Asia since 2007, first learned of Lin from Palo Alto friends. Though he does not follow the NBA, Chen hears often of Lin in the media. Chen, who was born and raised in Shanghai, China, until he was 12, is the CEO of a web 3.0 Internet startup funded by venture capitalists. He lives in Hong Kong and travels to Shanghai monthly for work.

I had heard of Jeremy Lin from former Palo Alto High School classmates as they often connect me with Lin because of our shared Paly and Harvard roots. But living in Hong Kong, I don't follow the NBA nor do I watch Lin. It's not surprising to see Harvard alumni excelling in many areas, from finance to literature to sports. But it's rare to see a Harvard basketball player to make it into the NBA. Even then, I haven't had any discussion with my Harvard alumni friends as we are all in our mid thirties and busy with the various commitments in our life.

People in Shanghai are proud to see a Chinese American excelling in an area which is not heavy with Asian recruits (other than Wang Zhizhi and Yao Ming). Many like to view it with a different lens. I've heard stories about Lin being underutilized because of his ethnicity, but I don't know if that's true. News about Lin is often played on Chinese CCTV news, but mostly within the sports section. Chinese people follow the NBA, but do not care about the NFL, NHL or MLB. Lin is highly recognizable among those 30 and younger and in first-tier Chinese cities. It seems like people in Hong Kong are less captivated by Lin as the NBA is not big in a former British colony except for the few American expats having a beer at sport bars.

In Shanghai, Lin is seen as an American Chinese. Given that his parents are from Taiwan, the political line of Taiwanese-American or Chinese-American may prevent Chinese from wanting to know him better as a descendent of Chinese. Chinese people feel proud of Lin, and maybe intrigued. But in their eyes, Lin is a Chinese-American, and the emphasis is on American. Lin would have little understanding about China and life in China. He has recently been given the role of Volvo's spokesperson. Volvo is interesting because it's a foreign brand, but acquired by a Chinese automaker—so like Lin, it's kind of in between two worlds.

In China, I don't see a greater significance in this aside from there being a successful Chinese-American basketball player. NBA fans are proud of seeing Lin. Non NBA fans don't care. Chinese people have excelled in many things around the world, so to hear the latest fad is fun, but not significant in the longer run. China will not change its education policy or sports program to produce athletes like Lin. In an education-centric culture in which people are practical about improving life through making more money, Chinese people don't see becoming a successful basketball player as a viable (given its low probability) route to success.

Chapter Two

THE WRITE GUYS

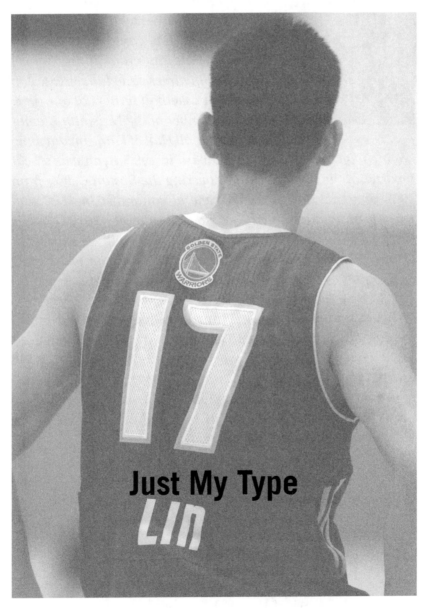

Just My Type

FOR THE LOVE OF IVY

BOB RYAN

Bob Ryan is the longtime columnist for the Boston Globe *who specializes in documenting the game of basketball both collegiate and professional. In fact, Ryan is sometimes called the greatest of the great basketball writers of our time. He is a member of the Naismith Memorial Basketball Hall of Fame media wing having won the* **CURT GOWDY*** *award in 1996. Ryan was a beat reporter of the* Boston Globe, *covering the Boston Celtics from 1969 onward. He became a general columnist in 1982 and recently announced that he would retire after the 2012 Olympic Games in London. The London* **OLYMPICS*** *will be his eighth Olympic Games and during his career he covered more than 20 NBA Finals and NCAA Tournaments.*

I can't remember the first time I saw Jeremy Lin play, but I started covering Harvard games when Frank Sullivan used to coach. He's the guy who actually recruited Jeremy. He and his staff recruited him, as we all know. So my attendance at Harvard games goes back at least 10-11 years. I got to know Frank and then they brought in Tommy Amaker, I would see Harvard at least once a year, maybe more.

***CURT GOWDY** was a young announcer for the Yankees when Vin Scully "broke in" with the Brooklyn Dodgers. Gowdy was an All-American basketball player at the University of Wyoming.

*In the first modern **OLYMPICS** in 1896 athletes could take any performance enhancing substance they desired.

I was aware that he was a different type of Ivy League player, a very athletic guard and much different than the norm.

It is so hard to translate that against the general competition at the time to where he is now. Except! Except, that he did rise to the level of the competition in the big, non-Ivy League games, as he had 30 points against UConn and 27 against Boston College and that was very impressive. While that was noteworthy, I could never have foreseen anything like what's been happening.

At the most, it was conceivable that you would bring him to camp and he could make a roster. I was really happy two years ago that his summer league play had warranted attention and he played very well against John Wall, and he had an invitation to play for Golden State.

His story is so amazing.

By comparison, the only guy I can think of that might be close in comparison was Michael Adams, and he was good enough to get selected for an All-Star game.

...the only guy I can think of that might be close in comparison was Michael Adams.

Of course, Adams attracted attention by playing in the USBL for the Newport Gulls on the same team as Manute Bol. I went to see Michael Adams in his rookie year with the Washington Bullets. I wanted to do a story that would record for posterity that Michael Adams had actually played in the NBA, never dreaming that he would have a long career, set a record for consecutive three-point shots and get in an All-Star game. I never dreamed that would happen.

Now, some have compared Lin to Tim Tebow, but it is only true in the religious aspect. Tebow is one of the great valued players in the history of his sport. If you are writing a history of college football, Tim Tebow is going to be front and center. Some have said he might've been the greatest college football player of all-time. Regardless, he was a player of extreme notoriety at a high profile sport at a high profile school. He won the **HEISMAN*** and certainly, you can always so he's 'one' of the greatest players in college football, all-time.

To set the record straight, Tebow played football at the University of Florida at a high profile school in a state where football has a high priority in the acknowledged best conference in America where if you're going to play college football, there's no place you can go to get a higher level of competition or notoriety than the Southeast Conference. Tebow did what he did at the highest level of competition in college football. He played before sell-out crowds everywhere he played for the three years he started at Florida.

Lin over the years at Harvard, at the most combined, played before crowds that Tebow saw in three or four games. That is years versus games. At the most!

Jeremy Lin was unknown to most basketball fans. Period. He was only known to Ivy League fans and real junkies and that's a fact. He played on a campus where until two years ago the program was met with massive indifference. You could walk around the Harvard campus during a game and say is there a game on? What game? We've got a basketball team? Isn't that nice?

Lin comes from so far, from a different concept and space than Tebow, that the only comparison is to religion and nothing else. Tebow's other thing is stylistic. Can he do it the way he does it?

With Lin, it wasn't some weird, new style as a number of coaches have been geared to fast break and transitional style

---

*What **HEISMAN TROPHY** winner has made the most money? The 1959 winner, Billy Cannon of LSU, was arrested for counterfeiting in the early '80s and spent almost three years in jail. Technically, he is the only Heisman Trophy winner to ever "make" money.

and doing the things he does. You look at Lin's game and it's a little bit of (Steve) Nash, a little bit of this guy and a little bit of that guy. Tebow's football style was really odd. Jeremy's style is not odd; it's just a style that not everybody wants. But Lin's made it. Two years ago, I thought, 'He has actually played in an NBA game!' In 2012? Oh brother.

The other point of comparison is the level of competition and difference between a college guard in the Ivy League and the lesser known conferences in comparison with the players in the Big East, Atlantic Coast Conference, the **BIG 10*** and so on.

Generally, the first impression or the big difference to me are the bodies. I made this distinction not long ago because I've been going to games all season long, attending every school in New England, some 21 Division I schools and I've been to all of them just this season for at least one home game.

So, I was at a game recently between Quinnipiac and St. Francis of Brooklyn. St. Francis has a half-decent team in the upper echelon of the league and it was a nice little game. Then a day later, I was sitting at midcourt, right up front and center for UConn and Marquette. First of all, the bodies, just in general, are completely different. The big guy bodies, the guard bodies, as the Marquette players looked like running backs or an NFL safety. Anyway, guards in the lower levels of NCAA basketball are not built like that. Period.

The speed and the power and the force of the game are so different. After seeing it for just five minutes and drawing it in comparison to what I had seen two nights earlier, it was like a different sport. Harvard and the Ivy League would be in the same circumstances. It is most pronounced in the big guys, naturally, but Jeremy Lin's body is adequate. You might look

*By winning percentage, Indiana ranks 13th in all-time **BIG TEN** football standings behind the University of Chicago.

at him and wouldn't say, 'he's an NBA body' but you wouldn't say you have to give him a good meal, either. He's somewhere in between.

So, count me among the many who believe the great fortune for him is that he landed with the Knicks and Mike D'Antoni. D'Antoni is the perfect coach, slash system, if you want to call it a system. It is the perfect marriage of coach, the idea of the game, and Lin's particular skills. I believe there are so many coaches in the league that never would have wanted him, that he doesn't fit with what they want to do and couldn't live with the turnovers. But, they will cut his turnovers down, of course.

Plus, he's handling the ball so much and doing the things he's trying to do with the ball, the literal high-wire act of being a point guard with Mike D'Antoni. Mike D'Antoni doesn't want nine or ten turnovers, but he can live with four or five.

Lin has the right attitude and work ethic.

When he was assigned to the NBA D-League, he went with the right attitude and he wanted to prove something. Not 'PROOOOVE" something but to go and play basketball and learn the way they want you to play at the higher level, and not going down to the D-League to play with a chip on your shoulder because the team doesn't understand you or whatever. There is no way Jeremy Lin would approach his basketball career in that way. It's just a product of who he is.

Lin went to the D-League and he was able to progress and you have to look at that over two years. Now, he's playing the best basketball of his life and he's been preparing for it in some way. That's what it tells me and that's what he's told me. We should all take note.

Some 12 years ago, I did a story with Dennis Johnson when DJ was coaching in the CBA at LaCrosse, Wisconsin. I went to a couple of games, including a road game with them and I flew back from Ft. Wayne, hung around and talked to guys and half of them were totally delusional. We talked a lot, DJ and I talked a lot about how to change some of the attitudes and it's very difficult. Nobody will ever worry about that with Jeremy Lin.

The D-League is serving a purpose, a good purpose and for Lin it was perfect.

***

As the Lin story broke, Ryan was seeking a story angle for a column in the Boston Globe. *He decided to list the greatest players from the Ivy League and for this book project, he was asked to place Jeremy Lin somewhere amongst the Ivy League's best of all-time.*

Lin's already become the greatest Harvard player of all-time, as, I believe Wendell Gray was the last Harvard guy and he played for the Knicks in 1953 for six games. Arne Duncan never played in the NBA but he played in Australia! So, Lin is the greatest NBA player to hail from Harvard. Statistically, in a short amount of time, he blew all the other guys away.

It remains to be seen, but I think Lin would now crack the all-time 12-man team as he would kick Matt Maloney or Dave Wohl off that team as a guard. He's closing in on Armand Hill of **PRINCETON*** who would be the third guard of my mythical team after the obvious starting guards, Geoff Petrie and Brian Taylor, both of Princeton too.

Petrie's career was short, as I believe a knee injury KO'd him. He had about six years, but he averaged 20 points a game and he had two 51-point games, both against the same team, the Rockets. He was a very good player.

America's first televised sporting event was a 1939 **PRINCETON-Columbia baseball game. The star for Columbia, Sid Luckman, is better known as one of the all-time great quarterbacks.*

If you look at the whole team, you start with Bill Bradley of Princeton and the New York Knicks as the greatest and Jim McMillian of Columbia was a starter on the 1971-72 Lakers and, as Elgin Baylor retired and Jim McMillian went into the starting lineup and that night the Lakers started their 33-game winning streak. McMillian had a brief career, as well. He played with LA and Buffalo and he played for the Knicks eventually.

Rudy LaRusso, many people don't know, LaRusso was a very good NBA player, a four-time All Star. He was on all those **LAKERS*** teams that lost to the Boston Celtics. He started on the 1962, '63 Lakers teams to '65 and was the other starting forward opposite Baylor on those teams. LaRusso was the starting captain for Dartmouth and led them to two Ivy League titles in 1958 and 1959. He was the greatest big man in Ivy League history.

Then, it kind of drops off. John Hummer had a decent career, but the center is fun, the only guy is Chris Dudley who played 16 years in the NBA, taking up space, blocking some shots and he was a very good offensive rebounder. We all know he was a horrendous free throw shooter which is what he'll be remembered for, of course. But, he played 16 years and you cannot play 16 years in any professional sport if you do not have some value.

When I looked for back-up centers for my all-Ivy team, it was only Dave Newmark who played three years and Walter Palmer of Dartmouth.

James Brown was a very good player at Harvard and has gone on to a great career in broadcasting. He was drafted by the Atlanta Hawks in the sixth round and was a solid 6-6 forward, but he never made it.

*In 2005, Will Bynum of the **LAKERS** became the youngest player in NBA history at 18 years, 6 days.

IT WAS A BALL

NEW YORK POST

PHIL MUSHNICK

Phil Mushnick is in his 40th year with the New York Post, *where he started as a copyboy in 1972. He served as the* Post's *beat writer for the New Jersey Nets before becoming the paper's sports TV-radio columnist in 1982.*

What Jeremy Lin brought to New York for about three weeks was a resurrection of the great Knicks teams from 1970 and '73. I can't imagine anybody from those teams looking at a stat sheet. They didn't care about stat sheets, they played ball.

I had no problem with how big the story became. Was it overdone? Sure, but it was overdone for all of the right reasons. It was refreshing. The guy was modest, the guy wanted to share the ball. The guy wanted to return basketball to basketball. What are you wearing sneakers for, especially in the Eastern Conference? Bill Walton was a great passer. He would grab a rebound and look to make an outlet pass. In the NBA now, you rebound and you look for the point guard to hand it to. It was refreshing. It was refreshing to see guys being paid millions and millions of dollars unable to stop a guy who was getting the minimum who was just bouncing around. Again, you had the Asian thing, and he was an American. It was great, it was neat and it should be going on now. Look at the team they were winning with. This was a "minimum" talent pool.

The last guy the Knicks had with such a work ethic was the kid who went to Golden State, David Lee. I loved that guy. People would say that you're rooting for the White Guy and I would say, "No, I'm rooting for the guy who works his butt off every game." Remember how many balls he would tip and keep alive? He was like **DAVE DEBUSSCHERE***, he was keeping the ball alive. "It doesn't have to be my rebound as long as it's our rebound." I appreciate that, that's what a team game is.

But alas and alack, I think it's gone. It sounds so cruel. It can be restored if the stars get hurt again. Not if the stars align, but if the stars collide. Didn't you enjoy watching those games? If you had known that Lin was a Black kid from **AUSTIN PEAY*** who nobody wanted, he wouldn't have been any less entertaining. Yeah, so there was a little more sizzle because he was a Chinese-American kid, or a Taiwanese-American kid. But if he was an unknown from Dartmouth, White, Black, Yellow, it made no difference. It was a gas, look at what he was doing for the team. Look at how people were running off of the ball. Nobody stood still when he was out there, everybody was looking for a pass. It was getting to the point that when he penetrated the lane and he threw those wrap-around passes, in time, the second guy would have gotten that ball. Not just the guy that got the pass underneath, because they would

---

***DAVE DEBUSSCHERE** was one of ten athletes to play both major league baseball and in the NBA. The Chicago White Sox protected DeBusschere in the mid-sixties allowing the Detroit Tigers to claim Chicago native Denny McLain. DeBusschere was also head coach of the Detroit Pistons at the age of 24.

***AUSTIN PEAY** (pronounced PEA) is a college in Tennessee near the Kentucky border. Its most famous player was James "Fly" William from the Brownsville section of Brooklyn. During a 1974 nationally televised tournament game against Kentucky, Austin Peay fans held up a huge sign that read: "The Fly is Open. Let's Go Peay!"...Williams managed 29 points per game during his two college years. Later he was shot four times and served two prison terms. He was voted the #2 New York City playground legend.

collapse eventually. The guy coming off the wing was going to get the next pass and he'd be all alone.

The whole Asian angle was fun, I didn't see anything wrong with it. It got carried away in some places, some of it got a little out of hand, some of the photos in the front of the paper, not in the back.

The Lin Era could be over before it began. The Knicks are reverting to getting the ball to the guy who makes the most money as opposed to the guy who makes the team better. It seems that the life has gone out of the team, either get the ball to Amar'e Stoudemire or get the ball to Carmelo Anthony. Let them freelance and "you guys all back off and start loitering on the outside." When the ball goes up, somebody fall back on defense and somebody go up for a rebound.

> The Knicks are reverting to getting the ball to the guy who makes the most money as opposed to the guy who makes the team better.

What could have been now seems aberrational, it could have been a continuum. One of the things I've seen over the last 20 years is that the Eastern Conference seems to play that minimalist game. It's very easy to coach, it's very simplistic. We saw it with Patrick Ewing. I was never a big Ewing fan because I never, ever felt that he made the team better. The Ewing teams were all misappropriated. Ewing would rebound, he would hand the ball to the point guard, the point guard would walk the ball up the court waiting for Ewing to get back downcourt, then they would feed it to Ewing, even if it was at the foul line, even if he was on the wing. He didn't even have time to post up, everything just slowed up. The Knicks offense was a four-man loitering crew and they always ended up getting the same, long, horrible shot with two seconds left on the shot clock that they could have had with 20 seconds left on the shot clock. It seemed like it was minimalist basketball.

No one knew what to do unless there was a timeout. The end of Knicks games went forever because no one had any concept on how to play basketball, just how to, like, you do this. You have one job to do. Wouldn't it be great if you were only allowed one time out over the last three minutes, because then the coaches would have to coach based on what will happen, not based on what is happening. You'd think that the better coached teams would have the advantage in knowing what to do, and when to do it. I would love that. The smarter teams would have the advantage. The last three minutes of the game is clipboard time. You know how many times I tell my wife, "Honey, there's only 46 seconds left," and she'd be warming up the car. Fifteen minutes later I come out, saying "Game's over." She goes, "Over? You told me there were 46 seconds left."

The silliest thing I saw throughout the whole early Lin craziness was when the Knicks destroyed the Lakers. The Lakers gifted them that game. Their strategy was to give Lin the outside shot. What they did was they allowed him a free step to the left, right and center. If you pressure a point guard who runs the offense, at the least, you make him go left or right. They gave him a full step forward so it was like they gave him a head start and, of course, he crushed them in that game. People learned from that because it hasn't happened since. But that was one of the silliest things I ever saw. The silliest thing I've ever seen is not fouling at the end of a game with a three-point lead. The second silliest is not covering the inbounds passer when there's, like, three seconds left and a guy has got to throw a length of the court pass. The third silliest thing I ever saw was giving Lin room to get started with the ball. He had three options, left, right or center, instead of just left or right.

> It's over because egos and money will predominate over sensible team play in just about any sport these days.

I think it's over. I hope not, but I think it's over. It's over because egos and money will predominate over sensible team play in just about any sport these days. I watch the Miami Heat and they have three superstars in the lineup and nobody seems to be open. The opponents have to be double-teaming someone, someone's got to be open. One of their non-stars has to be open for a layup.

In an era when it was considered bad form to gloat and swagger and pound your chest they did seem to enjoy it. You don't see teams running off the court and really happy and juiced up. I really don't care how the Knicks felt when they started winning with Jeremy Lin, I care how I felt. I enjoyed the games.

If you look back and look at New York's favorite teams from the winter sports, who remembers those Rangers who won the Stanley Cup? There were no set lines, they ended up playing Vancouver...a team of throw-ins against a Rangers team that was a bunch of throw-ins and was all broken up the next year.

But look at those two Knicks teams, which essentially stayed together for four years or five years. Look at those four Islanders teams that won four straight Cups and essentially stayed together for those four years. The thing that they had in common was their teamwork. The teamwork was so obvious and so extraordinary that we loved those teams. Those were the kind of teams that gave rise to the sense that New York is a sophisticated sports town as opposed to passing out towels to people to wave at the games. That's how we can distinguish ourselves, that we can understand that. Now they don't want us to understand that. "Hey, we're just one superstar away," how long have we heard that now? "We're just one superstar away." It turned out we weren't one superstar away, we were one free agent away. We were one unclaimed free agent away. Now, it's over. Or I think it's over.

What if Lin penetrated, threw a pass into Chandler, and when they collapsed on Chandler, Anthony comes flying in from the wing and gets a little push pass and lays in the ball? How easy would that be? But it's not going to happen. Carmelo needs to dribble a little bit, same with Stoudemire. They could play very easily off of Lin if they would be subservient to it, but there was a sense that these guys had never played that way. We played that way, we were taught to play that way. That's how we played in the rec league, one-touch passes, bounce passes, pick and rolls, get back on defense, "don't stand there and complain to the ref, get back on defense." This guy brought it back, it was like a throwback, it was nostalgic. But I think it's gone. We're not going to start the four guys that work best with Lin, we're going to start and emphasize our highest-paid players. Even if it kills us.

I was curious about this story only, and purely, as a sports fan. I have never turned on a game and said, "Oh, I'm a TV critic," or "I'm a radio critic." I always turn the games on as a sports fan. Something will hit you one way or another about the tele- cast or the broadcast and then you write about it, good, bad and in between.

But I found that Knicks games, even when the Knicks were half-decent, in the sense that they were playoff contending, before the Dolan era really set in, I found them interminably dull to watch. It was like, why are you putting sneakers on? Nobody's running. Loitering. One-on-one clear out ball. Any- one could coach that, I could coach that. All right, we have the ball. Get it to **EWING***. Get it to Carmelo. Get it to Xavier McDan- iel and then you other guys run over to the side. Bring your man with you and we'll go one-on-one. I wouldn't pay to see that. Again, I'm afraid that it's over.

Patrick **EWING was the first athlete to appear on the cover of Business Week.*

I'm afraid that they freaked this kid out and they're going to pull the plug on him. Since Anthony is back the cadence has gone. The unpredictability has gone. The defense doesn't have to worry about Lin's next pass. The same thing has happened with Stoudemire, too. The only one who has really been willing to buy into this thing among their stars is Chandler, and he has an inside game anyway. He can benefit from this. I don't think that Anthony was going to make him a better player, I think Lin would make him a better player. I don't think that Stoudemire can make Chandler a better player. You have a great finisher in Chandler and you have Carmelo Anthony hoisting them up after three dribbles. Why have Chandler? Have David Lee. It's back to dreary ball.

The one thing we weren't getting with Lin was a guy hitting a three and then making all of these gestures to himself, it was "let's get back on defense now." That seemed to catch on, everybody seemed to buy into it. Now everyone's been bought out of it. It's hard.

Mike D'Antoni never impressed me but he's never done anything to un-impress me, except for the other day when he didn't foul Paul Pierce with a three-point lead at the end of the Boston game. Maybe he's not capable of this. Who is?

I hope it doesn't end like Kevin Maas for the Yankees. He came here and hit, like, 40 home runs in two minutes and then faded away. Anything like this? There was The Bird, Mark Fidrych. Something here? Somebody who kept doing it and doing it and was totally unexpected. Maybe Mark Gastineau, but he was such a self-promoter. Gastineau played at East Central Oklahoma or someplace. Victor Cruz maybe, but he's got Eli Manning throwing him the ball, who is pretty good. Lin was the quarterback. You have to look toward a quarterback, somebody directing the play. Over many years Jean Ratelle of the Rangers was a great center like that but he played with primarily one line with Vic Hadfield and Rod Gilbert. Stevie

Cauthen? Stevie Cauthen hit New York and everybody said who the heck is Stevie Cauthen? At a time when all of these **JOCKEYS*** were Hispanic, coming from South America and Central America, here comes this little ratty kid from the South. He was great. But money took him away too.

No, there hasn't been anything like this. It was such a flare, almost like an explosion. It was like a warehouse that you thought was empty exploded, and what a show. Next year doesn't everybody want someone like Lin in their pre-season camp? Why don't you have it like a shock troop, a horrible analogy, but we'll put five guys in at once and they'll run their butts off. You want in or you want out? Do something, do something to sustain this. That's the frustrating part. I'm not a Knicks fan, I'm not an anybody fan, but I like to watch good, team sports. Those Islanders teams were fabulous. Do something to sustain this. They're just going to let it wilt, it's going to dry up and blow away. I'd really consider a system with "you five out, you five in." What do they have to lose? Unfortunately there is going to be a caste system that develops, the egos won't allow it. There's so much money involved with sneaker deals and other bull. It's a shame.

How many years did we hear that we're one superstar away? Baron Davis was supposed to be it, before that Carmelo Anthony was supposed to be it, before that Amar'e Stoudemire was supposed to be it. And we're all such fickle fans here. Now LeBron James is a piece of crap because he left the people in Cleveland. But if he had come to New York it would have been great. It's really sad because this was more than just fun, it was good for us to see a team game restored to a team game. It was good to see. You know how teams back pedal on defense?

*In what sport was Chris Evert the leading money winner in 1974? The answer: **HORSE RACING**. The owner, Carl Rosen, named his horses after tennis players. The horse named Chris Evert won $551,063 with five wins in eight starts.

When Lin was in there for those first eight or nine games you saw guys turning and running down the court to get back on defense. They couldn't back pedal, they wouldn't have gotten there fast enough. It was great.

There's something that goes on in baseball now that never went on. After you hit a home run you were never able to slap hands with the first base coach because you were long gone. You were running. Now you don't have to run hard, just run in case somebody drops the ball. They'll say, "Well, he's got a bad leg," but when the guy drops the ball he's got to slide into second base. Now he's really got a bad leg.

If you watched the Knicks in those nine or 10 games, you didn't have to be fast to succeed, all you had to do was keep moving. It's like Jimmer Fredette. He's slow, but he's got such a quick move he can get his shot because he can take that first quick step. You can beat him in a race but he kept moving, which is how he always got his shot. He'd wear you down. You're faster than he is but he's quicker than you are. Lin had everybody running. That was great. And then they'd take a time out and everybody would have their hands on their knees, breathing hard, which is great to see.

There was one story that the print media got right, "What's going to happen when the stars come back?" The suspicions were well-founded and well-placed. They were logically placed. In your heart of hearts do you think Carmelo Anthony was sitting there saying, "Gee, this is great, I can't wait to come back and be a part of this?"

Tell Carmelo to run through side to side underneath the basket because somebody would give him a pick. Look at how many open corner jumpers they had that they could have taken at any time when Lin was in there. Everybody was collapsing, then you're looking to the right and he's gone to the left. It was wonderful. What he was doing was absolutely unique. Ernie DiGregorio played like that. He wasn't allowed to play like that but he used to play like that at Providence. It doesn't fit the formula. It doesn't fit what we've been watching for almost 30 years now, 25 years anyway. 25 years of this tedium. Bounce, bounce, bounce. There's a reason that the organ is going "doonk, doonk, doonk, doonk." That's what's going on. That's the pace of the game. Tedium. It's such a great game.

> "Lin had 23 points, eight assists, but he had nine turnovers." Let him have 20 turnovers. Even if they lose by two points, at least they'll go down playing basketball.

And they go "Lin had 23 points, eight assists, but he had nine turnovers." Let him have 20 turnovers. Even if they lose by two points, at least they'll go down playing basketball. They don't want to run. They used to. A lot of it has to do with coaching, so much of it.

Jeremy Lin's emergence certainly didn't hurt when it came to solving the cable dispute. Whether there would have been a hue and cry among subscribers if the Knicks were playing 38 percent basketball and boring the heck out of everybody? It helped. It would have been resolved one way or the other but the other shoe has to drop now, there will be rate increases. Neither Time Warner or Cablevision is paying for this. We're paying for this. That was inevitable. Did it expedite matters? It had to, they both had to come off a little bit. Everybody knows by now that in a cable dispute there is no one to root for.

I hate to be so negative on this but I just don't see the magic coming back. It's all a big part of the human condition, and, to be even further trite, it's the the times that we live in. I'd love to enact "you five out, you five in." How cool would that be? You'd have Novak be your shooting guard, Lin would be the point guard. Move. Move, move, move. That would be great. Why not? What did Groucho Marx say, "Outside of improvement no one learns a thing."

WHERE THE PAST IS PRESENT

JOHN HORGAN

John Horgan is a journalist who has spent more than 50 years writing about sports in the San Francisco Bay Area. He watched Jeremy Lin excel against top-level competition as a Palo Alto High School standout, and he calls Lin one of the premier point guards to come out of the Bay Area. Horgan believes Lin's impact as an Asian-American athlete is unprecedented. Horgan, a lifelong Bay Area resident, covered the NBA for 11 seasons. He currently writes a weekly column for the San Mateo County Times *and blogs for* Horgan's County Corner. *Horgan also had an abortive one-year career as a basketball player for the University of San Francisco at a time when his build was as slight as Jeremy Lin's as a high school senior.*

I look at Jeremy Lin in the context of Bay Area point guards who made their teammates better as high school players. In other words, they weren't just a scoring machine. They weren't just a pure passer. They made their teammates better. Obviously, Jason Kidd and Gary Payton are right at the top. They were incredible in high school, college and in the pros. Just below them, you have guys like Charles Johnson, K.C. Jones, Phil Smith and Phil Chenier. And I'll tell you what— Jeremy Lin is in that conversation. All six of those guys were really good NBA players—some of them are Hall of Fame NBA players. Jeremy Lin is a notch below them.

The ironic thing about Lin is that when we saw him play at Palo Alto High School, he was very thin, he was not physically strong and he couldn't really finish, but he still made his teammates better. He was a finesse, slicing, facilitating player. He had a way of putting the ball right where the guy needs it. It's intuitive. It's a gift. It's like Steve Nash. Jason Kidd was that way in high school. He's the one that reminds me the most of Jeremy Lin at that age. But Kidd was much better, much stronger, much more physical, a much better rebounder and a much better defensive player. Jeremy Lin on defense...I don't want to be critical, but not so much. I don't want to come down on him, but it's hard for him to play defense in the NBA. He's dealing with men in the NBA—grown men.

It's difficult to compare Lin to some of his Bay Area point guard predecessors because now basketball is a whole different game than it was 25 years ago. You don't have the motion offenses where all five people are moving, screening, screening away, moving without the ball. Now you have sets—where guys set up in certain spots. The ball goes to the point guard and then he creates something off a set. Lin is part of a whole new breed of point guard—he and Jason Kidd.

Lin reminds some people a little of Steve Nash, who is a **CANADIAN**[*] and played at Santa Clara University. Even Nash as a young freshman at Santa Clara—believe it or not—was physically stronger than Jeremy Lin was as an 18- or 19-year-old freshman at Harvard. Today with the Knicks, Lin is physically a different guy. He's broader, he's stronger. Physically, he can take a shot—take a hit—and handle it. That's a big deal in the NBA and it's a big deal in Division I college, too. His body has changed a lot, and that's made a big difference.

Watching Lin play in high school, I always got the feeling that he was mentally tough. He might not have been the strongest and most physical guy on the floor, but he was mentally tough. He was a great, great passer with tremendous judgment. But I can understand why USF and Santa Clara and St. Mary's did not offer him a scholarship. They looked at him and they said, 'He's not ready for this. He's not mature. His body is not

[*] Jack Donohue, Lew Alcindor's (Kareem Abdul-Jabbar's) high school coach at Power Memorial in New York City was also coach of the **CANADIAN** Olympic basketball team.

mature.' Now looking at him, they go, 'Whoa! He's put on some muscle.'

The high school he went to, Palo Alto, is a suburban school that is largely white. They do have a basketball tradition but they are not a powerhouse. He played under Peter Diepenbrock and his assistant coach, Bob Roehl, who is a very, very knowledgeable guy. Bob Roehl helped during Palo Alto's state championship season in 2006. Those coaches knew what they had in Jeremy Lin. I was struck by how they tailored their offense and their defense to the talents that they had. They didn't try to do too much. But what they did, they did really well. Lin was the coach on the floor. He was like a third coach. You had Diepenbrock, Roehl and Lin. It was a beautiful thing. It was old-style basketball.

> Lin was the coach on the floor. He was like a third coach. You had Diepenbrock, Roehl and Lin. It was a beautiful thing. It was old-style basketball.

Basketball has really changed. It's become way more physical and way more violent in many ways. It's very tough to officiate. Lin has been able to bridge the old style of fluid movement, passing, cutting without the ball, etc. Today's game is either one-on-one or two-on-two. He's been able to bridge that. The big debate in New York now is that the Knicks have this tremendous player, Carmelo Anthony, and he's a one-on-one guy. You give him the ball, you clear the floor and he goes one-on-one. The problem is that doesn't fit the style that Jeremy Lin is really good at, which is pick-and-roll and so on. New York is in a real dilemma. There was a story in the New York Times about this recently.

Looking back at Palo Alto's postseason games when Lin was a senior, individually, Palo Alto's opponents had better players. But Jeremy Lin made Palo Alto a better team. When you combine the coaching of Diepenbrock and Roehl with Lin and his teammates, they were a much better team than the individuals at California powerhouses **MATER DEI*** and Archbishop Mitty—especially Mater Dei. Palo Alto beat Mater Dei in the Division II state final. But at the end of the year, Mater Dei was rated No. 1 in California in Division II even though they were beaten by Palo Alto. I thought that was the greatest compliment to Palo Alto ever. Even after Palo Alto beat them, nobody believed it. It was great. It was ridiculous. It was wonderful. It just confirmed the team concept at Palo Alto. A lot of people thought it was an insult to Palo Alto that they were rated No. 2 even though they beat Mater Dei. It was really the ultimate compliment. They beat them, and they're still rated behind them by the quasi-experts. It was perfect.

Lin against Mater Dei, in particular, looked like a coach on the floor—running the show, directing traffic. He was a maestro in that game. It was like he was directing an orchestra. Mater Dei was loaded with individual talent, guys getting rides to Division I. They had to react to what this guy was doing, what this guy was directing on the floor. It was like watching a composer at an opera. It was great and it was shocking. It was really amazing. I sat there and thought, 'Holy crap. This is really impressive. This is what basketball is really all about.' It's not about individual players. It's not about one guy. It's about a team. Lin made his team so much better with his passing, with his intelligence and mental toughness. He was a terrific high school player—one of the best ever from the San Francisco Peninsula.

From a cultural perspective, it was almost like Jeremy Lin was out of our realm of experience. We have a lot of Asian ballplayers

***MATER DEI** is a sports powerhouse in Southern California. The Santa Ana school boasts former football players like USC quarterback Matt Barkley and Heisman winners John Huarte and Matt Leinart. Basketball alumni include Darryl Strawberry Jr., Miles Simon, Reggie Geary, and LeRon Ellis.

in San Francisco, San Mateo and Santa Clara counties. There are a tremendous number of Asian players, and many of them are very good high school players. From the standpoint of college coaches, and that includes junior college coaches, those guys are just not on the radar screen. Jeremy Lin was something of an aberration. First of all, he was 6-foot-2 as a senior in high school and he was a point guard. That's a little bit different than what we're used to. He was much taller, with fairly long arms. He was a different type of Asian ballplayer, which I guess is a compliment to him. College coaches didn't know what to make of him. He was out of the realm of everybody's experience. We all kind of shrugged our shoulders and said, 'Wow, that's interesting. Now what do we do? What do we do with this guy?' There was no pigeon hole for him. There was no easy way to categorize him. Most scouts want to pigeonhole guys. Is he a one? Is he a two? Being an Asian guy, I think he flummoxed everybody.

Think about it—Steve Nash went to Santa Clara, and Santa Clara didn't recruit Jeremy Lin. Wow. In retrospect, of all schools, how in the heck did they miss him?

> To Asian girls and Asian boys—Jeremy Lin is a big deal. He's a celebrity. He's an instant icon for Asian teenagers—

In the Bay Area, the Jeremy Lin phenomenon is a really big deal. In Lin's senior year in college, his team, Harvard, wisely scheduled a game at Santa Clara. Getting into that game turned out to be very difficult. It was a packed house. A huge number of Asian young people came to that game, and a huge number of Asian media came to the game. I recall that Harvard won that game, but it was a huge cultural event. To Asian girls and Asian boys—Jeremy Lin is a big deal. He's a celebrity. He's an instant icon for Asian teenagers—boys and girls in San Francisco, San Mateo and Santa Clara counties. There's no doubt about it. But that's a good thing because he's a solid citizen—he's a great student and apparently a really good person, great family and all of that.

I can't recall another male Asian-American athlete in a major professional American sport being a comparable icon. This guy is a native born Asian-American basketball player who is in the NBA. Has there been anyone like him in baseball? No. **HOCKEY***? No. Football? No. Jeremy Lin is a whole different enchilada. He's it. I'm talking about in the whole darn country. He is unique. So far, so good. How long it's going to last, I don't know.

This is a rare thing. How many Asian-American professional athletes are there? Think about the NFL. Unless you're a quarterback or a wide receiver or maybe a punt return guy—most players in the NFL are really anonymous. There are a couple of Asian guys in the NFL—there was a Cal guy, Scott Fujita, who played for the **COWBOYS*** as a linebacker. But nobody knows who he is. He's not a star. He's just another guy getting his butt kicked most of the time on Sundays, if I may. In the NBA, you're out there in your underwear—you're exposed. The NBA is an international game. The NFL is not. Baseball—I can't think of any native born Asian stars, guys who've made a big splash. Hockey? No way in hockey. **SOCCER*** is just a niche sport. Jeremy Lin is it. He's the only one. I can't think of another Asian-American guy who's made a splash like this guy. And it's huge to be in New York. If he was playing in Portland or

*Since 1994 each player on the **NHL** Stanley Cup Champions can have the Cup for one summer day…the Stanley Cup holds 17 beers (12 oz.).

*When the Dallas **COWBOYS** Cheerleaders started in 1972, each earned $15 per game—the same amount they receive today.

*More U.S. kids today play **SOCCER** than any other organized sport, including youth basketball. Perhaps, the reason so many kids play soccer is so they don't have to watch it.

Minnesota, I'm not sure that this would have happened. Being in New York has been a huge, huge thing because of the media. When he was here with the Warriors, nobody cared except the Asian fans. The Asian fans came out to watch him play at Golden State. But the media coverage was not overwhelming. Of course, he was on the wrong team. He was on a team that already had two starting guards. They already had a point guard—Stephen Curry. Lin was in the wrong place. They liked him here. The fans loved him—the Asian fans just ate it up here. But unfortunately, he was in the wrong place. Winding up in New York was perfect for five or six different reasons.

I'll give you another aspect of all this that strikes me. It's been over-hyped. We've gone way over the top with this thing. Let's talk when the season is over. Let's take a look at the big picture and let's look at next year. I'll give the guy credit, though. To score 38 points against Lakers is a big deal. Anybody who can do that in the NBA is really big. I still wonder if this is all going to continue or whether we've seen the best that it's going to be. Will he wind up being a serviceable, adequate guy who may start, who may not start, who has a reasonable NBA career? The whole thing has been blown way out of proportion. And God bless him, by the way. It's great. I love it. But I do think the New York situation has blown this way, way beyond what's rational. I know I sound a little bit cynical, but I need to see more. I don't want to disrespect Lin because I really admire what he's done. What he's done is wonderful. The question is, Can it be sustained? Once an NBA team prepares for you, oh boy—things get pretty difficult. I hope he sustains it. I hope he has a fantastic career, a long career. But I just need to see more. I'm not an expert, but I've been watching the NBA for 50 years. And man, that's a tough league.

HEY NOW, YOU'RE AN ALL STAR, GET YOUR GAME ON. GO PLAY

MARC SPEARS

Marc Spears, the NBA national columnist for Yahoo Sports, *grew up in San Jose, California—not far from Palo Alto. At the 2012 NBA All-Star Weekend, one Northern Californian—Spears—was assigned to cover another Northern Californian—Lin—and had to navigate a massive media crush of 1,800 media members, including 321 who represented the international media contingent. They all wanted an exclusive interview to gain some insight into the experience from Lin's perspective. Spears shared his thoughts after the All-Star Weekend was in the record books.*

I saw Jeremy Lin in his game before the NBA All-Star Weekend, the Knicks against the Miami Heat in Miami. It was interesting. When he was with the **GOLDEN STATE WARRIORS***, nobody wanted to talk to him and then before the game against Miami in the pre-game, the public relations guy with the Knicks yells out, 'Jeremy won't be taking any questions before the game.'

I chuckled and thought that things have really changed dramatically. Shortly after that, the NBA put out a press advisory that Lin would have his own press conference on Friday of

---

*The teams with the most losses in the four major sports: The Phillies (over 10,000 losses), The **WARRIORS** (NBA), Blackhawks (NHL), and Arizona Cardinals (NFL).

the All-Star weekend, prior to the Rookie-Sophomore game which is basically unprecedented.

The kid seems like a humble kid, so I was worried for him and hoped he didn't get some kind of ego. The reality was that the Rookie team availability was so early in the morning and the interest in him being so high, it definitely behooved the NBA to have a separate deal for him right before the game where more media would be in attendance.

When I think of all the memories I will have from that All-Star weekend, I will remember a fan showing me a picture of the great Bill Russell giving some words of wisdom to Jeremy Lin. I'm sure Bill Russell doesn't stop to speak to just anybody, but he found time to talk to Jeremy Lin.

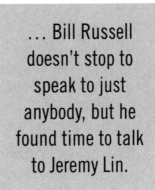

... Bill Russell doesn't stop to speak to just anybody, but he found time to talk to Jeremy Lin.

It had to be an amazing experience for Lin. He went from obscurity to the point where you had Blake Griffin, Kyrie Irving, John Wall, Ricky Rubio and a lot of great young players with great stories, including Griffin being an All-Star, but the story I wanted to write about was Jeremy Lin. Everyone wanted to talk to Lin. Outside of maybe Dwight Howard of the hometown Orlando Magic, Lin was the biggest story of the weekend. He made a game that a lot of people ignore into one of interest in the Rookie challenge.

I tell this to everyone. When I was at the *Boston Globe*, I didn't know who he was. I heard about him and I returned to the Bay Area right before Lin's senior year and I heard there was a kid from Palo Alto that was playing for Harvard. But, I didn't think much of it because I was covering the NBA and he wasn't going to be drafted very high. In fact, he wasn't drafted at all.

The thing that stood out for me was when I saw him play against John Wall in the NBA summer league. That when I thought, 'this dude can play a little bit.' I started noticing there was something to the hype coming from Harvard and Boston. But, I was thinking that maybe he just had one really good game. But then the Warriors signed him.

The Warriors were hoping for an Asian star. If ever Yao Ming was healthy and became a free agent from Houston, they would have been heavy on Yao Ming. They liked Yi Jianlian but when they signed Jeremy Lin, it was a big deal. I've never seen them hold a press conference, ever—he might be the only player in NBA history to go undrafted and have his own press conference after he signed and it was packed.

There were local media there and Asian media there and that was combined with the fact he was a local guy. They had added an Asian player and it was important to this area of California where there is a huge Asian fan base. Other than Stephan Curry and Monta Ellis, he was the fan favorite. And, it wasn't just the people who were Asian. It was all kinds of people, standing up clapping and all excited as they were rooting for their hometown guy.

But what I saw that year and what I saw in 2012, it's two different guys. Everybody I talk to says he has a lot more confidence, but the other thing is that he has an amazing work ethic. **KEITH SMART*** told him he had to work on his mid-range jump shot and not to rely on his driving abilities and he took that to heart.

There were others who worked with him, former Warriors assistants and the strength coaches all worked with him during the season last year. I remember going to games early and Jeremy was out there working on pick and rolls with Coach Pierce and Coach Silas. The work ethic was definitely there and

***KEITH SMART**'s shot to win the 1987 National Title for Indiana came at the very same minute that the movie "Hoosiers" was up for an Oscar....Keith Smart was an usher in the Superdome as a Boy Scout, the arena where he made the shot to win the title.

he went from having a shot that players would laugh at because it had such a hitch in it to having a very steady jump shot that nobody saw because there was no summer league this past year and really a limited training camp. Mark Jackson, the head coach of the Warriors, doesn't even know what he lost because he never got a chance to see him. You wonder,

> ...he might be the only player in NBA history to go undrafted and have his own press conference after he signed and it was packed.

if summer league had taken place, the Warriors might've kept him.

I did one story about him when he started to hit it big and it was from the Warriors' perspective and from the Rockets perspective on why they let him go. I also did a story, going back to his high school. I tried, at one point to just get a comment through his agent on why Lin thought the Warriors let him go. It was kind of funny, one minute he's in the Warriors locker and nobody wants to talk to him and then I couldn't even get a quote from him. I did understand that that time, that Linsanity had grown out of control and there were a lot of people pulling him in a lot of different directions. I'm sure his agent was trying to be a little protective of him, under the new circumstances.

We all thought that it would cool off eventually. During Lin's first week of stardom, it wasn't like they were playing the elite of the NBA elite, but, hey, he had big games against Dallas and the Los Angeles Lakers and that certainly deserves the credit. I thought at some point it would cool off.

I thought he would turn into a guy that they would not need to score but to distribute. I envisioned him being a player to average 10 to 15 point but to get double digit assists every night. But now, because of his popularity, assuming he will re-sign with the Knicks, he will be a starter in this league for a long time. Face it, he's a great passer and he can thrive in the offense the way Steve Nash did with the Phoenix Suns.

Lin is playing the same way. He is driving and kicking it out. Neither guy is really that athletic or can jump very high, so I think he should be watching Nash a lot more. Steve likes to pull up and pass. Maybe Lin will incorporate that into his game.

Lin has the same kind of work ethic as Nash. Next year, you'll see a better Jeremy Lin. He'll work on his weaknesses. He'll always become a better and better player.

Marc Spears on Covering Lin at NBA All-Star Weekend:

When the time came for Lin to meet the national media at the official NBA media availability session, held at the Hilton Hotel in Orlando, all of the other 2012 All-Stars and all-Star Weekend event participants were assigned to eight-foot tables scattered around the hotel ballroom. Over the years that system worked well for the NBA to stage media conferences for Yao Ming, Shaquille O'Neal, Charles Barkley and even Michael Jordan, but there were too many media outlets in hot pursuit of Lin. So, Spears clicked on his tape recorder and captured the main session which was so jam-packed that the NBA had to organize an area, much larger, to allow Lin to address the throng. In past **ALL-STAR*** games, the only time a player had his own "big stage" was, coincidentally in Orlando, twenty years ago when Ervin "Magic" Johnson played in the 1992 NBA All-Star game a few months after announcing his retirement from the NBA, after he learned he had contracted the HIV virus.

*During the debut of VH1 in 1985, the first image to come on screen was Marvin Gaye singing the national anthem at the 1983 NBA **ALL-STAR GAME**.

The scene had to be surreal for Lin. A few weeks earlier, he was playing in a relatively empty gym for the D-League's Reno Bighorns. Now, he was walking up to a podium to speak into a microphone that would carry his words to an international audience in 215 countries around the world. He was being treated with the same set-up that the likes of Magic Johnson had experienced at the peak of his worldwide fame.

Here is a guy who was ranked 467th out of 500 players coming into the NBA season. After his first week as an NBA starter with the New York Knicks, his ranking shot up to 69th. Some people look at the overall ranking as an indication of one's success in the league, but Jeremy does not seem too worried about that. He's not worried about the numbers; he is just glad that he is progressing. He's more focused on the team and their improvement.

As the interview progressed, questions were raised as to why Jeremy may have been overlooked by college recruiters and NBA scouts.It may have had something to do with his ethnicity; the fact that he is an Asian-American and the fact that he would have to prove himself over and over again. This is something that Jeremy embraces, and it gives him a little chip on his shoulder. He is proud to be an Asian-American.

Jeremy spoke about his choice to wear the #17 on his Knicks uniform, as he had worn #7 in the past. Some people thought he may have chosen #17 as a tribute to a player from the past-someone like Chris Mullin from the Golden State Warriors. Truth be known is that Jeremy had chosen the #7 in the past because it was one of God's numbers that He uses throughout the Bible. He chose #17 because the "1" was to represent Jeremy and the #7 was to represent God. He had the #17 in the D-league and he has #17 with the Knicks. Now, everywhere he goes, he feels God will be right there next to him.

Questions were raised about Mike D'Antoni and the New York Knick system of pick and rolls. Jeremy loves the system and feels that it is a perfect fit for his game. He thinks that Mike D'Antoni is (was) an offensive genius and he loves the way the system is designed. He cares a great deal about his teammates and he talks about those who have been most supportive-those who have been kind of "a coach in his ear". There is obviously Landry Fields, who does most everything with Jeremy. And then there is Carmelo. Lin reported Carmelo has definitely taken Jeremy under his wing as he talks to him during most timeouts and gives him advice. He wants Jeremy to keep being aggressive and to keep doing what he is doing. With time, they will learn how to play off each other. The other two players that really stand out are Tyson Chandler and Jared Jeffries. Tyson is an unbelievable leader-the way he plays and the way he carries himself. He is a total professional. As far as Jared is concerned, some people consider him to be one of the most underrated players on the Knicks. He is an absolute "team first guy" and his defense is unbelievable. He has been instrumental to Jeremy and has given him a lot of advice while helping him make the transition.

As far as Jeremy's life changing and with the sudden rise in stardom, he is just trying to stay focused on basketball.

The schedule helps because the games come so fast. He enjoys being around his teammates and is just trying to tune out all the outside distractions. He wants to make sure that he doesn't change as a person and that he doesn't let any of this get to him. His mom and dad always taught him—not just in basketball, but in life—to always give his best effort, to follow his dreams, and to do everything in God's glory. It is a motto that he has adopted...for everything in his life.

THE WRITE STUFF

DAVE D'ALESSANDRO

Dave D'Alessandro was an NBA beat writer for 26 years covering both the New Jersey Nets and New York Knicks for the Bergen Record, The National, *and* The Newark Star-Ledger, *where he currently works as a columnist.*

You really have to start with how in the heck did everybody overlook a guy with this kind of skill set? Even to this day we're hearing that he didn't bring a jumper to the table, yet I haven't seen him miss a clutch three yet. I haven't seen him miss a pocket jumper yet. I haven't seen him shy away from contact in the lane yet. He's got pretty much every offensive shot a point guard needs and on top of that he's got extraordinary vision and the ability to play at every speed and toughness. So, if you just go down the checklist, one through 20 or whatever it takes, of how many attributes are required for a guy to become an effective NBA point guard, he knocks off pretty much every box you'll ever need.

Of course we saw him slip a little bit in Miami but that's a case of not being familiar with the speed of the game, that appeared to be pretty obvious. He was just so darn indecisive, but that's one game. I feel firmly that you still start by asking how did everybody miss on him? As far as the phenomenon, that's a different subject. I'm just more mesmerized with how a kid with that kind of talent fell through the cracks like that.

The fact that he's an Asian-American from Harvard are certainly two factors at the top of the list when it comes to it being a "spectacle," and that's great. When marketing strategies for the league are being discussed they're always talking about

> You really have to start with how in the heck did everybody overlook a guy with this kind of skill set?

increasing their audience, both domestically and abroad. This certainly covers a pretty wide berth, between the Asian continent and the eggheads. That's got to be part of the phenomenon. He's entering into two fan bases that you wouldn't normally hear a whole lot about. I don't know whether the league is nervous about losing a certain amount of popularity on the other side of the world. With Yao Ming obviously retiring and Yi Jianlian now the 12th man in Dallas there weren't a whole lot of reasons for the Asian fans to take as great an interest in the NBA any more. When those two were in the league it was reported that hits on NBA.com increased by 25 percent. Even though Jeremy is not Asian per se, being Taiwanese-American, you find a greater appeal with players with the same background as yourself. That's one of the reasons why in that part of the world the spectacle started to catch fire.

There has not ever been anything in basketball that's been comparable to this. I didn't cover the league during the **BILLY RAY BATES*** phenomenon for the Portland Trail Blazers in the late '70s but I don't really think it's the same thing. The Billy Ray Bates thing was for a half a season, this is a different kind of animal. Jeremy is not just the type of guy who will excite the crowd with athleticism, but he is also a kid with a kind of background that people tend to find appealing. It doesn't hurt that you can put him in front of a camera and he has a story to tell and he can speak in complete sentences, which is what people want to see nowadays.

***BILLY RAY BATES**' NBA career was shortened by a fondness for alcohol. When the Portland police pulled Bates over late one evening, Billy Ray pulled out a note from a friend in Mississippi that read: "It's okay for Billy Ray Bates to drive. I've ridden with him and he's a very good driver." Bates never had a real license.

As far as other sports, I don't know if there is a comparison but I'm told that Fernandomania was like this with the Dodgers in Los Angeles in the early '80s. But that's it for the NBA. I don't think that there's ever been anything quite like this.

You can see how his unselfish play has affected the team in a few areas. I've only seen one game when Carmelo Anthony was there and even though he shot horribly he was trying to do the right thing. It is pretty clear that when Jeremy's on the court, even though he's given a lot of freedom to keep his dribble as long as he wants, he's able to hold it and make plays. He has the kind of game where guys find it infectious to share the ball. They certainly want to run along with him. They certainly seem, at least, very confident that he's going to get it to them when the fast break draws the double-team and that he will find them on the drive and kick. When you do that, that alone is pretty infectious. After awhile everybody pretty much wants to emulate a style that makes everyone want to reciprocate. I've seen it in Landry Fields and I've seen it to a certain extent in some of the big guys like Jared Jeffries or Amar'e Stoudemire. They all look a little more willing to look around before they look at the rim.

It's hard to know how Jeremy is dealing with this until you spend time in his skin. Only his family would know, only he would know. From a media perspective he is certainly accommodating enough, he's accessible enough, he's affable enough. Whether that continues and whether that's enough? Probably not. This is New York. You probably already saw that he had to admonish the Taiwanese media because his grandparents couldn't make it to work without being hassled or interrupted. Maybe it's a little bit different in our culture but probably not. Two straight weeks on the cover of **SPORTS ILLUSTRATED*** is

****SPORTS ILLUSTRATED** rated New York City circa 1966 as the worst time and place to be a sports fan. The Yankees, Knicks and Rangers finished last, the Mets escaped last place for the first time and the Giants were 1–12–1. The best time and place to be a sports fan? Philadelphia, 1980.

extraordinary, that used to symbolize being the number one sports star in the country. It's going to be a challenge. He's handled it fine so far but this is all so new to everybody and everybody's charmed by it. He does look a little bit tired, I would say a little bit burned out. If it reached the point where it interferes with his work routine or his life I don't know if you can blame him for dialing it back or not being as cooperative as the media wants him to be. I can't blame him for that, that's the nature of the beast. You can understand how much a guy should be required to share of himself and sometime you have to pull in the reins a little bit. I don't really know how to balance it but I'm sure he's learning on the fly.

His media access is really something that might have to be handled at the league level. I don't think that beat writers that have to file early stories are going to appreciate it too much, 10 minutes every two or three days, to actually craft something. It's just such a meat market and stories that can be turned into what we call "readers" in the newspaper are so few and far between for the NBA. I'm not sure we're ever going to get that back with the sheer volume of media in this market. You walk into the Knick locker room it's absurd, you can barely breathe. Where these people come from I have no clue. Now, with the Chinese media, it will probably double or triple or quadruple and it's probably only going to get worse. I can certainly see that the beat writers who have spent an awful lot of their time and energy following the team and traveling with the team and trying to report something original about the team will need a lot more than they're getting.

I do see him having a long NBA career. Whether he finds a niche that continues to inspire a frenzy among New Yorkers, I don't know. It's going have to come back down a little bit. But he's going to be lock-solid pro for a very long time. The issue I have here is how many great point guards besides Deron Williams has he matched up with so far? John Wall is just not there yet. Jose Calderon is solid, slightly better than average. Every night it's going to be relentless and more than most people can really handle. There are a lot of great, young point guards in the league and everybody seems to have one. Before too long we're going to get a better idea of where he ranks. As long as he continues to aspire to make the team better, makes plays and hits a decent percentage of his shots, then they will accomplish their goal and the team will take another positive step. Do we know what their real ambition is at this point? The playoffs aren't enough, the conference finals isn't enough. Is he the point guard that is going to take you to The Finals, ultimately? I guess we're going to find out. It could be a fun journey, it could be a crushing disappointment. It's something we're all going to be watching pretty carefully with a certain amount of raised expectations.

I live in Fort Lee, New Jersey and we are in the Time Warner cable coverage area. Due to a dispute we didn't get Knicks games until mid-February, we missed the first six or seven games of this excitement. I don't know what was going on elsewhere in town but I just know that my neighbors, both Anglo

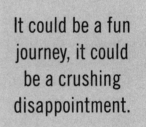

It could be a fun journey, it could be a crushing disappointment.

and Asian, were upset that they weren't given a chance to see this. They wanted to know what the fuss was all about. Whether or not they missed the frenzy that went by, I don't know, but I'm sure they're going to see what the kid is all about.

Jeremy almost had to be the one to resolve that dispute. If you're running a cable company and you're getting constant angry phone calls and you see that you're missing out on an opportunity to pull in a pretty big rating on one of your channels, you've got to be an idiot not to resume negotiations. Absolutely, he certainly helped solved it.

COVERING JEREMY LIN IS LIKE PLAYING HOOKY FROM LIFE

FRANK ISOLA

Frank Isola has been the Knicks beat writer for the New York Daily News *since the 1995-96 NBA season. He also appeared as a reporter and commentator on NBA-TV, SNY, The YES Network and TNT.*

Everything just fell into place and luck plays into it as well with this story. The idea that he wasn't good enough to be an NBA player has taken on a life of its own. Golden State liked him a lot. The only reason that they got rid of him was because they wanted to make an offer to DeAndre Jordan. Houston liked him and the only reason that they got rid of him was because they had three guards that were under contract. In the NBA, contracts dictate whether or not you can make a roster.

The Knicks season then started on Christmas and Iman Shumpert injured his knee in the second half. Suddenly there became a need for a point guard and the Knicks actually thought about bring in Nate Robinson for a minute, but Jeremy Lin was the guy they really wanted. They brought him in but it's not like they brought him in and he's playing right away. He was basically brought in as an emergency player and as a practice player. If Baron Davis had come back at the time they thought he was going to come back Jeremy Lin might have never been given a chance to play. They sent him down to the D-League for about a week since there weren't going to be a lot of practices and they thought they'd give him and Jerome Jordan a chance to play a little bit at that level.

It really started in a game against Houston, which was the week before the **SUPER BOWL***. They played against Miami on a Friday in Miami. They lost, but they were actually pretty competitive in the game, that was the game in which Carmelo Anthony didn't play. The next night against Houston Jeremy Lin came in in the third quarter. It was surprising that all of a sudden Mike D'Antoni played him. You could tell that he was a little rusty, he looked a little nervous. But the one thing that you did notice is that he was going to the basket and he was being very aggressive. Then, after the game, Tyson Chandler, who just a few months earlier had won a championship with the Mavericks, is pretty impressed with the state of affairs with the Knicks. Out of nowhere he said "the one good thing that came out of this game is that Jeremy proved that he could play. I really think that he can help us." That always stuck out in my head that he said that.

You go a week later and he finally got that chance against the Nets and once again circumstances played out. Teams weren't really preparing for him. Then you look at the teams that they played against, a struggling Nets team at the time, they played Utah, which is a terrible road team, they played Washington which is just a terrible team, and then things started to snowball from there.

The Lakers game was interesting because the Lakers were coming off a win the night before in overtime game against the Celtics and Derek Fisher can't guard anybody...38 points, that's really the game that put him on the map because even though the Lakers aren't great any more he scored 38 points against them and he outscored Kobe Bryant. Then, all of a sudden, everybody takes notice.

*Danica Patrick has starred in more **SUPER BOWL** commercials than any celebrity—10.

All of the reasons that people talk about regarding why this is such a big story are factors. People like the underdog story. People identify with the story of him sleeping on his brother's couch, especially New Yorkers. Everyone has been in a situation in their life where they're, not where they're down and out but maybe between jobs, and you have to sleep on somebody's couch. It makes a very human story, that's part of it. People like the story of perseverance after he got cut twice in December. And you can't discount the racial aspect of it, too. He's Asian-American. The fact that he went to Harvard. There just aren't a lot of Asian-American players in the NBA. That has a lot to do with it.

All of the papers are trying to find out something about him, an idea of where he's living and all of this other nonsense. It just becomes such a global story that they're bothering his family over in Taiwan. The Knicks are pretty limited with their access to begin with and the *Daily News*, we don't get one-on-one access with anybody, we're not afforded that privilege. So there's really nothing I can do about it anyway. There's pressure every day on the job so I don't think that Jeremy Lin makes it that much different. He is a pretty low-key guy, not that he's boring, I'm pretty sure he's a regular guy. But it's not like you're covering Ron Artest or Dennis Rodman or Charles Barkley where at any moment he could say something outrageous. It's actually quite the opposite which actually takes away some of the idea of pressure in covering this story. I always felt the same way about Patrick Ewing, I liked the fact that Patrick was always boring because you never had to worry about him saying anything to anybody else.

I don't think that we've seen anything like this story in the internet age, in terms of what is basically a coming out of nowhere story. I do remember the baseball player Kevin Maas, who played for the Yankees in the early '90s. He came up and all of a sudden he started hitting a lot of home runs. That became a pretty big story in New York. But that was before the internet, before 24-hour sports news, before ESPN started covering everything like it's the greatest story that's ever happened. It's a unique story from that standpoint. I still remember the guy from the Portland Trail Blazers, Billy Ray Bates.

> ...before the internet, before 24-hour sports news, before ESPN started covering everything like it's the greatest story that's ever happened.

This is different, it came at a dead time. The story really started to take off after the Super Bowl and before spring training and before the start of March Madness and the NCAA Tournament which is really a dead period for sports. Jeremy Lin, this story, was going to be big at any time of the year but at the time that it happened there was nothing else going on and that fed into it as well. If this was a black guy that went to Penn and was doing this for the Utah Jazz or the **MINNESOTA TIMBERWOLVES***, this would be a big NBA story, but it wouldn't be like this. The fact that he's Asian, the fact that he plays for the Knicks, all of that makes it a much bigger deal in my opinion.

Mike D'Antoni really liked Jeremy Lin. In terms of them being a different team he definitely changed the attitude of the team. I really noticed it in Washington and the interesting thing about that was that Amar'e Stoudemire was not there because he was in Florida mourning the death of his brother and Carmelo Anthony did not make the trip because he was hurt. I just found it interesting that without two superstars the Knicks seemed to be having more fun than they've ever had. It's not that they don't like Stoudemire and Carmelo, it's that the other players have a lot of pride and wanted to show and prove to people that they can win games without those two

*In 2009, during a promotion called "Reading to Succeed Night", the **MINNESOTA TIMBERWOLVES** handed out posters with "Timberwolves" misspelled..."Timberwoves."

guys. I thought they were going to get killed when you look at their starting lineup. It was Lin, Landry Fields, Bill Walker, Jared Jeffries and Tyson Chandler. So maybe that's more of a reflection of the Wizards, but it was apparent that the Knicks actually seemed to be enjoying themselves. And a lot of that had to do with Jeremy Lin. And when he had that dunk, the Knicks were on the road and the building went crazy, the players on the bench went crazy. It was nice to see in the NBA. A lot of these guys hate their jobs, they don't really like playing basketball anymore. Sometimes it's refreshing to see guys that actually enjoy it.

> When Steve Nash was drafted by Phoenix he didn't play in his first year....it's not like just because you don't play in your first year that you can't play in the NBA.

He showed he can play in Mike D'Antoni's type of system...with Woodson, we'll see. He has been taking a lot of shots, too, so his stats are a little inflated due to the amount of time he has the ball in his hands and the amount of shots he's taking. I definitely feel that he's a rotation player in the NBA but teams obviously thought that before. When Steve Nash was drafted by Phoenix he didn't play in his first year. I'm not saying that he's Steve Nash, but, it's not like just because you don't play in your first year that you can't play in the NBA. He can definitely play and be a rotation player. Whether he can be a starting point guard on a championship-caliber team?

Am I enjoying it? It's great for the fans, it great for the Knicks organization. My thing is that I like it when the games are competitive, when the games are close I enjoy that. I don't like blowouts either way. But it's also more work and I don't know, I just don't find doing more work more enjoyable. I love being at the games. The games are fun as you can tell, there's definitely an energy in the building. I thought that the game in

Toronto was pretty cool because even in that game he hadn't done much until the fourth quarter. He then scored the 12 points and had the three-point play that tied the game, and then he hit the three-pointer that won the game. It was interesting, when he had the ball and was dribbling out the clock, I don't think that there was a person in the building that didn't think he wasn't going to make the shot. I was never so confident about anything in my life, that he was going to make that shot. And that part of it is fun. But having more reporters around, I don't find that fun. That's just me. Maybe other people will probably lie to you and tell you this is the greatest, but they're just lying to you.

It's fun that it's something different to write about and it's nice that you're able to cover an athlete who is humble, a guy that is very respectful, a guy that cares about his teammates and takes his job seriously. There are a lot of guys like that in the NBA but this guy really sticks out. I like the fact that he's not arrogant, that he's not a jerk, and you consider how he is an inspiration to people. Going to a good school like Harvard you can work at your craft. The guy has got a lot of options in his life. If it didn't work out with the Knicks, if he ended up quitting basketball, he still would have had a pretty good job somewhere. Now the guy is set for life. I wish I had trademarked the word "Linsanity," then I would be set for life.

I don't remember where the term "Linsanity" started. I know the fans were tweeting it during the game against New Jersey, "Linsanity," "Linning," and all of this other stuff. So a lot of people had come up with it.

So, yeah, I'm enjoying some of it, but, no, I'm not enjoying all of it, but maybe I'm just miserable.

> I wish I had trademarked the word "Linsanity," then I would be set for life.

THE BOAST OF THE TOWN

SAM HITCHCOCK

Sam Hitchcock is an outstanding young writer with newjerseynewsroom.com. He has written for the MentoMan, the Times Herald Record, *and the student paper at his alma mater* **MIAMI OF OHIO***. *During the early stages of Jeremy Lin's rise to stardom he spent a "night on the town" to sample the frenzy for himself.*

At my young age, I realize there's a lot I've missed. I effectively missed Magic Johnson, Larry Bird, and Joe Montana. The two greatest athletes of my two favorite sports, Michael Jordan and Wayne Gretzky, retired when I was nine and ten. (I like to pretend Jordan never played for the Wizards, and you can't convince me otherwise.)

During the time I actually spent studying in college, I acquired a side dish of history to complement my journalism degree, but I can't claim to survey a sports scene and understand completely how it fits into an historical context. Still, I am happy to be around to savor the historical cultural phenomenon that is Linsanity.

My idea was to go to a Jeremy Lin "hotspot" in Chinatown and observe the support for the resurrected New York Knicks as they played their biggest game of the season yet in a matchup against the Miami Heat.

So here I was, sitting by myself in Nom Wah Tea Parlor, a half an hour before game time, with signed autographs of Joseph Gordon Levitt, Kirsten Dunst, Andrew Zimmerman, and the credulous Michael Rappaport, hanging above my head. Not sure what to expect, it ended up being a

---

*Do you confuse **MIAMI** (Ohio) with Miami (Florida)? Miami of Ohio was a school before Florida was a state.

fascinating experience, and reminded me of a moment from my childhood.

When I was younger, my mother used to read to me, and one of the books we read together was "Wait Till Next Year," by Doris Kearns Goodwin. Through the eyes of a child, Goodwin describes the anticipation and exultation of being a **BROOKLYN DODGERS*** fan in the 1940's/50's, mired with the disappointment. She experienced this collective adulation of the Dodgers with her neighborhood, and their bonding came through radio.

By 7 p.m., the TV hanging in the right corner of Nom Wah had the channel showcasing the Knicks-Heat contest on at full volume. Earlier, the restaurant had contained multiple families with young children as well as young New York yuppies with no interest in the game tonight. On cue with the TNT music humming, they began to drift out of the restaurant.

The first to enter Nom Wah who clearly was here to view the game was a middle-aged Chinese man wearing an Iman Shumpert jersey by the name of Chris Tan. He quickly took a seat, his eyes glued to the screen as announcers moved through the pre-game hype. I ordered some taro steamed dumplings (a delicious combo of pork, shrimp, mushroom, and dried sausage in a tapioca starch wrapper) and asked my waiter for a beer recommendation.

The atmosphere and setting of Nom Wah is curious, reminding me of a New Jersey diner in a lot of ways. The tablecloths are red and white checked, although tea leaves are interspersed into the design.

At tip-off, I started to feel the buzz. A young Asian woman in her early 20s entered and sat down, asking to be at the front

---

*Only 6,700 fans attended the **DODGERS**' finale at Ebbets Field in 1957. The park—built 44 years earlier—had a capacity of 32,000 with only 700 parking spaces. An apartment building now sits on that site.

table closest to the television. Tan's table began to fill up when his friends Peter Ackerman and Joven Buano grabbed seats, all three ordering beers while the momentum built.

Miami is the best team in the NBA at defending the pick-and-roll, and Lin is most effective when coming off ball screens with Chandler and Stoudemire. The game started with a cheer when Lin hit Carmelo for a perimeter jumper, and a collective "YEAAAAAAH!" came from the two tables watching. At this moment on Doyer Street, a waiter from a nearby restaurant came in and looked anxiously at the TV; he stood in the doorway and watched through Lin's first two assists of the game and LeBron's first four points before departing. Carmelo and Amare were involved early, and they would need to be if the Knicks hoped to keep pace with the sizzling Heat.

A second waiter entered the restaurant and watched the Knicks give up six straight points before D'Antoni called a timeout at 10-4. The family, diner-style restaurant had acquired a much different feel as all the kiddies were gone now and a stampede of people tried to push their way in. The pattern was the same for all: walk in with speed, stop, locate the television, stare intently for thirty seconds to a minute, and allow the waiter to direct them towards the best viewing spot.

Enthusiastic appreciation came from the crowd when Bosh and LeBron were called for charges and Lin's layup fell. At this time, a man entered wearing a blue Nike jacket over a short-sleeve black t-shirt that said "Just Lin Baby." Later I would learn his name was Eugene Lee.

The biggest "ooooohs" and "aaaaahs" of the game came from Steve Novak's back-to-back three-pointers, both shots giving the Knicks back their lead. The restaurant was close to full, and with each applause, waiters stopped and people walking nearby poked their heads in.

This was a regular season game that drew people towards it like a vortex. The men and women represented various demographics, but all seemed to feel the pull and attraction of collective excitement and jubilation, and as typified by gathering parties at New Year's and Mardi Gras, a desire to find connection with strangers. Nom Wah had been transformed from a Lin viewing spot to a Lin cheering party.

Near me, a tiny Asian woman, no been taller than 4'5", was sitting with a diminutive couple. She squealed with euphoria at each Knicks basket, and hissed and grimaced with each Heat bucket. With the Knicks leading 36-34 at a commercial break, she clapped loudly, completely satisfied with New York's effort so far and unwilling to compromise or curb her enthusiasm— because Linsanity can have that effect.

With three minutes remaining in the second quarter, it became clear to the audience that the Heat would not roll over like some of the Knicks' previous opponents, and LeBron's huge drive with 2:29 left induced groans and murmurs from the crowd. The Heat were not the **HAWKS***. They were not the Nets, or even the Mavs. If the Knicks were going to beat the team with two of the best NBA physical specimens ever, they were going to have to play a perfect second half.

One of his table companions looked at Eugene Lee and said reassuringly, "Lin is trying, man. Lin is trying." Ironically, this was followed by Stoudemire losing the ball and Wade dunking it.

With the Knicks down six after Mario Chalmers hit a three, Melo got the ball for the last shot before halftime and sunk it. The tiny Asian woman shrieked.

*In March 1954, the Lakers and the **HAWKS** played a regulation, regular season NBA game using baskets that were 12' high rather than the usual 10'...the next night they played each other in a doubleheader. True facts, believe it or not!

At the half, I learned that Chris Tan works for Advocates for Children, a program that assists at-risk children. He and Peter Ackerman, a cosmetic surgeon in New York, fall under the category of previously disillusioned Knicks fans who have been caught up in what makes Lin's ascendance such an amazing story.

"The combination of it being New York, with Melo and Stoudemire out, and [the team] basically written off and this unknown comes in and completely reverses their record is pretty unbelievable," said Tan.

"I had gone to games here and there in the past," he continued, "but there always seemed to be a negative aura with Marbury and Isiah, along with some terrible executive decisions. Peter and I went to the game against the Mavericks, and that game had such intensity. The thing I love about Lin is he is not afraid to drive against any team. Yeah, he has a lot of turnovers, but even against Miami he plays confidently and doesn't seem afraid."

Ackerman was quick to add that the atmosphere from the Mavs game was palpable, and that his favorite part about Lin is that he gets the Knicks to play properly. "There were times at that Mavs game where you could close your eyes and think it was a playoff game," Ackerman said.

> I am so happy he broke the stereotype of Asians.

The second half had the feel of a young kid expecting a game system on Christmas and getting a knitted sweater instead, a lot of anticipation and disappointed exhaling. Lin had several opportunities to convert a three-point play, and with each, the room filled up like a helium balloon; yet, each one fell on the wrong side of the iron.

With so much anticipation for a good Knicks team this past decade, and so much failure to live up to expectations, the past two weeks have brought Knicks fans an addiction to the eruption. A game-winning shot is the ultimate eruption, but a three-point play, a huge drive slam-dunk, or a smart defensive play also can have that effect. Sadly, the Knicks fell short on all three of these.

In the end, the Heat harassed Lin the full 94 feet, defending the pick-and-roll and forcing six turnovers from Lin in the first half. Chalmers showed his versatility as a shutdown defender, picking Lin for four turnovers on the night. Ultimately, the Knicks' inability to defend the glass and rebound did them in.

When the game ended, I sought out "Just Lin Baby" to get his take, much to the dismay of the awkward, nosy waiter who apparently thought me discourteous. What I found in Eugene Lee was the bridge of sports and culture. What Doris Kearns Goodwin found in Jackie Robinson, I found in Lee through Lin. This is what he told me.

"I have been following Jeremy Lin since he played college ball at Harvard. I grew up in New York. I knew he was good, but I did not know he was this good. I am Taiwanese-American, and I am so happy he broke the stereotype of Asians. We get discriminated against if you go to a playground in New York City. I'm not saying it is intentional, but you will get picked last. When he made it to the NCAA at Harvard, I was very happy. He changed a lot of Asian parents' views of playing sports here in America. The Tiger Mom is a very real problem for Asian children, and he showed that you do not just have to succeed in school, but you can be a really good athlete.

"She stereotyped how Asian and Chinese people must be good at math or engineering, but will never be good at sports. He was a big star in California and did not get a scholarship, but Harvard gave him a stage to perform.

"I have been telling everyone that the timing, place, and the people are right. This is what gave him the stage to play in New

York. He is very humble and gave back. He was almost let go by Knicks, and now he is performing so well. When the Knicks signed him I could not sleep, the whole night I was dreaming of Jeremy Lin doing well, even my fantasy team name is Jeremy Lin. I picked him up in fantasy and my team is doing so great, I am so happy for him. His story has touched me so much.

"My wife is from Taiwan and we have two sons who play basketball. She knows that you can make it if you work hard and you believe in yourself. Don't let parents dictate what you need to do. Do what you want to do. One day I hope I meet Jeremy's parents because I think they raised him very well."

By the time Lee and I were done, the combo of soy sauce, Chinese hot sauce, and Tsingtao was starting to make my stomach hurt. Having missed the 10:45 p.m. bus at Port Authority that would take me home, I had time to reflect on the bigger picture.

The Jeremy Lin phenomenon affected me because it gives people a reason to feel optimism and ebullience. And for that Thursday night I was part of a collective cheering section that transcended race in a very New York style: a mix of young and old, male and female, Asians and non-Asians, rooting for the Knicks and hoping our vivacity would be rewarded. The omnipresent desire the entire night was for that helium-balloon moment: everyone holding their breath hoping something spectacular was about to happen.

Lin's effervescence and conviction on the court have changed the perception of so many Asian-Americans, while simultaneously causing other races to connect with them over a team and a sport. New York lost to Miami from a score standpoint, but a bigger victory was had.

AND WHEN THE SCALPERS GET ALL THE WAY BACK UP TO "BROKE", THEY'RE GONNA THROW A PARTY

ANDREW MOONEY

Andrew Mooney is a sophomore at Harvard and an executive board member of the Harvard College Sports Analysis Collective. He is the primary contributor to the Stats Driven *blog on* Boston.com.

Like a few other Harvard economics majors, Jeremy Lin's influence has provided his corporate employer with a tidy profit, but he hasn't forgotten about the little guy; Lin's play on the court has provided ticket scalpers with a bonanza of their own, as the hoopla that surrounds him has led to a surge in demand for Knicks tickets on the secondary market.

Using data compiled by ticket search engine SeatGeek, we've graphed the average price of tickets to four different Knicks games, from a loss to the New Orleans Hornets on a Friday to a matchup with the Atlanta Hawks five days later, and their fluctuations over the preceding two weeks.

As the hype surrounding Lin compounded, single-game ticket prices soared by as much as 258 percent, in the case of a Sunday matchup against the Dallas Mavericks, climbing from $140.57 on February 4 to $503.82 on February 17. The average rise for the four games was 208 percent, meaning the prices for these tickets effectively tripled since Lin assumed a starring role.

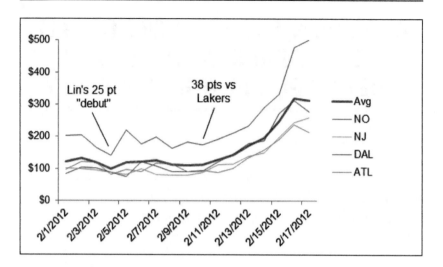

There exists a substantial correlation between Lin's performances and jumps in ticket prices. Over the 15-day period we examined, six of the top eight single-day price increases came immediately following nights on which Lin played, and the other two came once ticket prices (and Linsanity) had already begun their precipitous rise.

The graph also shows that prices did not move significantly until Lin's 38-point performance against the Lakers, which brought his international profile to its peak; the following day, Feb. 11, Google searches for "jeremy lin" reached their zenith worldwide.

How does Lin's influence compare with that of another significant acquisition for the Knicks, Carmelo Anthony? In the week before Anthony's arrival in New York on February 21, 2011, Knicks tickets sold on the secondary market for, on average, $128.51. After news of the trade broke, ticket prices rose to an average of $206.02 in the ensuing week, a 60.3 percent increase. Despite the smaller increase in ticket prices, Carmelo's impact upon them was instantaneous, whereas Lin's effect on prices took some time to gain traction.

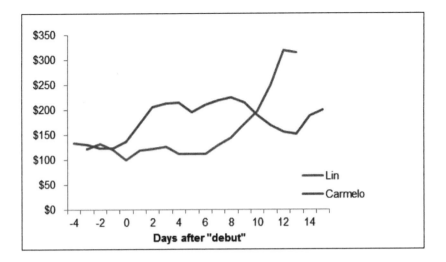

Ironically, after months of speculation and trade rumors, the addition of Anthony—a perennial All-Star and All-NBA selection—caused the price to jump less than the emergence of an unheralded rookie. It's possible that prices had already risen slightly, reflecting the expectation of a trade for Anthony, but the stark difference between the two suggests that the rise in demand is attributable to more than just basketball.

Consequently, perhaps the only phenomenon with which Linsanity can accurately be compared is Tebowmania, the similarly insufferable fad inspired by the one and only Tim Tebow, quarterback of the **DENVER*** Broncos.

And if ticket prices are any indication, Lin has actually created a greater spike in demand for his team than Tebow. In the fall of 2011, Broncos tickets moved from an average sale price of $143.20 before Tebow's first start to an average of $172.92 thereafter, a 21 percent increase. Even when we compare the pre-Tebow prices with their regular season peak in December, we find only a 57 percent increase.

*In the upper deck at Coors Field in **DENVER**, there is a row of seats that is painted purple all the way around the stadium to signify the mile-high altitude level.

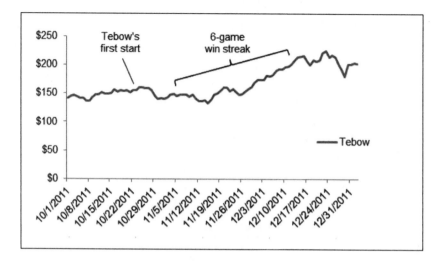

Has Linsanity officially displaced Tebowmania as the most intense craze in recent sports memory? Comparing ticket prices across sports is tricky, and larger football stadiums may make it harder to drive up prices. But given that both venues were essentially sold out prior to the teams' respective personnel changes, the 200-plus percent increase in ticket prices associated with the Knicks' addition of Lin puts Anthony and Tebow to shame. So yes, someone may have produced cultural madness greater than that which was inspired by Tebow. Time to move to Canada.

> Has Linsanity officially displaced Tebowmania as the most intense craze in recent sports memory?

Chapter Three

PUT ME IN COACH

**A Hard Way to
Make an Easy Living**

A COACH IS A TEACHER...
WITH A DEATH WISH

MIKE D'ANTONI

*Mike D'Antoni was in his fourth season as the head **COACH*** of the New York Knicks and was head coach when Jeremy Lin made his Knicks debut. He played at Marshall and was a second-round pick (20th overall) by the **KANSAS CITY/OMAHA KINGS*** in the 1973 NBA Draft. D'Antoni spent before four seasons in the NBA before embarking on a 12-year career with Milano in the Italian League. He coached in the Italian League for eight years, four with Phillips Milano, four with Bennetton Treviso and coached the Denver Nuggets for 50 games in 1998-99 before taking over the helm with the Phoenix Suns for four-plus seasons from 2003-08. D'Antoni resigned in the midst of Lin's breakout season.*

The whole story is that Jeremy Lin came here two years ago and went through a rookie workout before the draft and we liked him. We go, that's weird, an Asian kid,

---

*Mike Ditka's high school basketball **COACH** was Press Maravich. The team's ball boy was Pete Maravich, then nine years old...Jon Gruden was a ball boy on the last undefeated NCAA basketball team—the 1976 Indiana Hurryin' Hoosiers.

***THE KANSAS CITY / OMAHA KINGS** are now the Sacramento Kings. They started as the Rochester Royals before moving to Ohio to become the Cincinnati Royals. Their first few years in Sacramento they played in a temporary arena (ARCO) that was later converted to an office building. That arena/office building became the West Coast headquarters of Sprint when the new permanent ARCO Arena was opened.

Harvard and he's got some speed that we like. We like him. We told our scouts that as a coaching staff, they knew that we liked him. So out of sight out of mind, I don't know what goes on and then when Iman Shumpert got hurt I told Glen Grunwald that we've got to pick somebody up because if Toney Douglas shows up with a cold we don't have a back-up point. Grunwald says that they just waived Jeremy Lin and I said great, we like him, let's bring him in for insurance if somebody gets hurt.

By the time we got him at Golden State a couple of games went by, nobody got hurt and then Shumpert comes back. Now, he's like the fourth guard on a two-guard team. He doesn't really practice with us, we didn't really have any practices and when we did have one or two practices mostly it was Shumpert, Toney and Mike Bibby trying to figure who's the point guard, who's the second guy coming in off the bench. Jeremy's standing over there with me just in case somebody got hurt.

That goes on for about a month, the point guard play is not very good and we're coming down to the next Tuesday where we either have to guarantee Jeremy's contract or do we go look for another point guard? Well, I say that we don't even know if Jeremy can play, I haven't seen him, so let me take these two games, we'll evaluate him this week and then we'll make a decision. The first game against Boston we say, "that's okay, not bad." We did see things on the film that we liked. We go, okay, we'll give him another chance against New Jersey. And then it just exploded.

It was like, are you kidding me? We had this and we didn't even know it. I don't know if it was just the right timing, Carmelo Anthony and Amar'e Stoudemire were out, there were a lot of factors involved. It was a perfect storm. And he just took off.

It's not like he stepped up in practice. He never practiced. We would have seen him. We had a plan that we stuck to. We did it and luckily it just worked out. But there's just a lot of luck in there. We always like to say a kid deserves a chance but he wouldn't have gotten a chance, I don't care if he deserved it or not. We were doing what was best for the Knicks, it wasn't, oh, let's give Jeremy Lin a break. We were like, can he help us?

As far as expectations I just hoped he could kind of weather the storm a little bit. I mean, you never know, but not what we got. There's no way anybody knew that. You don't get cut twice and come out and dominate the league. You might come out and be a pretty good back-up but, my God, he was dominating. He went for 38 on national TV, that stuff doesn't happen. It's the most remarkable story I've ever seen, anybody who could go from that to that. He's still a rookie and he still has a lot of things to learn. The only thing I worry about right now is that people think he will just dominate the league. He's not going to dominate the league. Steve Nash doesn't dominate the league, there are nights when he gets killed out there. And there will be nights like Jeremy had against Miami when he's going to get killed. But he's a good point guard.

After New Jersey we knew he could play. After the next game you learn a little about his brain, his heart, his character. And then after three games in a row we're going, "No, this guy is really good." And then after the seventh game you go, "Holy mackerel, this is ridiculous." We knew after a couple of games that he was our point guard. That was settled. Now, what heights could he get to, could he do it against Los Angeles, we didn't know that.

> He's such a good story, he's such a good kid. It's everything that sports is supposed to be.

I've never seen anything like this, not even close. The greatest thing is he takes it in stride. He's such a good story, he's such a good kid. It's everything that sports is supposed to be, it's every book your read like the Chip Hilton series by Clair Bee, it's everything that you always dreamed about, every kid in the backyard dreamed about it. Everything. Harvard. Your Mom always tells you to study, well, look at that. Being a minority, an Asian-American, well, look at that. Everything, from obscurity, from hitting the big shots, it's just everything everybody ever dreamed about. It's a great feel-good story no matter if you're into sports or you're into business, whatever you're in. The story is the thing that drives it.

He's dealing with it great, he's perfect. And that kind of drives the story, too, because he's intelligent, he's settled, he's smart, he's mature. I'm sure he's going to go home and go, oh my God, I would be too. He's probably walking on air. But it's not going to change him as a person, he's too grounded for that.

When you have a point guard like that it changes things. The biggest thing is not just how he changed the team. He gave us hope that we could win and fulfill the expectations that we had before the season started. He gave us that hope and when you have that hope then you have renewed enthusiasm, the ball is shared easier and everything becomes closer. That always helps. It always helps that you're having a good time at your work environment. Everybody knows that the happier you are the better it's going to be. And he does lend to that. When your workplace is a better place to come to, you'll thrive.

His work ethic is off the charts, but most pro players are off the charts. Most pro players, their work ethic is incredible, especially guys trying to get into the league. So I don't think it's any more than what Toney Douglas did, what Landry Fields does, and all that, but it's very good. That's the type of thing that has sustained him until now, he's gotten better every year, every day. And that's on him.

My long-range projection for him is that he will be a starting point guard in the league and win a title.

I will really miss coaching him.

TAKE THIS JOB AND LOVE IT

PETER DIEPENBROCK

Peter Diepenbrock was Jeremy Lin's basketball coach at Palo Alto High School and remains a close friend of the Lin family. When Lin was a senior in 2006, Diepenbrock guided Palo Alto to a 32-1 season capped by a state championship. The coach toiled to help his gifted point guard understand the benefits of being a creator, and he saw that pursuit come to fruition during a senior season in which he considered Lin the team's offensive coordinator. Diepenbrock relishes how Lin began seeking his input as he matured, and he enjoys talking strategy with the Knicks playmaker. Diepenbrock, who teaches physical education at Palo Alto High School, is amazed that he is finally seeing the normally-stoic Lin thoroughly enjoy himself on the court.

My initial memory of Jeremy is when he first came to my summer basketball camp as a fifth grader. He was just real small but a very heady and confident young player. I got to know his family before Jeremy came to Palo Alto High School because his mother hired me to work with her older son, Josh, in his individual skills. Jeremy was supposed to go to our rival high school, Gunn, like Josh did. But I think he came to Paly in part because his mother saw that I was working hard and doing a lot of basketball in the community.

When Jeremy was a freshman, he played on the JV team. He was definitely one of the smaller players, but he had a much more advanced feel for the game than the other kids. The JV team did very well and he had a very good year, so at the end of the year I brought him up to the varsity for the playoffs. He didn't log a lot of time, but any time he did get he did very well.

As a sophomore, he was our starting point guard and he did OK. We had a very talented team, so Jeremy did not dominate. At that point, he was a good varsity point guard, but was still pretty small and pretty weak. I would say he had the big improvement in between his sophomore and junior years. His second year as a varsity player was when he really became a dominant high school player. And then his senior year, he went from being a scoring point guard to being a creator for others and running the show. His junior year, he was focused on scoring a lot more.

We had a really solid player-coach relationship. I would say Jeremy had similar goals to what I had as a coach, so we had a very strong connection on that level. I've had pretty good players in my past, but I would say that I trusted him more than any other player. I remember saying to him at some point in his senior year, 'Let's just be honest here. I'm the defensive coordinator of this team and you're the offensive coordinator. So you do your job, and I'll do mine.' So yeah, I had more trust in him than any other player.

> I've had pretty good players in my past, but I would say that I trusted him more than any other player.

When I think about our relationship, the main thing that comes to mind is the constant conversation of trying to get Jeremy to understand that his role should be to be a creator for others. We spent 11 months of the year together throughout the high school season and going to different tournaments, so over a long period of time we had a lot of good basketball conversations. And we watched a lot of video together. I'd tell him that scoring is great, but scoring is for a significantly lower-level player than for someone who can create for others. Just having him understand that point, that was a hard one. We struggled with that. Jeremy's personality, he was always a very confident guy and he had this incredible desire to win. A lot of the talks we had were about him learning that his teammates wanted to win, too, and that they were just as invested. He didn't need to feel like he had to do it all himself.

It was his senior year when that message really clicked. Part of the understanding came after he broke his ankle as a junior the night before our section championship game against Archbishop Mitty. That was an eye-opening experience for him. He says that that's what caused him to look at himself, to ask if he was being selfish and hurting the team. But during his senior year, he had five other seniors that he was very good friends with and that he had great relationships with. That helped with not caring who gets the credit, that type of thing.

> You have this kid who is so good… well, why is he so good? It's because he's playing all the time.

As far as when Jeremy broke his ankle in that pickup game, I never said anything to him about it. I heard someone say he was impressed or maybe surprised that I never pulled Jeremy to the side or yelled at him or something like that. But I knew the deal early on. You have this kid who is so good…well, why is he so good? It's because he's playing all the time. Are you going to pull him aside and get mad at him for playing all the time? That's who he is. So I never really talked about it. We just moved on.

Jeremy's competitiveness—that's the thing, that's the story. Jeremy was always playing, always working. And it showed whenever it was winning time in the fourth quarter. He had so many late-game heroics. He's the classic example of performing your best when it matters the most.

One of the funny stories I remember about Jeremy has to do with badminton. I love badminton and I always play in the gym, so I often get a group of kids together to play. The first time I played with Jeremy, I beat him. He didn't take too kindly to that. So he joined the school's badminton team, and then after that he beat me pretty good. I guess it was time well spent on his part. He didn't have a lot of respect for his coaches athletically, you know? I used to think it was funny that he was on the high school badminton team, too.

Jeremy was a pretty serious guy. He always had a lot going on in high school. He didn't have a lot of play time. He was either working on basketball or working on schoolwork or going to Christian school or working on the school paper. He had a very full schedule. He was always a very introverted youngster and he kept to himself.

The most incredible part of this whole story is how he's grown into this very mature adult that's more comfortable with himself. The appreciation and gratitude that he's shown me over the last five years, it's just unbelievable. Earlier, he was just your typical high school kid who was caught up in his own world. But it's been wonderful to see him mature into somebody that really gets it. It's funny—people always ask me if he was always like that. They'll say, 'You saw him as a fifth grader. Was he like how he is now?' I'm thinking, 'Yeah, I'm sure there are a lot of fifth graders praising their teammates.' It's just been an incredible experience to watch a kid who was caught up in his own stuff mature into who he is today. He totally gets it and understands that it's about teamwork and people working together, and he appreciates those who helped him get where he is. I would say our relationship is better than it's ever been. There's a lot of mutual respect between two friends, but also between a coach and a player.

Now we talk a lot about the Knicks and what's going on in present time. We talk about the last game and the next game. Obviously, I watch every game and I have lots of opinions and I let him know them. When he was with the Warriors last year and he'd only get in for the last 3½ minutes of a 22-point blowout, I'd still write him like a five-paragraph text. I'd talk about every decision that he made in those 3½ minutes, what he could've done better and what he did well. Earlier, when he went to Harvard, it was the same thing—just giving him feedback.

Now Jeremy's so much more receptive to my suggestions on ways to improve than he was in high school. One of the biggest shifts came after his freshman year at Harvard. Up to that point, he'd been successful pretty much his whole career, and he felt he really had all the answers for the most part. Like I said, it was a big battle in high school. Then he came back after his first year at Harvard, and he said, 'Coach, I'd like to work out with you.' So we go to the gym and he asked me about the triple threat and some other things. And I said, 'Now you want me to coach you? I've been here for three years! Now you want me to coach you?' The point was that he went off to Harvard and he realized that he needed to improve on some things that weren't up to snuff. He realized it, acknowledged it and took care of business.

Obviously, things have gotten crazy for Jeremy. How could they not have? But the thing that I constantly think about is how his mom and his parents have been talking about him being an NBA player since he was pretty young, so this might not be as overwhelming as it would for some other kids. His Christian faith and how devout the Lins are have really helped. They truly give a lot of credit to God and say this was God's plan. But Jeremy is just a different deal. Here's an example. I'm having lunch with him before the NBA Draft, and any kid in his right mind would be saying, 'Oh my God, if I get drafted it's going to be the greatest thing.' And he's looking at it and saying, 'How about this team? They run this offense. Or that team, they run that offense.' That's just who he is. To me, that was just so off the charts. You've got to be kidding me—caring about an offense or this or that. I'm thinking, 'Beggars can't be choosers.' But he's never looked at it that way.

At each level, Jeremy has gone in and figured out what his abilities are and what he's capable of. As soon as he did the NBA tryouts for the different teams, he realized, 'I'm definitely good enough to play with these guys.' Then it was no longer,

'Oh boy, wouldn't it be great to be on a team?' It was like, 'I can do this.' Then last year when he was on the Warriors, he wasn't happy when he got 4 or 5 minutes in a game. He was thinking, 'I can help this team. Why am I not getting more playing time?' Jeremy always has higher expectations. Right now, he's totally caught up in the moment, like, 'God, why didn't I play better last game?' Or, 'I had this turnover.' He's totally consumed with whatever he can do to play better.

At Palo Alto High School, there's just an incredible feeling of pride that one of our guys made it to the big time. The best way I can describe it is it's kind of a Super Bowl and a **WORLD SERIES*** put together as far as how it raises the community's spirit. It's just all anybody's talking about all the time.

On my end, it's been incredible. The best way I can explain it is I'm sitting in my office, I'm doing my P.E. thing, and all of a sudden the world crashes down on me. But it's been awesome and just so much fun to see him out there. It's just a lot of fun to have a relationship with an NBA player and to have a chance to have an effect on him and help him. And obviously, on a personal level, I'm proud my guy Jeremy is having this success. I've been very close with his parents, his brothers. It's just been an overwhelming, positive experience.

When I went out to **NEW YORK*** to see Jeremy play in the Mavericks game, I got to see his parents and catch up with them. They haven't changed a bit. Then I saw Jeremy at a restaurant.

*The last **WORLD SERIES** day game that was not played on a weekend was in 1972. The last day game ever was Saturday, October 25, 1987 between the St. Louis Cardinals and the Minnesota Twins. That World Series was the first ever played indoors (Metrodome).

*Al McGuire is the only man to have a brother and son play in the NBA… but former Miss America, Colleen Kay Hutchins has McGuire beat. Her brother, Mel, her husband Dr. Ernie Vandeweghe and her son, Kiki, all played in the NBA…and her daughter won an Olympic medal.

It's funny to be with a person you've spent so much time with, and now you're wondering if you can even see him in public without people going crazy. What a different experience that was. And then watching him do his thing on the biggest stage, where he hit huge clutch shots, it was just an incredible, incredible experience.

> There have been so many times like that where I'm sitting there watching and I'm like, 'Who is this guy?'

Jeremy's always been a stoic guy. He'd make these unbelievable plays, ones where 99 percent of kids would have a celebration or something, but he never did. It was like he was saying, 'This is just what I do, and it's not that big of a deal.' I just find it so interesting that the first time I've ever seen him really smile and have fun on a basketball court has been with the Knicks. Even with the Warriors last year, it was the same reaction anytime he made a good play—just a totally straight face. It's almost like he's just become comfortable with himself now that he's reached the superstar level. I don't know any other way to explain it. But it's strange for me to see. In one of his early games this year, he hit this three late in the shot clock and as he was jogging backwards he stuck out his tongue. They show it a lot on the highlights—his tongue had turned blue and he had this big smile on his face. There have been so many times like that where I'm sitting there watching and I'm like, 'Who is this guy?' It's just unbelievable how comfortable he is. He's just so comfortable with where he's at and what he's doing—it's blatantly obvious to me. That's why it's funny—everyone's wondering, 'How's he handling it? How's he handling it?' And I'm thinking, 'This is what he's expected the whole time and that's why he's been able to handle it so well.' It's like now everything makes sense to him.

EXPERIENCE IS WHAT YOU GET WHEN YOU DON'T GET WHAT YOU WANT

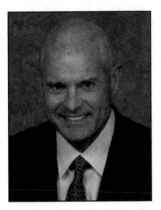

MARK GRABOW

Mark Grabow is in his first season as a player development coach with the Minnesota Timberwolves. Prior to that he served in a variety of capacities with the Golden State Warriors for 23 years working in strength and conditioning, player development and skill development. He worked very closely with Jeremy Lin during the 2010-11 campaign with the Warriors. Grabow graduated from American University in Washington, D.C., where he lettered for four years and served as captain of both the baseball and soccer teams. He later played professionally with the Washington Diplomats of the North American Soccer League.

In August of 2010, before training camp started and even though he wasn't drafted, Jeremy was the first guy to show up at the facility and get started in any kind of work with the coaches and myself. Every day, from that first day in August through the time he was with us, he was the first player to arrive every day, without fail. There was never a day when another player got in the gym before him. He was always the first one there, and he was always the last one to leave at the end of the day.

Early in the morning in-season he would get there and get all of his player development work done with coaches Stephen Silas, Lloyd Pierce or myself. Then he'd go into the weight room and do all of his strength work. So he literally had a practice before the practice, and then we'd practice as a team.

Then at the end of practice he'd get in a couple hundred more shots working with the coaches.

He was a player development coach's dream. That's the kind of a guy that you want.

He was a player development coach's dream. That's the kind of a guy that you want. He's a smart kid, he's a tough kid and he really uses player development coaches to the max. He's just one of those kids, he was never satisfied. If you had a little shooting game he would also make sure that he got to the target number that was established. He's a really conscientious kid.

But the things he's doing right now he was not capable of doing last year at this time. You could see flashes of it, but he still wasn't able to do it. When he went to the D-League...a lot of players take that as a demotion. He had a positive attitude and put up really good numbers with Eric Musselman at Reno. He utilized it well, got a lot of minutes and would seek you out and make sure that all of the things were covered every day.

The player development coaches worked on his strength, we worked on his ball-handling, his shooting, pick-and-roll situations, and what's happened now is that the game has gotten a little bit slower for him. He's able to read things. They're giving him a lot of different coverages right now. Last year he couldn't recognize the coverages or didn't know quite how to react. As the game has gotten a little bit slower he's seeing things a little clearer, making the right decisions so he has different options. He's put in so many pick-and-roll situations that he's figured it out.

He has gotten stronger, he's 10 or 12 pounds heavier than last year. He put on some really good weight during the lockout and he developed a little in-between floater, a little Tony Parker floater ,and his jump shot has gotten better. If you back off on him he's going to make a jump shot. If you get up on him he can go past you. He can get to the rim a little bit and he can take a hit a little bit better and finish. The added weight has helped him. Any time you add a little bit of weight and strength it gives you some confidence. That's one other thing that has jumped out at me as to why he's been successful.

One thing about him, he does everything at game speed. You find a lot of players when they're working out, they're saving themselves for the practice. Everything he did was game speed. That is really, really important, especially from an application perspective. Whenever you do a drill you want to do it at game speed once you've mastered that skill. So he got the conditioning aspect out of it as well as the skills aspect at the same time. He didn't take any drill off.

We had some really great players over the years at Golden State like Chris Mullin, players who would never take a drill off, and he was like that. He really applied himself in every, every drill. In the 23 years I worked there he was in the top five workers, along with Chris. There were a few others in there, but just the fact that he's in the top five, I worked with a lot of players over the years that have come and gone. Jeremy's approach and the way he applied himself every day, he never took a day off, he never took a drill off and that's something that's in him. He didn't need me to tell him about game speed. He was just a pleasure to work with and he's reaping the benefits right now.

His success is just a confluence of so many different things that happened in the past year. But I really believe that if he doesn't put that time in in the gym working on his shot, working on his handle, working on his pick-and-roll recognition, all of that stuff isn't happening right now unless he does all of that in preparation for that.

His story is already out. People have seen it, they've heard about it. Every player is different. Some players, when they go to the D-League, look at it as a demotion. They look at it like, "gee, when am I going to get back here?" I don't think anybody told Jeremy when he was coming back, Jeremy just went out and balled. And when he did come back he was better. His confidence had grown, he was handling situations better on the ball. He really, really benefited by his time in the D-League. You're just not going to get better sitting on the bench and watching or playing two-on-two with an NBA team. You've got to play. He really maxed out and that's what you want.

If you recognize where he was a year ago versus now you can see that he had a good base of support. What he didn't quite have was strength yet to absorb some hits. The league is very physical, you have all of these people grabbing on you, pushing on you, always trying to run you out or hold you off. There were times when Jeremy looked, I don't want say frail, but he wouldn't put his head down. He was never afraid. Even though he wasn't that experienced he never had a fear factor, he was fearless. And if you knocked him down he would brush himself off, get back up and go at it again. He was fearless in that respect.

Physically he needed a little bit more meat up top to hold guys off, to take a hit in the lane, to lower his shoulder and turn the corner. His lateral movement is very, very good. I've trained a lot of tennis players on the tour, some very, very high-level players. When he moves laterally he can really, really motor. He really has great lateral movement. That's something that he just had.

We had him in the weight room and he squats really well, he's got really good hip flexibility, he's got really good under-pinning, a really good base, and he's utilized all of that. Now he's added some weight up top. He's put his upper body strength and his lower body strength together. Whoever has tweaked his shot, it has gotten better. He had a couple of flaws in it. He's just put it together now.

Stephen Silas and Lloyd Pierce were the assistant coaches who had him first. I would take him later. They would do specific skill work like pure ball-handling, pick-and-roll situations, turning the corner on a pick-and-roll, streaming out, splitting it. They put him in a number of those situations, then worked on his trying to get to the rim or shooting little floaters so they're doing a lot of work there. They did a lot of two ball dribbling drills, working on his handle with his right hand and left hand. They did a lot of spot-up shooting, a lot of little pull-up shots, coming off of a screen and turning the corner. That was with those coaches.

I would stay 20 to 30 minutes, sometimes pre-game, post-practice or pre-practice because he wasn't getting a lot of minutes and we had to keep his fitness level up. I put the ball in his hands and combined the skill aspect with conditioning so we did a lot of drills where he was curling off of pin downs, just repetition of those, shooting his floaters, running the baseline into turnouts, shooting pull-ups and one-dribble breaking the defender down and getting into the lane. I did a lot of conditioning work with Jeremy after he worked with the pure skill guys. We would also do a lot of pre-game running, just sideline-to-sideline, pure conditioning.

He had a couple of shoulder issues in the pre-season so we always had to make sure his shoulder issues didn't pop up. We did a lot of shoulder work from a preventive standpoint and, obviously, we did a lot of core work. We also did a lot of lower-body work, a lot of squatting.

We all really, really worked with him on a lot of different floaters in between, getting to the rim, little rainbow shots, little touch shots, off the glass, straight on, off of different legs, spinning the ball, getting to the other side of the rim, reverses, reverses on the other side. You're always trying to put a player through drills with

I'm sure he's looking at a lot of film with Kenny Atkinson, the Knicks player development assistant coach, trying to find ways to adjust to what they're doing to his left hand.

contact, with an extra pad or an extra coach to apply contact, so he concentrate and finish. There was always a number of different game-specific drills for getting to the rim where you would draw contact.

He's now got that little runner off of one leg down the middle on the right side. Teams are pushing him to his left now, they are figuring him out a little bit. I'm sure he's looking at a lot of film with Kenny Atkinson, the Knicks player development assistant coach, trying to find ways to adjust to what they're doing to his left hand. If you looked at Dallas the other day they blitzed him on the pick-and-roll and strung him out and did a good job. They're throwing a lot of different coverages at him but he picks up things pretty quickly. He'll be watching film and he'll figure it out.

A lot of the attention he's received is market-driven. If he was playing in somewhere like Charlotte it would be a big story but nothing like it is right now in New York. It just shows you the difference between a big-market team and a small-market team. That's really a reflection of what a big-market team can do with a player.

He's a really well-grounded kid. When I saw him in Minnesota a couple of weeks ago we looked at each other and just laughed. I asked if he was doing okay and he said "yeah" and raised his eyebrows and shook his head. I told him to stay grounded and he said, "Don't worry, I will." I didn't even have to say anything because that's the way he is, very grounded. He's got his head on straight.

Jeremy is very religious and that is probably a way for him to stay humble. He attends **CHAPEL*** pre-game. Because of the

---

*Baseball **CHAPEL** was started in the 1960s by Detroit sportswriter Watson Spoelstra as thanksgiving for his daughter surviving a near-death situation. His grandson Erik, an Asian-American, is head coach of the Miami Heat.

path that he has taken, and he has been so, I don't want to say beaten down, but he's had to persevere so much going down to the D-League three times, being cut twice and almost a third time...it really, really humbles you. He's been at the bottom of the food chain for awhile so it gives him a greater appreciation of where he is and it's made him humble.

Never in a million years could I have envisioned this. I knew he had ability, I knew he was getting better. But to be where he is, it blind-sided everybody. It really did. However the planets aligned

> Coaches can live with mistakes when you're being aggressive, but when you're passive and you aren't confident and you don't look sure of yourself coaches won't trust you.

it just worked out for him. But so much of it is a reflection of how much work he put in. A situation presented itself and he took advantage of it. I'm sure that he realized, too, that he was on the cusp of being out of the league and going over to Europe or overseas or wherever he would go. He must have known it, too. I heard an interview where he said something like, "I knew I had to play my game."

He probably deferred a lot to other people when he got out there because he felt a little bit like he wanted to fit in and he probably figured it wasn't going to work. He just had to get more aggressive. Coaches can live with mistakes when you're being aggressive, but when you're passive and you aren't confident and you don't look sure of yourself coaches won't trust you.

But he went in there and he balled against New Jersey and right from there it just took off. He probably knew that he had to do something, not drastic but just maybe out of character from the way he has been in the NBA. In the D-League he was probably the man because he was aggressive and coaches put the ball in his hands. He deferred so much, possibly, that it took away from his aggressiveness. He realized that he had to change his ways a little bit to make it.

Any time you see a kid invest as much time into the game and max out...there are very, very few people who truly max out in this league. You know how much talent there is, but the question is how much do they max out their talent? You see a lot of kids who just don't. He has and he will continue to do that. He will not rest.

His first game, against Miami, they threw the gauntlet at him, they really went at him. Maybe he wasn't expecting it, maybe he had some fatigue factor. He'll figure it out. He'll use it as motivation and he'll watch a lot of film and figure it out. That's what teams are going to do now, they're going to run a couple of guys at him, they're going to push him to his left, really pressure him when he comes over half-court. That's what they're going to do in the second half to get him out of his game. With these other guys around him now, with Carmelo Anthony coming back and Baron Davis in better shape it's going to help him a lot.

His level of improvement probably won't be as drastic but you try to add a little bit more to your game and he'll do that. He's got to work on his off hand, his left-hand finishing around the rim, something like that. Whatever it is, whatever the Knicks development coaches want him to do, he will do. That's just who he is.

When he blew up I told him how happy I was for him and he hit me back and told me that he'd see me in Minnesota. I don't think there's a person who's not happy for him because they know who he is. I'm sure David Lee and all of the guys all feel good for him. He was a really good kid who worked his butt off and he wasn't a jerk. He was humble and he worked hard. He brought the donuts every morning whenever he was here. He was good and I'm really happy for him.

Some of the guys were tough on him as a rookie but he never got down. He took all of that rookie stuff but it wasn't anything drastic like in the old days.

Jeremy was a big deal here at Golden State. When he got into the game at Golden State in the pre-season the crowd went absolutely nuts. The other players all looked at each other like what's going on here? They had no idea, because he was a local kid from northern California and had won a state championship, that everybody in the crowd knew him. The players had no idea and Jeremy took all kinds of flack after that. There was a certain level of pressure on Jeremy when he got into the game, expectations were so high because people love him. When he'd start to bring the ball up you'd here something from the crowd so there was a pressure factor on him there. Jeremy in essence was the fourth guard and when he went into the game he didn't do badly. But he certainly didn't do the things we talked about. He wasn't capable of doing those things last year, he just couldn't do it. You did see that he did have the ability to play in the league, you knew that.

> Maybe another Asian-American will get a little longer look now because of Jeremy, and that's great. That's fantastic.

With Jeremy the thing that stands out is his persistence. His want, or, the other good word for it, his "burn". He's got a burn in him. Everybody uses it, has their burn and their motivation, whether they've been kicked around or whether their burn is to impress their peers, whatever it is. He has that burn in him. He loves the game, which you have got to do to have a burn.

People talk about the ethnic part of it. The funny thing is that coaches don't care about the ethnicity if the kid can play, they don't care if the kid is green or red or whatever. If a kid can play, he can play. It doesn't matter, it just doesn't matter. If you can play coaches don't care about the stereotypes or anything. Stereotypes are probably created by people who have never been in a locker room. Everyone knows that if you can play, people will find you and you will play.

Maybe another Asian-American will get a little longer look now because of Jeremy, and that's great. That's fantastic. But the bottom line is can the kid play. It doesn't matter, if you can play any sport. If you have the skill, if you have the want, if you're coachable and are you willing to sacrifice to be great? And he is.

His learning curve probably won't be as steep right now as it has been the past year but slowly, gradually, he'll keep working and getting better slowly. His turnovers will go down. The ball is in his hands so much and people are attacking him. He will improve.

When he was with Dallas in the summer league you could see some things. For some guys it doesn't come together until they're 28. For some baseball players it takes 1,000 **AT-BATS*** before they figure it out. Everybody's path is different, everybody's clock is different. It just is. There's no right way or wrong way but one thing that always rings true is that there is no substitute for hard work. There never has been, and never will be.

Orlando Cepeda used more **BATS than any player in baseball history. He felt each bat had exactly one hit in it. When Cepeda hit safely, he would discard the bat. He had 2,364 hits in his career.*

THESE SEVEN THINGS ARE THE TEN REASONS TO LOVE JEREMY LIN

ERIC MUSSELMAN

Eric Musselman, the son of former NBA head coach Bill Musselman, has been involved in coaching since 1989. The younger Musselman has extensive experience at both the minor league and NBA levels and has NBA head coaching experience with the Golden State Warriors and Sacramento Kings in addition to time as an assistant with the Atlanta Hawks, Orlando Magic, Memphis Grizzlies and Minnesota Timberwolves.

*Musselman served as the head coach of the NBA Development League's Reno Bighorns in 2010-11, where he coached Jeremy Lin for 20 games. The Ashland, __OHIO*__ native is currently coaching the NBDL's Los Angeles D-Fenders.*

My first impression of Jeremy Lin was that I thought he had great instincts. He had great toughness, he was one the best loose ball getters that I've ever been around, the way he'd go after 50-50 balls was impressive. He was a guy who was eager to learn, but he just needed some playing confidence. When he came to the NBDL level, he needed minutes and he needed encouragement to shoot the three ball. He just needed to play the point, and we actually played him at the 1-2-3, but he needed a lot of reps as a

*In 1976, Indiana, coached by Lee Corso, scored early to lead **OHIO** State 7-6. Corso called a time-out and had his team pose for a picture in front of the scoreboard. That picture was on the cover of the Indiana's 1977 football recruiting brochure. Ohio State won the game 47-7.

point guard. He was really good at the pick and roll and just handling the ball, being able to find the screen setter, but he needed to know how to read the other three people on the weak side.

Every time we had Jeremy, he got better. Guys going to the D-League for one or two games, I don't know if that helps them at all. But I know when guys get sent down and they play 20 games like Jeremy did, that's a body of work for the team to judge him or evaluate him on. It also gives a player a substantial amount of minutes.

It's hard on rookies in the NBA. The Warriors had a coach, Keith Smart, who was in the last year of his contract, and coaches try to win games. They had a lot of good guards with Stephen Curry and Monta Ellis, and it was just a bad situation for a rookie trying to break in and get some minutes. It was tough. But he was as good as any point guard in the D-League. At the D-League Showcase, we had 14 NBA teams come up and ask about him. Going into that Showcase, he had zero NBA trade value. Coming out of the showcase, he had a high trade value.

I didn't teach him how to be aggressive. When he was in high school, his team won the state championship in the state of California, it wasn't like it was a state that has little basketball. Then he played at Harvard, and every time he played a good team, he had a big game. When he goes in the Summer League, the biggest opponent he plays against, John Wall, he has his best game. I wonder what people were watching. He definitely got better with us, he definitely learned things, but his greatest assets are things that nobody teaches. Nobody teaches a guy how to go get loose balls. Nobody teaches a guy how to be tough. Nobody teaches a point guard how to be a great rebounder. He had all that, and that's what made him different from everybody else.

When he got minutes in the D-League, did he improve his decision making? Yes. Did he improve going left, which he needed to? Yes. Does he still need to improve going left? Yes. Does he still need to improve his three point shooting? Yes. But nobody taught him to dribble drive to the rim right. He's the best dribble drive right handed guy I've ever coached with the exception of Gilbert Arenas. All I know, is that when we had him, I thought he was the best point guard in the D-League, and if you're the best D-League point guard and you're a rookie, then you should be in the NBA.

> Nobody teaches a guy how to go get loose balls. Nobody teaches a guy how to be tough. Nobody teaches a point guard how to be a great rebounder.

There's a lot of guys that come on NBA assignments and they're not that good. They're marginal D-League players even though they're on NBA assignment. When a guy comes to the D-League on an NBA assignment they have a target on their chest. Other D-League players elevate their game and want to prove that they belong where that guy is. Jeremy Lin, guys were coming at him and he was going right back at them, and he was a rookie. It wasn't his second or third year. The guy has got great toughness, you can't make him switch, and the qualities that are the unteachable qualities are what separates him. And he's had those for a long time. He has NBA size, he's got great size for a point guard. He's a lot stronger than he looks, he's wiry strong. And he has NBA athleticism.

Sam Mitchell played for my dad, and he didn't make the NBA until he was 26 years old, and the guy ended up starting for the Timberwolves for a lot of years. I had Michael Williams way back when, and Michael went from the D-League to having a prominent role in the NBA. On last year's Reno team alone, Steve Novak is having an impact with the Knicks and Danny Green is in the rotation for one of the best teams in the

NBA—The San Antonio Spurs. So, I've seen other guys do this, but Jeremy's doing it in New York and he's been put in a situation where they needed help at that position.

The New York aspect plays somewhat into it. You look at a guy like Reggie Williams, when he was called up, and what he did with the Warriors, but the Warriors are West Coast and things go unnoticed a lot because of the **TIME CHANGE***. But over time, Reggie has not sustained what he did coming right out of the D-League. So there's definitely something to be said for Jeremy doing it in New York, but having said that, he deserves it. He's played incredible, it's been like a storybook, it's amazing. It's huge for New York, really. The NBA; with New York, Los Angeles, Chicago, Boston...I mean those are cities that really have a huge impact on television and everybody's business side of basketball. When those teams do well or when those guys have superstars or when those guys have draws, it helps the entire league.

> Forget how good of a player he is, he's an even better person. He's a great guy.

I try to watch every time he plays if we're not playing. I like watching him and Novak. I've texted back and forth with Jeremy. I want him to do well, I love watching him play. He's exciting to watch. My sons like watching him play, and he's a great guy. Forget how good of a player he is, he's an even better person. He's a great guy. When he got his airline upgrade seating, he would give it to a teammate. He would help carry the bags with the trainer. He didn't even flinch with any rookie chores, he just did whatever. He fit in with his teammates great. He was humble and never acted like he was an NBA player and the other guys were just D-League players. He fit right in in every aspect.

Half of the U.S. population lives in the Eastern **TIME ZONE.*

THEY SHOOT BASKETS, DON'T THEY?

DOC SCHEPPLER

Doc Scheppler worked extensively with Jeremy Lin as his shooting coach during the NBA offseason and lockout in 2011. Scheppler has coached high school basketball in the San Francisco Bay Area for 35 years and has run an individual basketball skills development business since 1986. He is a good friend and was the high school coach of Peter Diepenbrock, who later coached Lin at Palo Alto High School. Scheppler currently teaches physical education at Pinewood School, where he has led the girls basketball team to five state championships and 13 section titles in 17 years.

I first became aware of Jeremy Lin because of Peter Diepenbrock, the former Palo Alto High School coach, someone I've been close with for a long time. A few years ago Peter told me about this great eighth grader that was coming into Palo Alto. 'You have to see him,' Peter said. So I watched Jeremy play in a summer league game up at Skyline College, and I was immediately impressed with his vision, his presence, his ability to make plays and his ability to be fun to play with. In basketball, it's important to have people on your team who love to play, and Jeremy fit that description very well. He was a great passer and he could score a little bit. It was amazing that a skinny little kid that was about 5-foot-6 and 100 pounds could have so little fear playing against these 17- and 18-year-old men. I thought, 'Wow, this guy is going to be fun to watch.' You had no idea then who he would grow into—that he would eventually be a 6-foot-3, 205-pound rock with four percent body fat. Not to be racist, but Asian males just don't grow to be that big and long. As far as the upside to him at that point, I thought, 'OK, he's going to be a nice high school player because he's going to be 5-foot-9, a quick little guard that makes other people better.' That's basically all you thought of him at that point.

> Players can do things that capture everyone's attention— the flash and dash— but they don't really know how to make winning plays.

The negative things about him as an eighth grader were he was a little bit too loose with the ball and a little casual on the court. He didn't play with what they call a "high motor". He was loosey goosey. He had nice skills and was a nice player, but I thought he could play harder. It's like if you've ever seen Mike Dunleavy play. Guys like that just play at a certain energy level where you go, 'Are they really trying that hard?' So those were my first impressions of Jeremy.

I watched him play a lot in high school and saw him grow till he was about 6-foot-1 when he was a senior, although he was still a little bit thin. He had some special qualities—finding people in the open floor, the angles of his passes, the ability to make plays in the clutch, and having no fear of playing against really good players. He was the type of player that was never afraid to take a big shot—some players shy away from that. Even though he wasn't the best outside shooter, he still wanted the ball in his hands at crunch time. He had the ability to shine when he needed to be at his best.

The culmination of Jeremy's high school years came when he took his team to the state championship game. That was the Hoosiers-type game, the David vs. Goliath-type game. Palo Alto took on Mater Dei, a Southern California powerhouse. Even though Palo Alto was far from the most talented team, Jeremy led them to the state championship. Palo Alto played hard and played together, and they had a terrific coach in Peter

Diepenbrock. That team was a true testament of what a team can do when the players buy into playing the game in a winning way. That's doesn't happen often nowadays, even at the pro level. Players can do things that capture everyone's attention—the flash and dash—but they don't really know how to make winning plays. And that's where Jeremy is being really successful these days. He knows how to win. He knows how to make winning plays.

When Jeremy came home after his first or second year at Harvard, Peter called me and said, 'You're not going to believe this. Jeremy wants me to work with him on getting better.' We were thinking, 'Where was he in high school?' Jeremy wasn't the most coachable kid at Palo Alto. He didn't like to practice, but he loved to play. He didn't like the organization part or the repetition part. He didn't like standing around and running plays. But he loved to play basketball. He would go to the YMCA to play after practice because he felt he didn't play enough basketball then. Jeremy didn't like the nitty-gritty work, and that's probably typical of the high school male athlete. They like to play basketball, but they don't want to do the work that goes into being a successful player. But that's all history now.

Anyway, Jeremy came back early in his Harvard years, and I watched one of the workouts and added my two cents. Peter, his high school coach, was always frustrated with Jeremy's shot and his technique. It was always mediocre. He was OK, but he wasn't known for being a knock-down, gun-slinging shooter. He was known for his ability to attack the basket and finish at the rim. He also put other players in position to score, whether it be shooting open 3-pointers or getting his post players in a finish situation with his penetration. That workout was the first time I really saw him up close.

Then I went to watch one of his college games, when Harvard came out to play Stanford and they got their butts handed to them. It was something like 106-57, and Jeremy was held scoreless by a Stanford team that included Landry Fields, who's now his teammate with the New York Knicks. I'm sure Landry uses that against him. Later, when Harvard came out to play Santa Clara, Jeremy came out for warm-ups 45 minutes before the game and the place is packed with people wearing The Jeremy Lin Show t-shirts. At that point, what really caught my eye is that Jeremy had become a great screen-and-roll player. He'd always make the right decision in handling a ball-screen situation, and that's something that is a result of running that type of offense in high school and running it in college. At Harvard, he was played away from the ball but he still came off a lot of ball screens and found guys for open 3-pointers and found guys at the rim. That may be one small reason why he was able to step in and play Mike D'Antoni's system with the Knicks really well because it's all related to the point guard having the ball in his hands and making the decision after using the ball screen. Those were my impressions of Jeremy through college.

The summer after Jeremy graduated from Harvard, Peter went down to watch him play in the Las Vegas Summer League. Peter was giving me text message updates of how Jeremy was kicking John Wall's butt. Basically, he was playing so well and the place was going crazy for this Harvard kid. The next day, Peter texts me and says, 'He's getting three offers—from the **LAKERS*** the Mavericks and the Warriors. Stay tuned.' And then two days later, the Warriors signed him to a free-agent contract. Within the week that he signed, I told Peter, 'I want to work with him on his shot. You've had your chance with him. I have a thing in mind that could really help him.' And Peter said, 'Yeah, he's really up for that.' So we set some dates

*Bill Sharman, former **LAKER** coach, was once kicked out of a major league baseball game even though he never played in one. An outstanding outfielder in the "loaded" Brooklyn Dodgers farm system, he was called up to the major league club in September, 1951. During a Dodger game at Wrigley Field home plate umpire Jocko Conlan, tired of heckling from the Dodger dugout, ejected every player sitting in the dugout including Sharman.

before Jeremy was going to go work out with the Warriors in September, but in August he got an offer to go visit China with Yao Ming. So we never really got to meet and work. But we did have a conversation where I listed the things I thought he really had to do to become a great shooter—bringing his release point down and other things we ironed out in his work with me the next summer. So we never got a chance to work together then, but he still took some steps forward that were crucial in setting the foundation for me to work with him later. I emailed him a couple times when he was with the Warriors after I watched him shoot in the pregame, saying, 'You're on your way. Everything looks good. You've made the positive changes that will lead in to working with me. I'm so excited to work with you in the offseason.' And Jeremy was game for that. He told Peter, 'I don't think Doc knows how badly I want to work with him. I want to work with him four or five days a week.'

After the Warriors season ended last year, Jeremy's knee was bothering him. So we waited to work together until late May, at which point we arranged to meet at the gym. I didn't know that he'd had a surgical procedure done on his knee. He said he was rehabbing it and he said he could jump. So we just started the foundational things I thought were important for him to make the solid changes that had to be made.

The next day Jeremy calls and says, 'Doc, my therapist is upset. She didn't want me to start jumping until she gives me the OK. I'm not going to be able to jump.' So I said, 'Let's do this—let's work on your release and just perfect that.' So we shot free throws and worked on his release, worked on some technical things that didn't involve jumping at all. He also brought his younger **BROTHER JOSEPH***, who is at Hamilton College, and

*__JOSEPH LIN__ was a 5'11", 135 pound freshman on the 2011-2012 Hamilton college basketball team. He averaged just under three assists and just over three points per game.

said, 'Can you help my brother? Can you take a look at my brother?' So I worked with his brother, and that was also a small foundational step because Jeremy saw what I was going to do with him in these workouts once he was healthy. He saw the work in progress. He saw his brother immediately improve. With the changes I make in someone's shot, there's an immediate spurt in their shooting ability, then it plateaus and then it goes it up in incremental steps.

So Jeremy brought his brother over to my house for a month, two times a week, except when they went back to China. I worked with Joseph on his stuff, and I worked with Jeremy just on his free-throw release. And immediately, Jeremy gave me feedback from it. The young man is the greatest kid. He sent a text and said, 'I'm learning a ton. I can't wait to work with you more. Joseph loves working with you. You're helping him a lot.' And it was a 30-minute drive to my house. So his dedication was he'd go over to his upper-body workout and he'd do his rehab across the Bay in Pleasanton, and then he'd come over to my house and shoot with his brother. It was an 8-hour day for him. That was his focus. That was his goal.

When Jeremy finally started to be able to jump, that's when we put the technical work into play, the changes that we made. We made his jump shot quicker and more efficient. We brought his release down into a specific area next to his forehead—not exactly where I wanted it to be but I didn't want to make a major change. I said, 'Jeremy, as long as your hand is behind the ball, that's what's crucial. Look where my release is, and look where my elbow is. Now look where your release is.' And we moved his release three inches to the right. The other technical thing we worked on is that your wrist joint has to move throughout the sequential aspect of shooting the ball. In other words, it's not arm joint by arm joint. Your wrist is always moving. Improving that created a lower arc angle for his shot, which helped it become more consistent and more controllable from distance. Then we got rid of jumping so

high, and that made his shot quicker. We got him to release
the ball a split second sooner in relation to his jump so he was
able to use more leg power in his shot. And we gave him better
balance by spreading his feet out underneath his shoulders.

Once we got a consistent catch-and-shoot shot with those
changes, we started to work on more technically difficult shots
involving that catch-and-shoot—we worked from the triple
threat, worked off the dribble, worked on different situations.
So as time went on, he became very, very skilled at shooting
in all these different situations. That's after four months of our
sessions.

He'd work out at Sparta Performance Science in Menlo Park
for two hours, come to me and be dead. His legs would be
tired. We'd start our workouts with 50 shots from the top of the
key, and he'd make between 40 and 45 every time. We'd play a
game called Beat The Ghost where you have to make 21 shots
before you miss seven. We did a lot of different shooting drills.
You could see his tenacity. He wanted to win. He would make
17 of 24, lose to The Ghost, and he'd want to play again. He
would be unhappy when he didn't beat The Ghost. We'd figure out his percentage, and he'd be shooting like 70 percent.
But if he didn't beat The Ghost, he'd say, 'I'm not winning. I'm
not into moral victories, Doc. I have to beat The Ghost.' There
were days he'd kick the ball around the gym, get upset and get
himself exhausted. And we would play until he beat The Ghost
a couple times. He just wasn't satisfied. I had to keep reminding him of the moral victories and the strides he was making.
I wanted him mentally to make that transition from being a
great basketball player to being a great basketball player who
could shoot the heck out of the ball. I wanted him to have
a shot that was a weapon for him, not to just be somebody
who could take it to the rack and finish. The mental process
of that, to have the mind-set of a shooter, was the next step.
I knew he had the body of a shooter because everything was

technically sound. But he was very hard on himself in terms of his technique.

Jeremy was obsessed with playing this game called Free Throw Golf. It's a nine-shot contest where you alternate shots with your opponent. You get a birdie when you perfectly swish it. You get a par when you make it. You get a bogey when you miss. And one of your nine shots can be a bank for an eagle—but you only get one of them. At the end of nine shots apiece, whoever's the most under par wins. I'm a helluva shooter, so Jeremy would win a couple, and I'd win a couple. He'd win a couple, I'd win a couple. I had a tradition from a guy I used to play **GOLF*** with that you'd put a badminton birdie in your bag whenever you made a birdie during your round, and you'd keep the birdie until the next guy got a birdie. Then at the end of the round, whoever had the last birdie of the day got to keep the birdie in his bag until the next time you played. So I started a tradition with Jeremy that was similar to the Augusta National Masters **GREEN JACKET*** that whoever won at Free Throw Golf got to keep the birdie. I would display mine in the back of my Camry, right in my back windshield, so everybody would see that I had the birdie. Jeremy wouldn't display it that egotistically, but he would remind me all the time, 'I've got the birdie, Doc. I've still got the birdie.' To this day, he reminds me that, right now, he has the birdie. The score is 18-14. My comment is, 'Well, you should be able to beat a 58-year-old white guy at free throws when you're 23.' We go back and forth with the banter. It's a lot of fun.

*While playing **GOLF** in 1567, Mary Queen of Scots was informed that her husband, Lord Darnley, had been murdered. She finished the round.

*The Masters began in 1934. But no green jacket was awarded until Sam Snead won in 1949. The winner can take the **GREEN JACKET** home for one year. When Jack Nicklaus won in 1963, he was so heavy that Augusta borrowed Thomas Dewey's green jacket to put on him.

In our second-to-last session, which was the week Jeremy's NBA training camp began in December, we were working out at Pinewood School, where I teach and coach. We put on a shooting show like you wouldn't believe. I eventually won 8-under par at Free Throw Golf in nine holes. The best you can get is 10-under. So I got six perfect swishes plus a bank shot for an eagle. Jeremy had a 7-under. I believe he had eight perfect swishes and a missed bank to lose. We had kids watching us. When I won, I took a lap around the gym with my arms up. Jeremy's such a competitive guy that he dejectedly, but in a kidding way, walked to his car in the parking lot to get the birdie. As he gave it to me, he said, 'I'm getting this back tomorrow. I'm working with you tomorrow.' The next day he kicked my butt, and I had to go to my car and get the birdie. I gave it back to him and gave him a hug. Two days later, he was going to get his first workout with the Warriors. A little later, after I locked up and left the gym, there's the birdie on the door handle of my car. Basically, it was the poignant interchange between a coach and a player that signified, 'This was for you. It's my birdie, but I'm winning this because you're helping me.' It was just such a classy, selfless act that I drove right to his house. His car was parked out front, and I put the birdie under his windshield wiper with a note that said, 'It's all you. You earned it. You're the best shooter in America.' It was like that end of the line when you work with somebody and they're ready to show the world how good they are. We worked for four months, 3-4 times a week, interspersed with his travel to Los Angeles, China and New York. We spent a good 150-200 hours in the gym together. It's just such a special time with the relationship that you make. I cherish it to this day.

Now we exchange texts regularly. We talk about his shot. We talk about other things. Jeremy is very inclusive in the success he's having now with his AAU coach, his high school coach, his high school teammates, his pro teammates, and it's just a great phenomenon. We still have goals for his shot. He's still not putting into play a lot of the shots we practiced religiously during that time. They're still not a part of his game yet. When somebody has a playing style they've used for a long time and then they learn something new, it's just not possible to put the new things into play and go from there. He's not that super human. Let me tell you—he's the best learner I've ever worked with in terms of grasping things quickly; in terms of listening, watching and accepting correction; in terms of being a coach-able, humble guy. He'd say, 'Just tell me what you want me to do, and I'll do it.' And that's something he wasn't in high school. Back then, he was a typical stubborn male. Last summer and fall, he was on a mission. One of our goals was for him to go into training camp and earn a spot on his team, to earn as many minutes as he could. We knew leaving the gym on our last day together that he was completely prepared to do that. We knew how much he'd improved. I knew he had the head and the body of a shooter much more than he had before.

Those are the things that I was really pleased with, and those are the things Jeremy gives me credit for. After he made that shot at the end of the game against the Toronto Raptors, I sent him a text that said, 'BAAAM!' except I used 12 B's, one A and 95 M's. Then I said, 'You're a ghost buster!' That was the term we used when he beat The Ghost. And he sent back, 'That was all you, Doc. I wouldn't have made that shot unless I worked with you. You gave me the confidence and you kept after me. So thank you.' He tells you he loves you, he thanks you, he keeps asking for feedback. Sometimes when you're all excited about somebody, you can nitpick to death about their game— the turnovers he makes, how I want him to look for his shot more. So I really have to be cognizant of not overdoing that. I tell him, 'Stay in the moment. Keep getting better. It's only just begun. The sky's the limit. We know how good you can be.' I also see some technical things that I text him about. I said, 'Please feel free to tell me to Shut the .---- Up anytime you want because I don't want to be a pain to you.' He came back and said, 'No. Please. Share.' So I sent him a three-page text about this, this, this and this. And he said, 'It all makes sense. Thank you very much.' That just tells you who Jeremy is. I mean, c'mon. He's a pro now. He has the accolades of the NBA and the world. And he still listens to a high school girls coach who coached his high school coach? Now keep in mind I'm a very successful girls coach. My Pinewood School team has won five state championships and 13 section titles in 17 years. So it's not like I'm some slouch. I was a great shooter when I played. I've coached basketball for 35 years and I've worked individually with players for 25 years. I know my s--- better than any NBA assistant coach, and that has been reinforced with my favorite student. Jeremy has told me, 'The stuff you've taught me, I'd never learned those things before. It all makes sense.'

> He has the accolades of the NBA and the world. And he still listens to a high school girls coach who coached his high school coach?

Jeremy doesn't like to fail. Motivation is a strong emotion. His hard times last year with the Warriors created a motivation that was extremely strong. That's a great life lesson for all of us. If you don't like the way things are going, don't whine, don't complain about it, fix it. Don't cry about it; get better. That's the goal even if you had a successful year—just get better. Look at the great ones—the Jordans, the Johnsons, the Birds. Look at LeBron James this year. His motivation was higher because he was embarrassed in the Finals last year. He didn't have a post game, his shot wasn't that great. But after losing like that, it creates a more powerful motivation to get better, to not fail. That's exactly what was created within Jeremy. His work ethic and his attention to detail improved as he matured as a human being. It wasn't something he had in high school. He loved basketball but he wanted to do it his way. When he realized that probably wasn't going to be good enough, he had to really buckle down to get better. The things he had to fix were his shot and getting a little stronger and being more athletic, and that's what he really concentrated on in the offseason. He has an unbelievable work ethic from the standpoint of wanting to get better, not being satisfied with losing. He doesn't like moral victories and he had to be reminded of the significance of those things. He was on a mission. That was the thing—he was on a mission. People are motivated by a lot of different things. Jeremy isn't really motivated by the money or attention. He's very motivated by proving people wrong. He's motivated by winning.

> He's very motivated by proving people wrong. He's motivated by winning.

Jeremy needed some reminders that the process to getting better isn't just about winning a drill. It's about going through the trials and the tribulations, the good days and the bad days. The goal is always the same. That's been a consistent theme even when he's been on top of the world— you need to get better. When things weren't going his way, when he went through the hard times with the Warriors, the Rockets and the first bit with the Knicks, I told him, 'Jeremy, they can't take away how much better you've gotten. You're a much better player now. They can't take that away. You'll always have that. You just have to find a situation where you can show it. It might not be this year. This might be your moral victory year.' And he said, 'Doc, I'm not into moral victories. This was supposed to be my breakout year.' So that drove him. And look at that—halfway through the season, this is his breakout year. The beauty is that he did everything right in his work and with his mental approach. He stayed positive. The most important thing, the hardest thing for any athlete, is when you do get your chance, embrace it. Enjoy it. Play without care. Don't be rushed. Don't be tight. When he finally got his chance to get some consistent minutes, he performed at the highest level that any human could. That's one of the great, great athletic qualities that he has—he performed his best when his best was needed. His best was needed to keep his job. He's understood, 'I need to make this shot so my team wins. I need to make this play so my team wins. I need to play well to play more.' Having coached for a long time, it's very hard when you have players on your bench who are prove-it-to-me players. They're the ones who you tell, 'OK, you've got 2 or 3 minutes. Show me what you've got.' Sometimes with kids, they screw up by choking. Or sometimes they screw up by doing too much. It takes a rare bird to be able to perform really well in that situation. Some will say, 'I never really get a rhythm on the floor; I'm only in there for 3 minutes.' But Jeremy Lin, he eventually got his 2 or 3 minutes in crucial time, and he turned his team around.

The other aspect of how well he's doing in New York comes from something his high school coach told him way back when. Peter said, 'The beauty of basketball is taking your game to the next level. It's a lot harder and more intricate to set up other players than it is to score yourself. It's a higher level. It's a deeper meaning.' That was a similar thing to what I told his coach in high school when I saw Peter hog the ball at an open gym. I just told him, 'Peter, it's no fun for other people to play with you. The goal of the game is to be fun to play with.' Well, Peter took it to a new level when he described it to Jeremy. He said, 'You're at a whole different level when you're involving your teammates, when you make others like being on your team.' Look what Jeremy does for the Knicks. Those lessons were learned in high school. They were ingrained in him during those teachable moments, and he embraced that. Look at the looks on the Knicks' faces now. Before Jeremy played, they were a bunch of one-on-one losers. But now, they love this guy. It's not because he has this vibrant personality. He's just a nice, kind, humble, easygoing kid that people get along with because he's such a good person. He doesn't have the swagger; he doesn't have the street cred. But people love him because he is who he is, and he's very honest about it. Any human being embraces that. There's a lot to Jeremy Lin other than just the skills he developed.

JEREMY LIN'S MILLION DOLLAR SECRET

PHIL WAGNER

Dr. Phil Wagner developed and instituted the fitness and nutrition programs that Jeremy Lin used to great success during the 2011 NBA offseason. Dr. Wagner owns Sparta Performance Science, a training facility in Menlo Park, Calif., that is built on a foundation of science. Sparta's force plate gave Lin a 'fingerprint' of his nervous system and enabled Dr. Wagner and his staff to build a comprehensive program that Lin determinedly followed for four months. Dr. Wagner cites numerous ways Lin's training has been evident on the basketball court—including that Lin increased his vertical jump 3½ inches and that he handles more like a Porsche than a motorcycle this season.

Jeremy Lin came to us at Sparta Performance Science in the summer of 2011 at the suggestion of Doc Scheppler, who was working with Jeremy on his shooting. We've worked with a lot of NBA players and we've also helped out a lot of local basketball players in the Bay Area in connection with Doc. When Jeremy first came to Sparta, he mentioned that he had some knee injuries in the past and he was looking to try to get rid of them. He also said he wanted to add a lot more explosiveness to his game because he felt that was something that was holding him back.

Jeremy identified those goals and we started working together right away. First, we tested him using our technology, which is the force plate. The force plate measures how much force you're putting into the ground. From there, we were able to assess why he felt like he was lacking that explosiveness.

Basically, the force plate measures three things—how quickly you can produce force, how much force you can produce and how long you can produce that force for. All of that helps identify where you're prone for injury, what you do well and what might be a weakness. What we found with Jeremy was that he really lacked the ability to create force quickly. Jeremy came in and was very flexible. When we first tested him with the force plate, he actually produced force over a long period of time very well. He was really flexible and really light, so he was strong for his body size. All the workouts we set up for Jeremy

> He also said he wanted to add a lot more explosiveness to his game because he felt that was something that was holding him back.

centered around heavier weights and lower repetitions—just working on power. We weren't really working on endurance or flexibility; mostly strength and power. Actually, we were trying to tighten him up. The body's main system of working athletically is using the stretch shortening cycle—when you stretch your muscles and tendons, you get a reflexive snap back. That's what allows you to jump really high and run fast and basically keep doing movements over and over again. So if you think of Jeremy as a rubber band, he was able to stretch back really far because he was flexible. But he didn't have that snap. So as a result, we had to make that rubber band thicker, without having to take away from that ability to stretch.

With most basketball players, we have to work a lot on mobility—just range of motion, being able to descend all the way down into a full squat where your butt is almost on the ground. Most basketball players struggle with the mobility side, not so much the strength side. Jeremy struggled a lot with the strength side, but he actually was really flexible. Most basketball players right away are doing a lot heavier weights than Jeremy was doing, but they don't really get much heavier because they have to spend so much time staying flexible. On the other hand, Jeremy came in and was flexible, but he needed to get bigger and stronger. So we had him do a repetition of the same movement over and over again, just a lot of training his body to get stiffer and bigger and stronger.

Jeremy squatted really heavy for about one to three reps. When he first came to Sparta, he was squatting 50 kilos, which is about 110 pounds. And when he was leaving, he was doing 110 kilos. So he more than doubled his leg strength. That's a lot even for a high school kid, let alone for a guy who's playing at the highest level. For a pro basketball player, 110 kilos, which is 242 pounds, is extremely high. On the flip side, 50 kilos when he first came in, is extremely low. Most guys are in that 80-90 kilo range.

In addition to the squats, Jeremy did a lot of heavier dead lifts and a lot of upper body pull-ups. But he definitely squatted the most. The program sounds kind of boring—I mean it's not very sexy. There are no exercise gimmicks. There's no variety of movements. The workout is just heavy, very direct lifting of weights. It's certainly very technical to lift those kinds of weights that heavy. We would squat 10 sets for 60 minutes. So for an hour, all we would do is squats. It was very directive, it was very boring, it was very heavy and he made incredible gains.

One of the things he had to be careful of was he couldn't go shoot with Doc Scheppler or go play five-on-five directly after training at Sparta just because his legs were so jello. Doc and I just coordinated it that if he was going to go shoot over there afterwards, Doc would make him work mostly on his release point rather than his ball movement and dribbling.

Other than squatting and lifting heavy weights, Jeremy did some work on our slide board, a lateral explosive exercise that doesn't involve landing. But that was few and far between for him because he moved really well side-to-side. What we were trying to do with all of that heavy loading was make sure that his trunk was stable when he was moving side-to-side, which I believe is one of the things you see with him on the court now. When he's moving to the basket, no one's knocking him off course.

We also gave him the upper body programs to do on his own, which he did in the East Bay. At Sparta, because I'm a physician, we use our science and technology to design and individualize the whole workout program. Most of our athletes live outside of the area, so

> He was elevating 12 more pounds 3½ inches higher. So he's jumping higher with more weight.

we give them two days of workouts to do on their own. Those upper body workouts help support what they're doing here. So when Jeremy was over in Pleasanton, he was doing variations of pull-ups and presses and trunk work to strengthen his abdominals.

We were looking to improve his force output, so one of the stats we throw out was he increased his vertical jump 3½ inches. That was because he put more force in the ground. The force plate works off Newton's third law—for every action there's an equal and opposite reaction. So when he got stronger in squatting he could put more force down into the ground and therefore could get more force back up. That caused him to get up 3½ inches higher. To say his power went up is accurate because he's jumping higher. But then you also add on the fact that he got 12 pounds heavier, and then his power really went up. He was elevating 12 more pounds 3½ inches higher. So he's jumping higher with more weight. Practically, that was a carryover from squatting more—his power went up and his vertical jump went up. Everything is based off that ground reaction force. So if he's trying to shut down a driving lane defensively, he's got to push left really hard to move right. You've got to push in the opposite direction you have to go, and that's where the slide board really came in. Some of the stats we have from our slide board are that his lateral quickness improved 32 percent. It improves because he's able to push more side-to-side, which caused him to move quicker side-to-side. It's based off that ground reaction force philosophy.

Nutrition was also a big, big part of Jeremy's program. We provide the stimulus to get bigger by squatting and lifting, but if you don't meet that stimulus you're not going to optimize the improvement. In talking about getting Jeremy to become a bigger, thicker rubber band, the big part we had to work on with him with was improving his protein intake. His diet was not terrible, but it was really high on carbohydrates and subsequently low on protein. He was a big Jamba Juice guy who loved smoothies. They're loaded with calories which are really dense, which is good at times, but it was to the point where it was inhibiting his ability to eat more protein. As a result, we had to take those out of his daily regimen and increase his protein and vegetable intake to help him recover faster. Because he was doing so many workouts, the vegetables provided a lot of vitamins that helped him recover and the protein gave him that stimulus to get bigger through all the lifting.

> It's just a guy who really took more responsibility for his own improvement than anybody else.

We really emphasized with him—eat more servings of vegetables. He was eating zero when we started, zero vegetables a day. Our goal was eight servings, and he increased it up to six servings a day. His protein was getting up to about 200 grams, which was about one gram per pound—that's what we wanted. Earlier, he was around 100. The only time he did meet the eight servings of vegetables a day was when he went to China to play an exhibition in Taiwan. Because they have so many vegetables in all their meals he was able to eat those eight servings, but unable to eat the protein requirements. But that was only for a brief period when he was gone.

Jeremy's motivation was extremely high. We've seen two lockouts in a short period of time with the NFL and the NBA, so it's been interesting to see how the athletes in those sports respond to that. It really favors those athletes that are self-motivated, and Jeremy is certainly one of the athletes in that category. You really have to go search for ways to continue to improve when a team cannot provide it for you. Jeremy sought out a strengthening program with us, a way to improve his shooting with Doc Scheppler, and he tried to schedule and find his own games of five-on-five. So he really had to be his own agent and coach and handler, and he spent most of his day in the car. It was amazing—he had to shuttle from place to place, organize his own schedule and optimize it. That's really what you're seeing now with Jeremy's success. It's just a guy who really took more responsibility for his own improvement than anybody else.

Jeremy was very focused at Sparta. There was a very quiet determination about him when he was training here. We train a lot of pro baseball players, so he was working alongside a lot of baseball players during that time, not other basketball players. He was certainly friendly to these guys, but he was quiet in the sense that he really had something to prove and you could tell there was a little bit of angst or frustration. Between the NBA lockout going on and his uncertainty in the game, there was total determination that he was going to work as hard as he could to put himself in a position to be successful.

We talked about how frustrating it was with the day-to-day uncertainty with the lockout. He just wanted to get back into the game of basketball. At some point, he had a ticket to go back over to Italy to play. He pretty much conceded the NBA wasn't going to happen this year—that was one of the peaks in how frustrated he'd get. It was tough because he worked so hard in the offseason and he scheduled so many of his own workouts that he figured he'd have a chance to be able to prove how much dedication he had and how much commitment he had made. He was getting frustrated that the harder he worked and the longer he worked, the less likely it seemed that the season was going to happen.

Jeremy's one of the more competitive athletes I've ever met... about everything. He was just as competitive with himself as he was with other people. He knew what his previous best was in everything, from squatting to slide boards to jumping. So everything was a competition, whether it was with another person or himself. And everything was geared toward... everything was a mini-game almost. Even with us, I remember many times where he would just start calling us out, the coaches, trying to bait us, to get involved in whatever he was doing. He just thrived on that competitiveness.

We have records in our facility for different age groups—male and female. Jeremy was even competitive with high school females even though he is more athletic than them. We have female records up there that have stood for a few years, and he was excited when he broke those. He would actually tell the female athlete something like, 'I just broke your record.' He obviously wouldn't say it in an arrogant way, but it's like he was saying, 'I'm competitive. I don't care who you are or what age you are or what gender you are.' He would always bring that competitiveness to the table. That was one of the only funny anecdotes that I saw with Jeremy. Most of what I saw in him would just be raw determination. When I think back on Jeremy's offseason, that's it. My most frequent memory of Jeremy is him sitting on the bench we had next to our weightlifting racks, totally drenched in sweat, his head between his knees, breathing, just saving his energy before his next set came up. We'd do everything on a timer, so there's a certain work-to-rest ratio that we prescribe based on the athlete's needs.

We can look at the force plate to summarize Jeremy's progress objectively. Jeremy's onset of tension, that ability to develop force quickly, was his biggest improvement. It went up 16 percent, which is why his vertical jump went up. His lateral quickness went up. It's just that sheer rate of force development. And that rate came from being able to squat more weight. So if you look at it like a flowchart, he squatted 120 percent more because he went from 50 to 110 kilos. And that squat improvement led to a 16 percent increased rate, which led to a 3½ inch higher jump and a 32 percent increase in agility.

> Comparing Jeremy to other NBA athletes, flexibility-wise he is off the charts for a basketball player.

Comparing Jeremy to other NBA athletes, flexibility-wise he is off the charts for a basketball player. He is excellent. In the other strength categories that translate to all athletic movement, he's above average for an NBA player. Jeremy worked the most on being able to develop force quickly. By increasing his rate of force, that really carried over most to his quickness because when you have good range or good onset of tension, you can react to stimulus really quickly. What we see a lot with people like Jeremy when they come in is that they jump really well off one leg, but it's hard for them to jump off two. That's because the two-leg jump is quick and short, whereas a one-leg jump is long and smooth. One of the first things that Jeremy realized in his training was, 'Man, I can really jump a lot better off two feet now.' That's a rate-force jump versus timed jump. A timed jump is a dunk contest—I'm going to start at the half court and take these long strides and then take off from the free-throw line like **MICHAEL JORDAN***.

***MICHAEL JORDAN** was the Assistant Captain of the 2009 U.S. President's Cup (Golf) Team.

People talk about body control so much in basketball, and really body control is a sexier word than strength. The stronger you are, the better control you have in traffic, when you're off balance and when you want to head in a certain direction. The best thing I saw with Jeremy when he started playing this year was that his body control was significantly better. He was a stronger, bigger guy, so he just had better body control. The best example is probably LeBron—he's the strongest guy in the NBA, and he has the best body control. We talked a lot about the rate of force, the onset of tension, which really has to do with how stable you are—your body control. That's what Jeremy lacked when he came in. I likened him to being a motorcycle—certainly fast and maneuverable, but definitely not stable around the turns. With his work at Sparta, he transformed into more of a Porsche—where you can maintain that speed and maneuverability but also be a little more stable when you're changing directions.

> I don't think we'll ever find another NBA player that commits for that long and as consistently as he did.

Looking at Jeremy's improvement subjectively, I don't think we'll ever find another NBA player that commits for that long and as consistently as he did. There are a lot of factors involved in that. Jeremy was extremely determined to play in the NBA, and that's always the most important aspect. At Sparta, we see a lot of intellectual athletes because we're right by Stanford. We do a really good job of getting those types of athletes to buy in because we're so science-based. He really bought into everything we're doing because we explained the *why* behind everything. And then the lockout was probably the third aspect—just having more time to be able to work with him. So his certain determination, the buy-in from the science and the lockout, that was kind of a perfect storm to maximize his offseason. I don't think I'll ever have another length of time like that to improve somebody because of the lockout. But if we had 100 other NBA guys like that during the lockout, 99 of the other 99 guys wouldn't have turned out like Jeremy.

We've had a lot of successful athletes in the professional ranks, but it's really hard to find somebody that's risen so quickly. But more importantly, Jeremy is just such a good person. I cannot think of any other pro athlete we have or have ever had who would compose himself the way Jeremy did in younger groups, with high school or college kids. When he worked out with high school and college groups, people would have no idea that he was a pro basketball player. He didn't talk about it, he didn't behave like it. He was just like another athlete going out there and enjoying himself. He has such a humble personality. Because of that, it's so great to see him have this kind of success...and that's why so many people can relate to him—it's because he's just so down to earth. He's just a guy who you'd want to go have dinner with or go get coffee with. It was just a fantastic experience for us to work with Jeremy, and it seems like it's worked out pretty well for him, too.

Right around the NBA All-Star break, Jeremy let me know that he's going to come back this offseason and that he's going to bring his brother. That just shows Jeremy's determination. He's thinking, 'I had a good offseason—it put me on the map.' Most people are thinking that this is the Jeremy Lin season, right? But he's looking at it a lot differently, like, 'This is the start of my NBA career as opposed to the peak.' It wasn't like he was waiting until the end of the year to decide what he's going to do for his next season. He was already eyeing the next season while he was still focusing on this one.

He still has some physical room for improvement, which is great because that means he can get better. Mentally, I don't think he can get much better because he's so grounded spiritually and emotionally and he has a great support system. That's great because those are obviously the hardest things to improve on.

IN CASE YOU'RE EVER ON SPORTS JEOPARDY

In 1955, the Syracuse Nationals beat the Fort Wayne Zollner Pistons in seven games in the NBA Finals. The Pistons did not play any games at home during the Finals because their home arena, The Allen County Coliseum had booked a bowling tournament. The Pistons played their "home" games in Indianapolis. Two years later, the Pistons moved to Detroit.

Late hamburger king Dave Thomas named his company after his daughter, Wendy. Wendy was once a babysitter for John Havlicek's children in Columbus Ohio.

In the 1970s, Kentucky basketball recruited 6-foot 10-inch Parade All-American Bret Bearup from Long Island. After a high school game, Bearup was approached by an up-and-coming coach who said, "Hi Bret. I'm Jim Valvano, Iona College." Bearup looked down and said, "You look awfully young to own a college." Bearup is now the top honcho at the Denver Nuggets.

The band, Pearl Jam, was originally named Mookie Blaylock, after the former Oklahoma and NBA player. They recorded their first album, "Ten" (Blaylock's number) under that name. In 1992, the band Mookie Blaylock changed their name to Pearl Jam after a hallucinogenic concoction made by lead singer Eddie Vedder's great-grandmother, Pearl.*

When Steve Alford was a senior in high school in 1983 in New Castle, Indiana, his high school team averaged more people in attendance per game than the Indiana Pacers.

During one off-season, Celtics center Dave Cowens drove a cab in Boston. He claimed he took only one passenger the "long way because the passenger was an obnoxious Knicks fan.

Bob Iger, the CEO of Disney, is married to former NBA sportscaster Willow Bay. Iger made 52 million dollars in 2011.

Bob Gibson played basketball with the Harlem Globetrotters several off-seasons...In 1972, Bill Cosby signed a lifetime contract with the Globetrotters for one dollar per year. In 1986, the Globetrotters gave him a nickel raise. Cosby made several appearances with the team and is an honorary member of the Basketball Hall of Fame.

The current Madison Square Garden opened in 1968 and is the fourth Madison Square Garden in New York history. It is the oldest arena in the NHL and the second oldest in the NBA—behind Oracle Arena, home of the Golden State Warriors.

Chapter Four

CALIFORNIA HERE WE COME

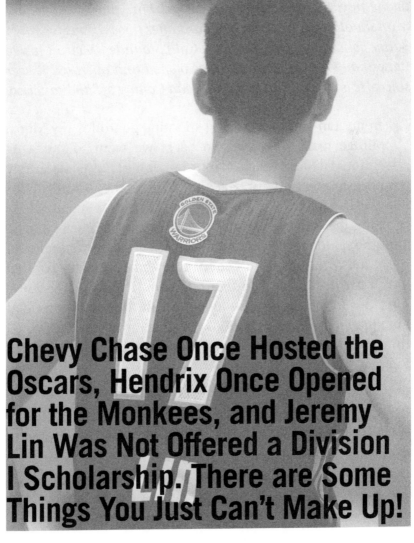

Chevy Chase Once Hosted the Oscars, Hendrix Once Opened for the Monkees, and Jeremy Lin Was Not Offered a Division I Scholarship. There are Some Things You Just Can't Make Up!

A PLAY-TONIC RELATIONSHIP

JIM SUTTER

Jim Sutter coached Jeremy Lin's Amateur Athletic Union (AAU) basketball team for six years and remains one of the star guard's confidants. Lin joined Sutter's Metro Mirage Basketball Club when he was in fifth grade. The San Francisco Peninsula-based team advanced to the AAU national championships four times in the next five years. Sutter directed Lin's positional switch from shooting guard to point guard after two seasons together. Sutter, who lives in San Carlos, Calif., founded Metro Mirage Basketball Club in 1992 and has owned and operated it ever since. He is a plumber for the City and County of San Francisco.

Jeremy Lin was the starting shooting guard for my Metro Mirage team the first two years we went to the AAU national championship tournament. He was definitely our best shooter and our best scorer. But at the 12-and-under nationals, when he was in sixth grade, we had some problems bringing the ball up the court. So I made the decision that after the national tournament, I was going to move Jeremy to point guard and make him our primary ball-handler. I wanted to put my best athlete in that position. But I was also looking at his future. When you looked at how Jeremy was one of our smallest guys and you looked at his mom and dad, you'd think, 'He's going to end up playing point guard anyway down the road because of his size.'

Jeremy bought into the switch. He wanted to be supporting the team. He wanted to be the guy. He's a great kid. One of the ways I presented it to him was by saying, 'You're going to make everybody around you better.' There were times during his seventh and eighth grade years when he'd come up to me and say, 'Can I play some two guard today?' And I'd say, 'Nope, you're the one.' Without a doubt, the team benefited from Jeremy moving to point guard the first year. His seventh grade year was a growing year for the team because we had a lot of moving parts, but a year later we made it to the eighth grade AAU national tournament. And the next year, in ninth grade, we went to the national tournament again.

I had experience working with other talented players that were point guards so I had more than a fair share of set plays that Jeremy benefited from. A lot of our plays involved screens for him—high on-ball screens, the same stuff he's run with the New York Knicks. Those plays gave Jeremy the opportunity to come off that screen, look to attack the basket or pull up and shoot a jump shot. Or there was always a second wrinkle in the play that had somebody else that could be coming open, so it gave him an opportunity to read that stuff, to read what was going on.

One of the reasons Jeremy was one of the smaller kids growing up is because he was the youngest kid on the team. He was born in August of 1988. Jeremy played in the AAU nationals at the 11-, 12-, 14- and 15-and-under levels, but at all those national tournaments he was not actually that age until after the tournament. Because of his age, where he was born and the grade he was in,

One of the reasons Jeremy was one of the smaller kids growing up is because he was the youngest kid on the team.

he was always playing up a level. That's why he's so young now at 23 years old. He turns 24 in August and now he's literally one of the younger guys in the NBA, even though he played four years of college. But playing with and against older kids for all those years was obviously a huge benefit for him.

When we played at the 11th-grade level after taking a year off, Jeremy had some pretty nice talent around him on our team. Our starting center was 6-foot-8. We had a kid, Blake Schultz, who went on to play at Williams College and become the Division III player of the year in 2010. Those types of teammates help any kid blossom. When you've got more talent around you, you get more of a feel for the nuances of the game. We played a lot of teams and we played a lot of good kids. As a 17-and-under team that summer, we played against Kevin Durant and Ty Lawson, who both played for the DC Blue Devils. We lost to them by five points. Earlier, at the 11-and-under level, we played against Derrick Caracter, another future NBA player. This is something that people have lost sight of. Jeremy was involved in AAU, which allowed him to play against all those talented kids and to see them play. He played in so many important games with Metro Mirage from fifth to 11th grade. We traveled to play in **FLORIDA***, Tennessee, Nevada, Virginia, and Texas. There's no doubt in my mind that all that prepared him for what he is now.

One thing that has always been evident in Jeremy's development is he's got that balance about him that there's never a moment that's too big. A large part of it is just his discipline of playing ruthless on a basketball court. I've seen it from a young age—whenever his team is up against a good opponent or whenever he's facing tough competition, he glows. Plenty of talented kids will shrink or go and hide in that situation. But Jeremy has always played well. He's focused.

Take that AAU game when he matched up against Ty Lawson in Las Vegas. Lawson, who would go on to play at North Carolina, was considered one of the top five point guards in the country. And Jeremy truly, honestly did not have a problem with him. Jeremy was all over the floor and he was drilling threes. He was never fazed. Jeremy physically could handle the on-ball pressure given by anybody.

---

*The **FLORIDA** Marlins have won the World Series twice but have never won their division—the NL East. The Marlins are the only team that travels north for spring training...In 2012 they changed their name to the "Miami Marlins."

Jeremy knows when it's a big moment and he's always ready for that big moment. As a kid, his Metro Mirage teammates gravitated to him because of how he played and how he treated them on the court, as a team. He made sure everyone was going to get their looks. But ultimately, when things came to crunch time, Jeremy was one of a couple of the kids that we'd give the ball to. Do you remember the game-winner he hit for the Knicks against the Toronto Raptors? That was one of our old plays called Step Up. Basically, the point guard has the OK to walk right up to the top of the key and shoot a three. In that Toronto game, the defender backed off on him, and he just shot the three.

That's a shot he took numerous times when we were in knock-down, drag-out fights throughout his AAU career playing for me. He hit a huge three for Palo Alto High School in a championship game at the end of the shot clock. It's something he's always done. He's always come up big. I've never seen him throw the dice and come up craps. He doesn't throw the double ones. When things are in his realm, he always comes up with seven. Look at what happened when he took it to John Wall in that NBA summer league game. I remember talking to him the night before, and I said, 'This is your big stage right here. You've got to do it now.' He just said, 'I know.'

> It's no secret that Jeremy put in a tremendous amount of hard work to get to where he is now.

It's no secret that Jeremy put in a tremendous amount of hard work to get to where he is now. His motivation has always been his straight desire to be the best kid, to be the best player out there. He wanted to be a guy that played in college. Early on, it was always looking at the scorebook afterwards. He'd look at it like any other kid would. He wanted to see how many points he scored. It's something that every kid and parent are always looking at, especially once the kid starts playing well.

For any coach, it's the easiest thing in the world—if you're teaching them something and they're getting better and they can tell they're getting better, they just want to do it again. As some people would say, they're drinking the Kool-Aid. They just want to keep eating what you're giving them. With Metro Mirage, I made sure we focused a lot on the team aspect of the game, and Jeremy always wanted more. That was just his flat-out desire. He just wanted to keep getting better. I made sure the fundamentals were really ingrained in him, but then he'd work on everything a lot more on his own. The dribbling drills we did constantly, he would be doing the same work over at the Y with his brothers. A lot of that mind-set is his upbringing, his discipline and his will to succeed. He's just taken it to a completely different level.

You have to understand, Jeremy focused so much on sheer fundamentals. I spent an awful lot of time with him on triple threat basketball—dribbling, shooting, passing. I went out to see him play 10 or 12 times at Harvard, and I remember one of the conversations we had while walking the streets of Cambridge. He just looked at me and said, 'Coach, all I'm doing is the triple threat stuff that you ingrained in me as a kid. That's all I do now. I'm so grateful that you taught me that.' As a coach, it makes you well up a little. He's taking these tools and using them to succeed at the next level. He's the one that put in the amount of work needed to play at that level.

So much of what I see with Jeremy right now in the NBA has roots in our old AAU practices. One of the things I teach is attacking the defender's shoulder. All kids, they get the basketball and they try to go around the defender trying to get to the basket. I teach 'Attack the shoulder.' It's very simple, the defender's either going to let you go or he's going to foul you. There's obviously the third possibility where the defender might be quick enough to take an offensive charge, but I don't talk about that. I've had phone conversations with Jeremy in the last 3-4 weeks, and he says, 'All I'm doing is attacking the shoulder, coach, just like you taught me. That's all I'm doing.' Some of the guys in the NBA don't necessarily need fundamentals like that because they're so darn athletic. But those are some of the big reasons why Jeremy is succeeding.

It's funny how Jeremy didn't get the college recruiting attention. Part of it goes back to losing that AAU game to Kevin Durant and Ty Lawson at the Main Event in Las Vegas. That was essentially a sweet sixteen game in that tournament. If we won that game we would have been in the elite eight, and we would have gotten all the college coaches showing up for the game. Half of our team probably would have gotten Division I rides by winning that one game.

Losing that game by five points was one of the toughest things. At one point, we were down by 12, and then we actually came back to grab a two-point lead. By not winning that game, that's where Jeremy gets lost and probably one of the reasons why he wasn't recruited. I'm not saying college coaches weren't showing up for all the Durant and Lawson games. But in the top eight, you're just going to get a lot more guys watching.

> ...Jeremy didn't get the college recruiting attention. Part of it goes back to losing that AAU game to Kevin Durant and Ty Lawson...

No one wants to talk about it, but the college coaches screwed up. Jeremy was right in front of those guys' noses and they didn't see it. Those tournaments are essentially meat markets. The coaches get enamored with the 6-foot-8 kid, the super-fast player and they're locked in. They only get one game and they're locked in looking at one kid. At some point, I heard some coach say that he didn't even know which AAU team Jeremy played on. Everybody gets enamored with the team name, and if they're watching someone else they're not focusing on what's going on in front of them.

That same year, when we were playing 17-and-under, we went down to Southern California for the Best in the Summer tournament. We played two games the first day. That night, a kid passed away after suffering a heart attack on the floor at Loyola Marymount, and they cancelled the tournament at that point. We would have probably played two or three more games. So it was a perfect storm that prevented Jeremy and our other guys from being seen. Something awful happens where a kid dies on the basketball court, and the last opportunity slips away for some kids to be seen by college coaches.

The biggest thing that Jeremy's got over a lot of guys is stuff you can't measure, and that's how he was missed. The sheer discipline, drive, hard work, focus—there's no way to test them. And that's how he slips past a guy who's trying to recruit a kid for his college team. You just have no idea what's really going on in front of you because you can't measure it. Jeremy was a little thinner than everybody, and it's sad enough people would say, 'He's Asian, so how good can he really be?' He's got something. It's just something that you can't measure—that's my best explanation for it. That's exactly how he was missed by college coaches. How did Stanford miss him? He was playing right across the street at Palo Alto High School. They didn't have enough scholarships so they offered him a walk-on spot.

> The biggest thing that Jeremy's got over a lot of guys is stuff you can't measure, and that's how he was missed.

Regardless, I think going to Harvard was one of the best things for Jeremy academically, socially and basketball-wise. To be honest, to get away from mom and dad was another good thing—and there's nothing wrong with that. If he'd gone to Stanford, he would have been real close to home. Mom would have been right there the whole way. There were just a lot of pluses with him going away to Harvard, including a tremendous education. He obviously couldn't beat that. And he got to play right away.

Jeremy got offers to walk on at Stanford and **UCLA***. But at those schools, it probably would've been very similar to what you saw with him in the NBA with the Golden State Warriors and Houston Rockets. They had him at the end of the bench. Jeremy was like the fifth point guard in Houston when he got picked up by the Rockets. He was the fourth point guard when he got picked up by the Knicks. All he was looking for was that window of opportunity. And when he finally got it, he busted through the window.

The first time Jeremy and I really discussed his hopes of playing after college was toward the end of his junior year at Harvard. We sat down at this pub in Cambridge, and he was all ears. I told him, 'You've got one year left. If you want, you may have a chance to play in the NBA.' Jeremy goes, 'I want to play.' I said, 'I know you do.' When we talked, it wasn't so much that we talked about it; it was that it was assumed. He wanted that opportunity. He knew he was close.

From that point on, Jeremy was saying, 'I need to get to work even more.' I connected him with this speed guy I know, a quick coach named Victor Hudson who was working with guys who were applying for the NFL draft. So Jeremy spent time with Victor, getting quicker. Then I met with Jeremy one day and we went for maybe a two-hour workout. We worked on a wide range of things, triple threat stuff, giving him thoughts and ideas of what he could be working with. I'm sure Jeremy was doing the same stuff with Peter Diepenbrock, his Palo Alto High School coach, who was opening the gym for him at Palo Alto or at Cañada College. Jeremy has kept his coaches real close to him. He's got a tight-knit group of guys that he

*Kareem Abdul-Jabbar's role as Roger Murdock in "Airplane" was originally written for Pete Rose.

listens to. He doesn't go to the outside realm and let other people in. He's very introverted in that way. So he was using me and Peter as his information—for ideas and connections. Peter had helped him get into a summer pro-am league earlier. And Jeremy was just gobbling it all up. He'd say, 'What else do you think I need?'

Last year, when Jeremy was mostly sitting on the bench with the Warriors, we talked about him just wanting the opportunity and not getting it. He was not frustrated, but he was getting disappointed. It was hard. There was no doubt it started to wear on him. He just wanted to play. Jeremy said it before and it's true—he was playing it safe at times. When he got sent down to the D-League last year with the Warriors, I told him straight up, 'You need to dominate down there. If you don't compete down there, then this is their way of saying good-bye to you. It's an easy out on their part.'

Getting sent to the D-League last year and then again this year with the Knicks hardened him, there's no question. He needed to go down and take control of games. And that's what he did last year with Reno and that's what he did when he went down for two games with New York this year. He said he rolled his ankle in one of the games but in the other he went for a triple double. We didn't speak when he got sent down by the Knicks, but I'm sure what went rolling through his head was, 'I've just got to go down here and dominate; otherwise it's over with. I may not have a chance to latch on to some other team if I get let go by the Knicks.'

Jeremy and I have exchanged texts back and forth ever since everything exploded this year. I make comments and he writes back and says, 'Yeah, I've got to stop doing this,' and stuff like that. He makes it sound like, 'Thanks for watching.' I'm sure he's getting the information from the Knicks coaches. But he's got me and Peter watching the games, and I'm sure Peter's sending him similar texts to what I'm sending him. I talk with

Jeremy every once in a while. But I don't want to bombard him. He's got so many things going on at this point.

What I see with Jeremy now in the NBA is exactly what I saw—he's just on a bigger stage. Don't get me wrong, it's completely surreal sometimes when I'm watching SportsCenter and they're talking about Jeremy Lin. But what I'm seeing on the basketball court is what I'm used to seeing. We averaged about 35-45 games a year for six years, so that's somewhere close to 200-300 ballgames. And we had practices 2-3 times a week from fifth grade on. So everything I see him do is all stuff that I've seen before.

Playing the way he plays, that's not surprising as much as just seeing his name up on the screen or listening to the radio and hearing, 'Jeremy Lin and the Knicks go to Boston.' Sometimes I can't believe what I'm listening to. But him playing the game this way doesn't surprise me because he's done all this on every level in one way or another.

> ...that's not surprising as much as just seeing his name up on the screen or listening to the radio and hearing, 'Jeremy Lin...

THE SON ALSO RISES

KIRK LACOB

Kirk Lacob is the Golden State Warriors Director of Basketball Operations and the son of team owner Joe Lacob. He grew up a short distance from Jeremy Lin in northern California and began playing basketball with and against him in elementary school through their summers while they were in college.

This really has been a surprise. Obviously, it didn't start with us by any means but Golden State was a pretty significant step in his NBA journey because we were the first team he played for outside of the summer league. We have a personal history going back with my family and him and we're extremely happy for him. We're proud of him. He's a Bay Area native as well so there's such pride in having him do so well. Overall all I can say is that we're really, really happy for the guy and it's great for the NBA, great for the league. and I hope the story continues and goes on and who knows what happens next.

I've known him since we both were in the third grade, the first time we played against each other. He grew up in Palo Alto and I grew up in Woodside, which is about 10 minutes away, and we played against each other in a number of different youth camps.

When I was in fifth grade we played in a regional tournament and his team actually beat mine by 51. For me it was a big moment in my growth. He was the heart and soul of that team and, later, with his high school team.

For me he was really a rival for a lot of the time because I played point guard and he played point guard. We both thought we were pretty good. I wanted to be better than him and his team would usually win. I always thought I would grow up to be taller than him to be honest. I would grow and every year I'd come back and he was an inch taller. And just a bit better.

I always wanted to beat Jeremy. It was amazing to play against a guy like that who just improved every single time out there and really gave it his all. I remember at one point my Dad said "You got to beat him, you can be better than him."

He was the guy I wanted to beat, I always felt that he was my rival. I don't know if he ever felt the same way, but, to me, he was the guy I wanted to beat. The reason was because his team always seemed to win and he was the point guard. It always meant a lot when a team won because it meant the point guard was probably pretty good.

He just had an unbelievable calm and control about him. He was one of the kids who understood where he wanted to be and he never really got rattled. Especially when you're playing AAU ball at a young age and coaches put a full-court press on you, it's very hard for the kid not to get rattled. And there were a lot of bigger, quicker, more athletic kids and he always just remained very, very calm. He was always very good late in games because he played the end of the game just like he played the rest of the game. It didn't seem to matter to him.

He was one of those guys that you didn't think would get by you or you didn't think he would get by that bigger, more athletic guy on the other AAU teams, but he did. You didn't think he was a great **SHOOTER*** and yet he kept hitting shots. On the

*The only person to **SCORE** back-to-back fifty-point games in the history of Long Island High School basketball is Jim Brown, the NFL legend...Jim Brown was selected in the 1957 NBA draft by the Syracuse Nationals.

defensive end he was very annoying, frankly, he would really get into you and he never really stopped, he was go, go, go all of the time.

> No one predicted he would become the size he did because if you look at his parents and even his two brothers, they're not nearly as tall, they're not nearly as big.

I always thought I would wind up bigger than him but he was always just about an inch taller than me. We were both very skinny, he was very, very thin growing up. No one predicted he would become the size he did because if you look at his parents and even his two brothers, they're not nearly as tall, they're not nearly as big. Part of that is a testament to his really unbelievable determination to get to the point where he wanted to get. He got very few looks in high school at first because of his stature, he couldn't have been more than 6-0, 6-1 and like a 155, 160 pounds. You look at him now and he's 6-3, 205.

He was always just a little bit better and not just compared to me, but compared to everyone else. If you had watched one game and watched a guy play, then watched a completely different game with Jeremy in it, you would think the other guy was better. But when they would go head-to-head Jeremy would beat that guy.

Jeremy attended Palo Alto High School and I attended the Menlo School. They're about five or 10 minutes apart, both right in the backyard of Stanford. In fact Palo Alto is literally across the street from the campus. If you're at the football stadium you can see Palo Alto High School across the street. Menlo School was a smaller private school, we were California Division IV. Palo Alto was a mid-size public school, extremely good academically. It's one of the best in the country actually. They were a public school and they were in a different league than us.

It's strange that I grew up playing against him so much on the AAU circuit and yet we never played in high school in a real regular-season game.

We scrimmaged them before the playoffs were starting in our senior year. My head coach at the time was Kris Weems, who played at Stanford and is actually on the Warriors staff now. Kris had worked a lot in the summer with Jeremy, he was a player development coach in addition to his high school job. We scheduled a scrimmage just a couple of weeks after the regular season ended and we were getting ready for the sectional playoffs. We knew they were very, very good. They had lost once all season, and we were quite good as well. I had all of these guys on my team who had played with Jeremy and the rest of us had played against him. Again, it was a measuring stick. We were small, our entire lineup was between 6-1 and 6-3, so bigger guards could go in the post. Coincidentally neither center stood taller than 6-1.

I'm sure no one thought either of us would be real contenders. I actually thought it was a very, very fun, exciting scrimmage. The fact that everyone knew each other made it more competitive. We played them dead even. I don't really know if they kept track of the score or not but for me part of it was going up against Jeremy. I remember that even in a scrimmage the guy was super competitive. He didn't want to really ever take a play off, he pressured me a lot, then I would try to pressure him a lot.

After we finally got eliminated in our playoffs in Division IV we started to follow them and they kept winning. They won the section and the Northern California championships and we started watching the games and going to the games. These were kids we grew up with and it was really, really exciting to see them do well.

I remember in the state championship game they played Mater Dei, who had a 7-footer by the name of Alex Jacobson who is at Arizona right now and had committed by then. Their point guard was Kamyron Brown, who was a four-star recruit then and has since transferred. Taylor King was a five-star all-area kid who went to Duke and Villanova. The Wear twins were freshmen on that team, they're now at UCLA and they were at North Carolina. Andy Brown is now at Stanford. They were an incredibly talented team and they were ranked number four in the country. I remember being at a friend's house for a family get together and we all gathered around the TV and watched the Palo Alto state championship game. On one hand we couldn't believe these guys were doing what they were doing, but on the other hand we knew just how tough they were.

It was a close game going into the fourth quarter. I remember thinking, "everybody's talking about this Kamyron Brown kid and Jeremy is killing him, he can't get by him". Jeremy would just score at the opportune time. He banked in a three with no time on the shot clock with about a minute to go to give them a five-point lead. That sent them on to win by five or seven, somewhere in there, and they won the state title. We were actually all jumping up cheering because we were so excited for those guys. Little did we know it would get so much more exciting later on for the rest of us.

We were all looking to play basketball in college and, frankly, we all came out of a wealthier suburban neighborhood. Blake and I played at a smaller, private school while in Jeremy's case, playing at a very academically-focused public school, people don't really look at you the same. The amount of recruitment was much, much lower. All of us wanted to go to Stanford, we all wanted to play, it was all our dream. I hadn't really talked to him about it because, in a sense, we were all competing. We all made very different decisions, which, now, is unbelievable because of the path it took the three of us on.

Stanford offered me a walk-on spot. I was choosing between playing Division Three or going to Stanford or trying to walk on at Duke. I don't know whether Blake or Jeremy were offered walk-on spots or if they wanted a scholarship. But Jeremy ended up going to Harvard. It was a relief to me knowing that. It would be tough to compete against him to make the Stanford team and to get playing time in the future.

> We were all looking to play basketball in college and, frankly, we all came out of a wealthier suburban neighborhood.

Blake actually went to Williams College, a Division Three powerhouse that won a national title while we were in high school. So we took three very different paths.

I was a walk-on my freshman year and ended up starting a club program at Stanford. I was a practice player in the spring and the summer with the team. Jeremy would come back over the summer and play with the Stanford guys and I was in those groups. It just seemed over the years that Jeremy got better and better.

We watched Jeremy from afar, Blake and I would talk about it. He came back to play Stanford our sophomore year. I was a student at Stanford and had finished playing on the **VARSITY*** level. I was still very close with Landry Fields, a great player at Stanford. They were all talking about Jeremy Lin, "he's doing really well". The entire team, all they could talk about was "we're going to shut down Jeremy Lin, he's not that good." And they did. It was the worst game of his college career. He was embarrassed to be in front of his friends and family and play so poorly.

***VARSITY** is the British short form for the word University.

By senior year Jeremy has made the **ESPN*** Top 100 list. Harvard had an upset victory over Boston College and he was starting to get on the map. Landry Fields of course, was having a really, really good senior season at Stanford and Blake was averaging over 20 a game at Williams. He ended up being the D-3 National Player of the Year. Jeremy came so close to putting Harvard in the NCAA Tournament for the first time in 50 years. I'm just sitting there thinking, "Wow, imagine if they had all ended up at Stanford." The three of us could have all been there together and the starting lineup would have been Jeremy Lin, Blake Schultz, Landry Fields. Now Landry and Jeremy are the starting backcourt for the Knicks.

When I got involved in the Warriors Blake had gone overseas to Germany to play and was having a pretty good season. Jeremy was on the Warriors by then and his parents came up and said that the three of us should start a blog so people can follow the path that the three of us have taken. We all made such different college decisions. Jeremy is now in the NBA playing for his hometown team, Blake's playing overseas and is probably going to go to med school afterwards and Kirk, you're working for an NBA franchise which is clearly your dream. Who knows what's going to happen in this sport, it would be interesting to chronicle it. We never ended up formally putting something together.

I never saw any racism but I'm sure when they played in the big national tournaments kids talked trash to him. It really would not have surprised me because it would even happen

---

*There have been almost 400 self-serving *SportsCenter* commercials. The only athlete to turn down an **ESPN** ad was Bill Buckner. ESPN wanted to shoot him alone in a utility closet covered in dust. An anchor would open the closet, push some mops aside, and there would be Buckner. The anchor would ask Buckner if he was okay, and Buckner would say, "No, I'm not good." The anchor would then turn out the light and walk away.

to me and I'm not Asian-American, I'm white. At one point I wore sports goggles and I really got it from some guys. But I doubt it really ever rattled him or bothered him. I remember him saying, "Honestly, I am Asian-American, but what I really am is a basketball player. I'm very proud to be Asian-American and I really want to embrace that, but I'm also just a basketball player. That's what I want to be known as."

> I never saw any racism but I'm sure when they played in the big national tournaments kids talked trash to him.

There were other good Asian-American players, I think there was another one on his AAU team who at one point may have been a better player in some people's eyes. He was bigger, he was stronger. Unfortunately, that kid was 5-10 in the sixth grade and never grew. He went to another high school in Palo Alto and I played against him. He was still 5-10 our senior year in high school. There were other good Asian players. Obviously, the Bay Area has a very, very large Asian population. I guess in this part of the country it doesn't matter as much, it really wasn't surprising to see an Asian basketball player. I don't think we've seen one on the college level.

I do honestly believe it hurt his college recruitment, I really do. There are plenty of guys who are very skinny and lanky but they'll take you because they see your ability to get bigger, or they'll see your athleticism or your speed. Why wouldn't you give him the same benefit of the doubt?

We're still good friends. I hadn't talked to him a whole lot his senior year in college, I mostly saw him during the summers when we were in college. When he was playing in the summer league that was right around the time we took over the Warriors and he'd had that terrific fourth quarter against John Wall. I'm very, very much a basketball junkie and watched tons and tons of the summer league games. I actually begged my Dad to take me on a trip to Las Vegas for a week so I could go watch the games. Part of that was that I knew that Jeremy was with Dallas and I wanted to see him play. To see someone you know get an opportunity like that is really unbelievable. I saw him and I always thought he was good but I never knew if he was good enough to be an NBA player.

The Warriors ended up offering him a contract. He joined the team and we rekindled our friendship. I was careful not to be clearly too close to him because I didn't want to hurt him in the eyes of the other guys. It was clear that my Dad did like him and you never want to put a guy in a position where other players feel like someone is being favored. I feel a very big connection to the young guys, I still do. I run our Player Development now for the Warriors and I'm very involved as the GM of our minor league team for us.

> It was clear that my Dad did like him and you never want to put a guy in a position where other players feel like someone is being favored.

When Jeremy went down to Reno last year I would go and visit him every time. We felt that was very important and not just to Jeremy, we feel it is very important to spend time with those guys. I took him out to dinner down there just to check on him and see how he was doing. I knew that he was not having an easy time of it. He was a great soldier about it. If you told him to go to the D-League, he wouldn't necessarily put his head down but he'd let you know he wasn't happy about it.

He'd say, "I understand, it's in my best interest." I talked to him and said, "Look Jeremy, you know I'm not going to lie to you. You need to play."

I would spend time with him down there and we would talk about different things. He would ask me "Honestly, what are my chances?" He was a guy who just so badly wanted to get there and I do remember a conversation we had right before the lockout. I knew I wasn't going to get to talk with him for at least a little bit and he said "What do you want me to do this summer? I'm really excited about next year, getting an opportunity. Is there anything you think I should be doing?"

I told him, "Jeremy, just keep working hard, you'll get your opportunity." He looked at me and said "I'm telling you one thing Kirk. I'm never going back to the D-League. I will not, I can not go back to the D-League." I know he's said this now in interviews but I really remember him saying "I will not go back. I will do anything that is humanly possible not to go back. I was very appreciative of my time there, I think I learned a lot and I'm actually happy that I had the opportunity to get better with Coach Musselman. But I'm never going back. That's my goal and I'm going to stick to it."

That's just a testament to how he is. I don't want to put him on a pedestal and say the guy has a complete never-say-die attitude. He has his own doubts and he's mentioned that in the press. He had his doubts about himself and there were times when he would complain about things.

But he has a very, very intense competitive drive, he really does. He wasn't happy at all when the Knicks sent him down. I've talked him to him since he was no longer a Warrior. I stayed in touch with him while he was in Houston and then New York. I try not to get too close to the situation because I can't tell him, you know, this could happen or that could happen. He is very respectful about things. He says "Hey, if you can't talk about it to me, feel free not to talk about it." We've talked off and on.

When he first started playing in New York I sent him a couple of congratulatory messages, he and Landry, saying "hey guys, it makes me really happy to see you guys do well." He'd respond with "thanks, it really means a lot that you're still keeping in touch." I know the D-League, being down in Erie, you can tell that he was absolutely crushed. He was incredible the one game he played there. He was really, really incredible.

I've sent him congratulatory messages saying, "Hey, you're doing a great job, keep it up, congrats," or "my brother says 'hi', he's really happy about it. How's your brother doing?" That type of thing.

The first game he played with the Knicks was when the **KNICKS*** came to play the Warriors in Golden State. I know people forget about that now but when he first got signed by the Knicks he was already at home in Palo Alto. He didn't have to travel to meet the team, he just went to practice the day before we played them. I went down and talked to he and Landry before the game on the floor just to catch up with those guys. I try not to bother him with things going this crazy because he doesn't need any more distractions, he's got enough people trying to flock to him. All I want to tell him is to continue and hope you do well.

The attention is tough for anybody. He does have a good head on his shoulders. He understands. He's very sincere when he says things like "I understand that there's a big story about me but I don't really want it to be all about me." He's being sincere when he says that. He's really not an arrogant person. He's got a little bit of cockiness but he's not a selfish person, definitely not super self-absorbed.

He went through a lot last year here and I always felt a little bit bad for him because I really wanted him to succeed. I thought he could do it, though obviously not to this extent. I know it was very tough and in some ways I think it toughened him up.

*It is true that former NBA **KNICKS** Coach Pat Riley never played college football, but was drafted by the Dallas Cowboys. His father Lee Riley was a major league baseball player. His brother, Lee, Jr. played seven years in the NFL with the Eagles, Giants and New York Titans. It is not true that Pat Riley combs his hair with a pork chop.

Being around your family and friends and local media in the San Francisco Bay Area, which has such a large Asian population, he got so much attention all of the time here. The crowd would go crazy every time he checked into games. I'm sure there were times when other players on our team, veteran players, didn't think it was warranted.

It might have made him a little better prepared for this. New York is a completely different animal, don't get me wrong. He's in the center of the spotlight now. But he had a taste of it when things were going tough, too, here. Early last year was a tough period for him and he went through a lot of people wanting to talk to him all of the time. He was having trouble with his own feelings about not playing while people are talking to him about this and that. At some point writers starting writing about him being just a marketing ploy. He had to sit there and read that and he's like, "This stinks, I wanted to play for my hometown team. Now they're saying that I'm not a real player."

There is no way I would have predicted that Jeremy would be on the cover of back-to-back **SPORTS ILLUSTRATEDS*** and featured on the cover of Time, absolutely not. I knew that with his background if he became any sort of NBA player it would be a pretty big deal in the media. No one could have predicted this. For his first 10 games he was averaging like 24, 25 points and 9 assists. Nobody does that. He broke records. You can't predict anyone to do that, let alone somebody who went undrafted. I don't care what the record is before, for a guy to go undrafted

---

***SPORTS ILLUSTRATED** first published in 1954 and its first swimsuit issue was in 1964. The *Sports Illustrated Swimsuit Issue* has 52 million readers, 16 million of them are females...12 million more than normal...In 1955, S.I. selected horse owner William Woodward as their Sportsman of the Year. Woodward's wife shot and killed the unfaithful Woodward before the issue went to press. S.I. then selected World Series hero, Johnny Podres.

and put up the numbers he put up? And not just put up numbers. Guys put up numbers at the end of the season when you're out of the playoffs. He was putting up numbers in the middle of the season and winning games for a team that wasn't winning much before.

The only thing I can add is that there's a lot of people out there who I read about trying to take credit for Jeremy's success. I get a lot of people e-mailing me saying I did this for Jeremy, I did that for Jeremy, you should interview me. Look, the guy who did this was Jeremy Lin. This guy worked unbelievably hard to built the body that he's built, to build the skill set that he's built.

> All of the credit should go to Jeremy. He worked hard and when his time came he took complete advantage of it.

People were making fun of his shooting stroke last year. At one point a scouting report I read on him said he was a below average athlete and a great shooter. I was like, I don't know who's watching him but that's not the kid I played with. He struggled to shoot, he had a funky shot, he was a very good athlete with good size, but he struggled to shoot the ball. He worked all summer with one great local shooting coach, a guy named Doc Scheppler.

All of the credit should go to Jeremy. He worked hard and when his time came he took complete advantage of it. We are definitely some of his biggest fans.

GYM DANDY

KEVIN TRIMBLE

Kevin Trimble and Jeremy Lin were teammates at Palo Alto High School and remain close friends. They first met when they played in a YMCA basketball league in Palo Alto, Calif., when they were 9 years old. At Palo Alto High, they won a state championship as seniors, stunning nationally-ranked Mater Dei of Santa Ana, Calif., to complete a 32-1 season. Whenever Lin returns to the San Francisco Bay Area, Trimble makes sure they meet up to play basketball, grab some late-night eats and play video games. Trimble is an audit staff associate at Ernst & Young and lives in Menlo Park, Calif.

Jeremy and I first played basketball together at the YMCA when we were in about third grade. It was in the summer, so it wasn't competitive at all. My dad was the coach of that team. So now I joke around with my dad, 'Oh, you made Jeremy the great player that he is.' I don't remember a lot from that time. But I talk with my dad and he tells me about how Jeremy could score on anyone he wanted to, whenever he wanted to, even in third grade.

Then in our sophomore year at Palo Alto High School, I started hanging out a lot with Jeremy. He was just a normal kid. There wasn't anything different about him. One of the things we did was we'd work out a lot away from our basketball practices. We'd always play this game called "Tip It" on a short hoop. We'd pretend to be NBA superstars and do crazy dunks. We'd play little games like that a lot. We'd also get late night shooting in together and then get food afterwards. In Northern California, everyone loves to go to In-N-Out for burgers, so we'd go there at 11 p.m. But now when Jeremy is back in the Bay Area, we have to go to Denny's because he says it's more nutritional.

We also like playing video games and poker, and enjoy just hanging out with the guys. We don't really go out on the town with Jeremy. He's not that kind of guy. Recently, Jeremy bought this Xbox game called Dance Central, and he said, 'Do you want to come over and play?' I'd never played before, and it ended up being pretty funny because we didn't know how to dance. Basically, you dance in front of a camera that senses your motion. So we'd dance in front of the TV for 2 minutes, trying to figure things out. Our friend Kheaton Scott, another Palo Alto High teammate, could actually dance, so he'd always win.

There's one joke from our high school days that we still give him crap for. He always gets mad when we talk about it, but it's fine. Our junior year, Jeremy was already the best player on the team. Meanwhile, Kheaton and I didn't play unless it was the last 3 minutes of the game and we were winning in a blowout. One day, while having lunch, we were joking around with our friends from the girls basketball team who had just lost a game. Kheaton and I are making fun of them because they'd lost, just like typical high school boys would. Then Jeremy comes in and he decides to make a joke at our expense. He goes, 'What're you guys laughing at? All you ever do is get me water.' It was pretty funny. And then Kheaton says, 'Maybe you shouldn't have said that.' It was one of those humorous moments, and we still give Jeremy crap for that today. That's the funny moment that always sticks out when I think of Jeremy.

What was it like to basketball with Jeremy? It was nice. It was easy. It was awesome. He made it so easy for everyone. He could take charge of the game. We could rely on him to have the ball in his hands, and it was fun to watch just to see some of the stuff he did out there. At the time, we knew he was definitely better than us. We knew he was going to play in college.

One game early in our senior year sticks out. We were playing down at this tournament in San Luis Obispo. Jeremy had some back pains in the preseason, and I guess his back wasn't feeling so well that day. It was our last game there, and we weren't playing for anything. It was like a third- or fourth-place game. At that point, we all just really wanted to go home because we were really upset that we'd lost for the first time that year. Anyway, we were playing this good athletic team from Bakersfield, and Jeremy just goes out there and throws out a triple double like it was nothing. Even though that game didn't really mean anything—it wasn't for league, it wasn't for a championship—and nobody wanted to be there, Jeremy played out of his mind to lead us to the win. And we didn't lose again after that.

When Jeremy was at Harvard, I didn't get to see him play much because I went to Wake Forest. But I'd try to follow the box scores to see how he was doing. No one was talking about him at the time because Harvard obviously doesn't get any press. One time, when Harvard had a road game at George Washington, I went up to see the game with our friend Kheaton Scott, who was at school in D.C. Even though Harvard lost, Jeremy played incredible. I'm sure that George Washington had no idea that this 6-foot-3 kid was going to come into their building and make them look stupid. Watching moments like that, it was just really cool to see how good Jeremy was. But even then, I still wasn't thinking, 'Wow, he's ready for The Big Show. He's going to be in the League.'

Even though Jeremy played for the Golden State Warriors right here in the Bay Area during his first season, it didn't really sink in that he was playing in the NBA. I'm not necessarily sure why. But when I saw him put on a Knicks jersey this year, that's when it really hit me. 'Wow, he's playing in the National Basketball Association. He's playing on the same team as Carmelo Anthony and Amar'e Stoudemire. He's playing for the Knicks right now, one of the most storied franchises in sports history.' That's when it was like, 'Whoa, this is actually happening.' Even though he wasn't really playing at that point, seeing him in the Knicks jersey made it real.

But no one could have predicted his meteoric rise. It's just incomprehensible what's been happening. An Asian-American coming into the league just doesn't happen, especially someone with his story. So obviously everyone's going to jump all over it. But it's just so strange that that's all everyone is talking about. Everyone knows who Jeremy Lin is. Even last year, you could have a conversation and say he was on the Warriors, and people would have no idea who he was. Linsanity—and I don't even like to use that word—it's just so incomprehensible how all of that happened. But it's awesome to see it. I just hope it dies down so he can focus on playing basketball.

A few weeks ago, some of my old teammates and my high school coach were planning to go to New York to see Jeremy play. I was on the fence about making the cross-country trip, and then Jeremy hit that game-winning shot against the Toronto Raptors. I heard about that shot while I was stuck in traffic driving home from work. I was on the phone with Kheaton, and he was giving me the play by play of what was happening. In the closing seconds, he's like, 'Jeremy has the ball at the top of the key. Five, four, three...' And then he stops. Then all of a sudden he just starts yelling, and I knew exactly what had happened. It was amazing. And after that play, I'm like, 'Well, we're going to New York now. We have to go.' So that night we booked our flights.

It was just incredible to see him play at Madison Square Garden. All of the old Palo Alto High players got to sit together at the game. It was awesome. We got to stand by the court beforehand to watch the players warm up, and then we got booted. We had to go up to our nosebleeds. Our seats were in the second-to-last row, and there were about 10 of us up there. Once

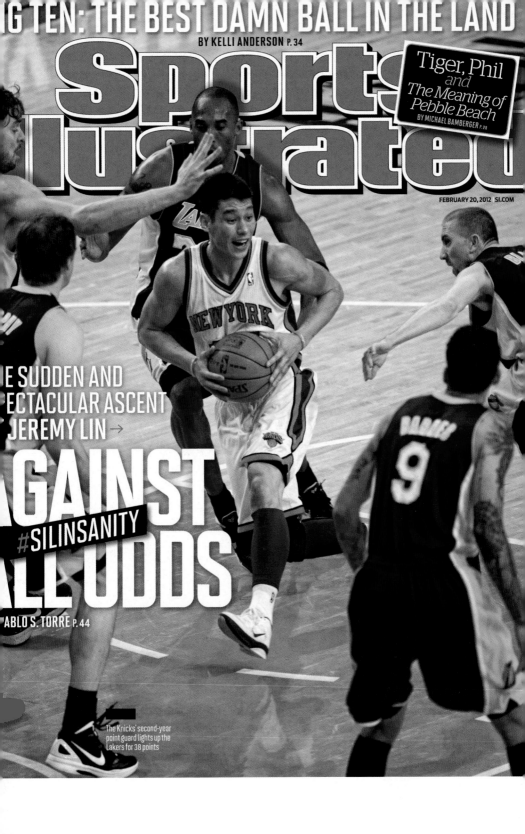

IG TEN: THE BEST DAMN BALL IN THE LAND

BY KELLI ANDERSON P. 34

Sports Illustrated

FEBRUARY 20, 2012 | SI.COM

Tiger, Phil
and
The Meaning of
Pebble Beach
BY MICHAEL BAMBERGER P. 28

E SUDDEN AND
ECTACULAR ASCENT
JEREMY LIN →

GAINST
LL ODDS

#SILINSANITY

ABLO S. TORRE P. 44

The Knicks' second-year
point guard lights up the
Lakers for 38 points

Jeremy Lin greets Yi Jianlian before a Knicks-Dallas Mavericks game at Madison Square Garden.

Jeremy Lin attends a Columbia-Harvard game with former Harvard teammates Dan McGeary and Andrew Pusar

The Best Sports In Town®

ALL LIN!

Amar'e who? Harvard hero saving Knicks

Jeremy Lin was overlooked by the NBA despite dominating the Ivy League at Harvard (right). Now that he has gotten a chance to play for the Knicks he is proving the Crimson produce more than just presidents. PAGES 72-73

The Best Sports In Town®

MAY THE BEST MAN LIN

Jeremy vs. Kobe tonight at MSG

PAGES 93-90, 83

The Jeremy Lin Show returns to the Garden tonight when the Knicks square off with Kobe Bryant and the Lakers. Lin, who has gone from bench-warmer to phenom in less than a week, has led the Knicks to three straight victories since being installed as the point guard by Mike D'Antoni.

NEW YORK POST

SUPER **ports** ATURDAY

FEBRUARY 11, 2012

LINSTANT KARMA

Harvard hero turns Knicks into fun bunch

Steve Novak and Jeremy Lin whoop it up in the Knicks' win over the Wizards Wednesday. Lin's energy and stellar play has brought life to a listless team. VACCARO, BERMAN / P. 54-55

NEW YORK POST

SUPER **Spo** SATURDAY

FEBRUARY 11, 2012

Jeremy scores 38 in Knicks' win over Kobe, Lakers

LINCREDIBLE!

New sensation Jeremy Lin celebrates his 38-point masterpiece in the Knicks' thrilling 92-85 win over the Lakers. COMPLETE COVERAGE / PAGES 55-52, 46

NEW YORK POST

SUNDAY Sports

FEBRUARY 12, 2012
★★ R

JEREMY WIN!

BERMAN, VACCARO, BONTEMPS / P. 103-99

Lin sinks go-ahead FT as Knicks notch fifth straight

Jeremy Lin went cold in the second half in Minnesota last night, going just 1-for-12 from the field. But he sank the go-ahead free throw with 4.9 seconds left in the Knicks' 100-98 victory over the Timberwolves, their fifth straight win.

TIGER MAKES PEBBLE PUSH
Makes move with 5-under third round: Cannizzaro / P. 87-86

POWER RANGERS
Down Flyers again: Brooks / P. 80

NEW YORK POST

SUNDAY Sports

FEBRUARY 12, 2012

LUCKY LIN

BERMAN
PAGE 103

D'Antoni: Jeremy got a bunch of breaks

It took a combination of injuries and poor play from Baron Davis, Iman Shumpert and Toney Douglas before Jeremy Lin cracked the Knicks' lineup. But Lin finally got his break, and he is taking advantage. "You have to have luck in this league," coach Mike D'Antoni said, "and he got a bunch of luck."

TIGER MAKES PUSH AT PEBBLE
5-under third round puts Woods in striking distance PAGES 87-86

SUNDAY Sports

FEBRUARY 12, 2012

POWER RANGERS
DOWN FLYERS AGAIN: BROOKS / P. 80

NEW YORK RANGERS

Knocks down
go-ahead FT
as Knicks notch
fifth straight

JEREMY WIN!

Jeremy Lin went cold in the second half in Minnesota last night, going just 1-for-11 from the field. But he sank the go-ahead free throw with 4.9 seconds left in the Knicks' 100-98 victory over Ricky Rubio and the Timberwolves, their fifth straight win. **BERMAN, VACCARO, BONTEMPS / PAGES 103-99**

PHIL ROCKS TIGER, WINS PEBBLE
LEFTY FIRES FINAL-ROUND 64; WOODS SKIES TO 75: CANNIZZARO / PAGES 66-67

MONDAY, FEBRUARY 13, 2012

NEW YORK POST

www.nypost.com

The Best Sports In Town®

Melo, Amar'e
have to fit in
with new
Knick star

LIN &
BEAR IT!

BERMAN, BONTEMPS
PAGES 68-69, 61

Jeremy Lin, driving to the hoop during the Knicks' victory Saturday night in Minnesota, says he doesn't expect any chemistry problems to develop when Amar'e Stoudemire and Carmelo Anthony return to the lineup. "We just have to find a way to quickly come together and ride this momentum," Lin said.

The Best Sports In Town®

VaLINtine's Gift

Amar'e will love playing with Jeremy

Amar'e Stoudemire will be teamed with Jeremy Lin in Knicks starting lineup for first time tonight when they visit Toronto. **COVERAGE: PAGES 67-62.**

The Best Sports In Town®

Toronto gripped by Linsanity

YO, CANADA!

Jeremy Lin, being sandwiched by the Raptors' James Johnson (left) and Jose Calderon last night, is drawing crowds on and off the court these days. Toronto issued 76 extra media credentials for last night's Knicks-Raptors game on Asian Heritage Night at the Air Canada Centre. PAGES 79-76, 3

NEW YORK POST · Page Six

WEDNESDAY, FEBRUARY 15, 2012 / Cloudy, 53 / Weather: P. 36 ★★ **LATE CITY FINAL** www.nypost.com · · · · · 75¢

Jeremy wins it in last second

COMPLETE COVERAGE: PAGE 3, SPORTS

THRILLIN'

WEDNESDAY, FEBRUARY 15, 2012 — **NEW YORK POST** — www.nypost.com

The Best Sports in Town®

Lin's 3-pointer with 0.5 left extends win streak to six

Jeremy Lin drills a 3-pointer over Jose Calderon with a half-second left to give the Knicks a 90-87 victory over the Raptors on Asian Heritage Night at the Air Canada Centre last night in Toronto.
Lin took over down the stretch, scoring the last six points as the Knicks rallied from a 17-point deficit.

PAGES 79-76, 73, 3

RANGERS BLANK BRUINS
LARRY BROOKS / PAGE 70

AMASIAN!

The Best **Sports** In Town®

Jeremy's trey at 0.5 extends Knicks' streak to six

THRIL**LIN'**

Jeremy Lin drives to the hoop during the Knicks' 90-87 victory over the Raptors last night in Toronto. The Knicks trailed most of the game, but Lin, who scored 27 points and handed out 11 assists, drilled a three-pointer with a half second left to push the winning streak to six. PAGES 79-76.

The Best Sports In Town®

Pass-happy Lin gets streaking Knicks to .500

DISH UPON A STAR

COMPLETE COVERAGE PAGES 69-64

Let the Linsanity continue. Jeremy Lin, wrapping a pass around DeMarcus Cousins, notched a career-high 13 assists to go with 10 points in less than three quarters as the Knicks won their seventh straight with the Harvard Hero running the show, pounding the Kings 100-85 last night at the Garden.

The Best Sports In Town

LIN THERE DONE THAT

Joba to Jeremy: Enjoy the ride

New York City is riding a wave of Linsanity, much as it did in 2007 when Jobamania gripped the region. The Yankees' Joba Chamberlain (inset) said Knicks sensation Jeremy Lin should relish his time in the spotlight, but understand that there are tough times to come. **KEVIN KERNAN / PAGE 67**

NEW YORK POST

Page Six

FRIDAY, FEBRUARY 17, 2012 / Clearing, 53 / Weather: P. 38   **METRO EDITION**   www.nypost.com   75¢

Bring 'em on!

NEW ORLEANS HORNETS · MAVERICKS · NETS · ATLANTA HAWKS

LIN'S KNICKS GO FOR MSG SWEEP WEEK   SEE SPORTS

GOV'S CLASS ACT

Gov. Cuomo scored a major victory yesterday when officials reached a "historic" deal with the state teachers union on a teacher-evaluation process. The move ensures more than $1 billion in federal education funds tied to a new rating system.

PAGE 7

Gets union to OK teacher evaluations

NEW YORK POST

SUPER Sports SATURDAY

FEBRUARY 18, 2012

CAN'T LIN 'EM ALL

Knicks' 7-game win streak snapped by woeful Hornets

The Knicks' Linsane seven-game win streak ended in unexpected fashion. A dejected Jeremy Lin scored 26 points but committed nine turnovers in the Knicks' 89-85 loss to the 7-23 Hornets last night at Madison Square Garden. The Knicks fell under .500 at 15-16. **COMPLETE COVERAGE PAGES 61-56**

SPRING TRAINING PREVIEW

YANKEES, METS FACE QUESTIONS IN CAMP / PAGES 103-98

SUNDAY Sports

FEBRUARY 19, 2012

COUNTER POINT

NEW YORK BASKETBALL

Jeremy no lock to keep starting job if Baron plays well

MELO LIKELY NO-GO VS. MAVS PAGE 79

Jeremy Lin's stellar play over the past two weeks may have saved Knicks coach Mike D'Antoni's job, but that doesn't mean Lin's job as starting point guard is safe. If Baron Davis plays well once healthy, D'Antoni said picking a starter "could be tough." **GEORGE WILLIS / PAGE 106**

SUNDAY

NEW YORK Sports

FEBRUARY 19, 2012

NEW YORK

WAFFLIN'
Jeremy no lock to keep starting job if Baron plays well

MELO LIKELY NO-GO VS. MAVS
PAGE 79

Jeremy Lin's stellar play over the past two weeks may have saved Knicks coach Mike D'Antoni's job, but that doesn't mean Lin's job as starting point guard is safe. If Baron Davis plays well once healthy, D'Antoni said picking a starter "could be tough." **GEORGE WILLIS / PAGE 106**

SUNDAY

NEW YORK POST Sports

FEBRUARY 19, 2012

DALLAS 41

CHAMPING AT THE BIT
Dirk & Co. next big test for Jeremy's Knicks

Jeremy Lin (right), Amar'e Stoudemire and the Knicks laid an egg vs. the lowly Hornets on Friday. Getting back on track today could be a tough task, as Dirk Nowitzki (inset) and the defending champion Mavericks, who have won six in a row, invade the Garden. **PAGES 107-105, 79**

www.nypost.com

The Best Sports In Town®

NEW YORK POST

CASHMAN KEEPING CLOSE EYE ON CC'S WEIGHT
KING, SHERMAN / PAGES 70-71

BERMAN, VACCARO, SERBY, BONTEMPS
PAGES 75-72, 59

WINSANITY!

Lin, Knicks knock off champion Mavs

Jeremy Lin and Steve Novak are jumping for joy after Novak hit one of his four fourth-quarter treys in the Knicks' 104-97 win over the World Champion Mavs yesterday at MSG. Novak scored 14 points in the fourth quarter, while Lin poured in a team-high 28 and handed out 14 assists.

NEW YORK POST **Page Six**®

MONDAY, FEBRUARY 20, 2012 / Sunny 46 / Weather: P. 20 ★ ★   **LATE CITY FINAL**   www.nypost.com • • •   75¢

Lin-phomania

Jeremy leads Knicks past champ Mavs

PAGES 3, 16 & SPORTS

The Best Sports Town®

GOD'S GIFT
LIN'S PRAYERS ANSWERED
VACCARO / P. 70
EXCLUSIVE

LIFE'S A BEACH

Knicks blow by Hawks on way to Miami

Jeremy Lin and Carmelo Anthony laugh it up during the second half of the Knicks' 99-82 rout of the Hawks last night at the Garden. The Lin-Melo marriage was much smoother than its clumsy first effort, but now comes the real test: a date with LeBron James and the Heat in Miami tonight. PAGES 71-68

THURSDAY, FEBRUARY 23, 2012   *NEW YORK POST*   www.nypost.com

The Best Sports Town®

HEAT'S ON CARMELO
GEORGE WILLIS / PAGE 68

Lin had his prayers answered in Miami

EXCLUSIVE: MIKE VACCARO / P. 71

GOD'S GIFT

A month ago, Jeremy Lin was mired on the Knicks bench and worried about his future. When he went to a pregame chapel service at the arena in Miami, where he and the Knicks will face the Heat again tonight, his lone prayer was not to be cut. The rest, as they say, is history.

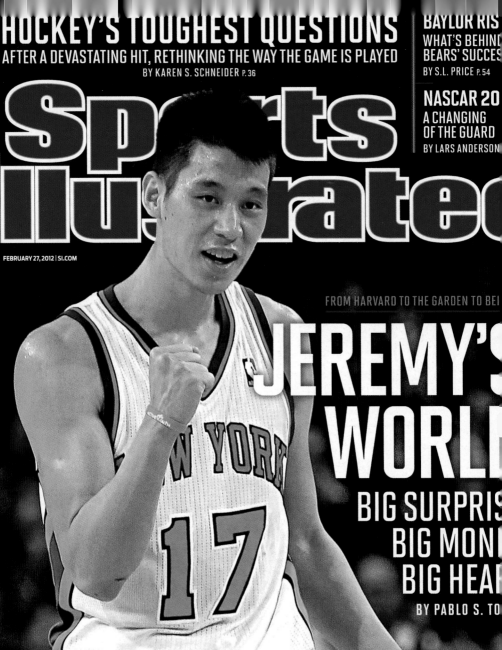

HOCKEY'S TOUGHEST QUESTIONS
AFTER A DEVASTATING HIT, RETHINKING THE WAY THE GAME IS PLAYED
BY KAREN S. SCHNEIDER P. 36

BAYLOR RIS
WHAT'S BEHIND BEARS' SUCCES
BY S.L. PRICE P. 54

NASCAR 20
A CHANGING OF THE GUARD
BY LARS ANDERSON

Sports Illustrated

FEBRUARY 27, 2012 | SI.COM

FROM HARVARD TO THE GARDEN TO BEI

JEREMY'S WORL

BIG SURPRIS
BIG MON
BIG HEAR

BY PABLO S. TO

Jeremy Lin leads the surging Knicks with 28 points and 14 assists in a win over Dallas the game started, Jeremy was just owning the floor. Whenever he did anything, we'd all stand up and scream and clap. It was amazing. I couldn't wipe the smile off my face. I was getting teary-eyed up there just watching him play. It was a once-in-a-lifetime experience. You just don't see your friend play in **MADISON SQUARE GARDEN***. That's not something that happens.

Kheaton and I, we always wanted Jeremy to be better with interviews. So we always try to analyze how good his interview is after the game. It's almost more exciting for me than watching the highlights, just to hear what he says. With all the interviews he's doing now, he's obviously gotten a lot better. It's pretty funny to watch. When he used to get interviewed, even when he first got to the NBA, I don't know if he cared too much. He'd give short answers and he didn't come across as the most personable guy. But now I can see the humor he displays with us when we're hanging out. That humor is coming out in the interviews. Now you can see how confident he is and how much more his personality shows. It's really cool for people to see that side of him as well, instead of just Jeremy the basketball player. Now he's just got to start dressing better. We can't keep seeing him up there wearing hoodies at the postgame press conferences. He's always wearing his New York fleece hoodie. He needs to get better with that. I haven't given him flak for that yet, but I need to.

> Now he's just got to start dressing better. We can't keep seeing him up there wearing hoodies at the postgame press conferences.

---

*When Boston Garden opened in 1928, its official name was Boston **MADISON SQUARE GARDEN**. Boston Garden was replaced by The Fleet Center and was demolished in 1997.

IF YOU'RE LUCKY ENOUGH TO HAVE JEREMY LIN AS YOUR STUDENT, YOU'RE LUCKY ENOUGH

MIKE MCNULTY

*Mike McNulty was one of Jeremy Lin's English teachers at Palo Alto High School. McNulty, who has been a **P.A. ANNOUNCER*** for Palo Alto basketball games, enjoyed watching Lin play all four years in high school. As a senior, Lin was a top student in McNulty's Literature of Sport class. Lin's unexpected rise to NBA stardom was a hot topic among Palo Alto students in that same course. McNulty, who lives in San Jose, Calif., has taught at Palo Alto for 20 years. He was previously a sports information director at Santa Clara University and Gonzaga University.*

I got to know Jeremy Lin through basketball to begin with. I've been a sports fan all my life, so I was always interested in the sports teams at Palo Alto High School, where I'm an English teacher. When Jeremy first got to Paly, we were pretty good at basketball. I remember his coach, Peter Diepenbrock, telling me that this freshman named Jeremy Lin was going to be a great player. Jeremy wasn't very tall at the time—maybe 5-foot-5 or 5-6 at the most—and he probably weighed 100 pounds dripping wet. They called him up to the varsity at the end of the year and we were in the Central Coast Section playoffs. Jeremy came into this postseason game as a raw freshman, and the opponent didn't bother to guard him. He

---

*The **PUBLIC ADDRESS ANNOUNCER** for the Houston Colt '45s (later the Astros) in their 1962 inaugural season was Dan Rather... the P.A. announcer for the Brooklyn Dodgers in 1936 and 1937 was John Forsythe, later a TV and movie star.

took three 3-pointers and he made them all. I've never seen anyone else do that as a freshman. That was the start of his career.

Over the years, Jeremy just kept getting bigger and bigger and bigger. And it was so much fun to watch him because he is a much different player than most of the kids you see in high school. He was so gifted in a lot of different ways. I got to know him fairly well through the course of watching games. I did a lot of the announcing for the basketball games.

Then when Jeremy was a senior, he took a one semester class from me called the *Literature of Sport.* I already knew him fairly well, and I got to know him even better there. I thoroughly enjoyed having him in class—he was a great student. I don't think you can have a much better high school student than he was. He's just a remarkable guy. He was the model student. He sat right in the front row, and he was an exceptionally good writer.

I can't imagine there was anybody in the school that he didn't get along with. He's got a great, even personality. You'd never see him get too high or too low. He was very consistent from a personality standpoint. He was very respectful. There were a lot of people on that campus that liked him—not just because he was a basketball player but because of the type of person that he was. You don't see students like him all the time, and we've had a lot of good students at Paly. Paly is an exceptionally good high school. He stood out because he was so consistent in so many ways.

One of the things that always impressed me about Jeremy is that if you hadn't seen him play basketball, you wouldn't know he played basketball. He was really unusual in terms of a high school student-athlete. He never called attention to himself—it was always about the team. That may sound somewhat like a cliché, but in his case it's really true. He was probably the most unassuming superstar that I've ever seen. Nothing fazed him. He's such a consistent person. Jeremy is Jeremy. He's such a good guy that he's one of those people that you look at and you say, 'There's got to be a flaw someplace.' But I don't ever remember seeing one.

When Jeremy was a junior at Paly, he was the key to one of the best performances I've seen in my life. We had a semifinal playoff game against Sequoia High School, a tough team with some good athletes. We were down 12-8 midway through the first quarter, and from there we outscored Sequoia 43-3 the rest of the half. And it was all because of Jeremy. I don't know what happened, but all of a sudden the switch got turned on and he did everything you could do in a basketball game. He shot the ball, his assists were incredible, he had a steal and a jam ... he basically just took over the entire game and it was over. I was sitting there with two or three people, and we were just stunned. I'd seen him play a lot of games but when I saw that, I just said, 'Oh boy, he's pretty good.'

The day after that game the team had practice, and practice was never enough for Jeremy. After it was over, he went down and played a pickup game at the Y. Unfortunately for a lot of different people, mostly for him, he broke his ankle. It happened when a guy was chasing him from behind. It was an accident, but he was out the rest of the year. Paly won the next game, the Central Coast Section championship game against Archbishop Mitty, but then they lost in the Northern California title game.

When Jeremy was a senior, there were so many games that he played where he was just dominant. The state championship game against Mater Dei ... I've seen a million games, but that was one of the most amazing games I've ever seen. Mater Dei had so much more talent than we did—just pure talent. They had six or seven guys on that team that eventually signed Division I letters. But because of Jeremy, we won the game. He did things down the stretch ... he was at his best when we needed him to be at his best. One thing that always jumped out at me, and you can still see it now in the way he's playing—he makes everybody better. Whatever team he's playing on—because of him and his leadership and his skill level—he always makes everybody better. And that's the mark of the great players. Not everybody does that. But the great players make the players around them that much better, and he's always done that.

During Jeremy's years at Paly, it was a completely different atmosphere in the gym then it was before or has been since. The last two years he was there, they were something like 65-3. It was ridiculous. It wasn't just him. It was the team overall. They had a unique group of people that played on those teams. The team's skill level, and certainly Jeremy's leadership and skill level, it attracted far more than just your crazy basketball fans. A lot of people from the community would come and watch just because of him and the guys that he played with. But he was the dominant player, there was no doubt.

> But the great players make the players around them that much better, and he's always done that.

Ever since everything took off for Jeremy in the NBA this year, there's probably been as much Linsanity at Paly as anywhere else. And Paly is a very laid-back school. It's the type of place where kids are not easily impressed. But they are very impressed with Jeremy Lin. It's been a very, very, very hot topic on campus. It's much different than normal. We have a very large Asian-American student population and he's obviously been a huge inspiration to that group. It's been really interesting for them to experience the success that he's had.

I teach a Sports Lit class, and a lot of it is about what's happening now. So we talked about Jeremy's situation for probably two weeks straight. The class is a little bit different. Every day we talk about a sports column. I have the students sign up and on their day bring in a column of their choice. They tell us who wrote it, they read the column and they explain why they chose it. And that spurs the class discussion. So we had a long stretch there where every column was about Jeremy Lin. It's a great situation for me because we have this ongoing phenomenon that's taking place in New York, of all places, and it involves someone who sat at a desk in that same class. It's really pretty interesting.

When Jeremy had his first big game against the New Jersey Nets, that Monday we started talking about it. It was like, 'Look what's happened. He didn't get a chance and now he's got his chance, and he had a great game.' It just kept building and building and building. The topics have varied. We've talked about the Asian-American connection; about the power of positive thinking.

I start each semester with an exercise. I have the students tell me, 'Why sports? Why do so many people get so involved with sports? Why do we watch it? Why are we so interested in it? Why do we buy all the jerseys and caps?' The kids come up with about 97 different reasons, but very rarely do they come up with the one I'm looking for. My final comment to them is, 'All of these reasons are good. But the one reason we love sports so much is because *You never know*. All the other parts of your life are pretty much predictable. But with sports you absolutely never know, and that's the one thing that fascinates people.' I said, 'There's probably never been a better *You never know* than Jeremy Lin.' If anybody tells you that they knew this was going to happen, it's a figment of their imagination because nobody could see this coming. Maybe he did but not many other people.

It's just so much fun to watch Jeremy have this kind of success. He's such a good guy. I've read everything I can get my hands on. The first couple of weeks, people were always picking on the things he didn't do well. The thing that struck me about that was that these are the so-called experts, and they obviously had no idea who he was and had no expectations of his abilities. So what you have to do is make excuses and explain why you didn't see this if you're the expert. I saw the game he played in the summer league against John Wall a couple years ago, and he was spectacular. Who knows why people make decisions on players? I've always thought there were a lot of scouts—college coaches or professional scouts—that are looking for that guy that's not out there. They're all looking for that guy that really doesn't exist. But in Jeremy's case, he's obviously been overlooked. You can get real nitpicky and say, 'Well, he doesn't shoot it quite as well.' You could play that game forever. But the bottom line is that he plays and he plays well and he's a winner and he makes everybody better. It's tremendously interesting to me to see how he's been received. You don't see this happen too often if at all in the NBA—and he has completely screwed up all the people that are supposedly in the know. It's really funny to watch.

ALL IT TAKES IS ALL YOU GOT

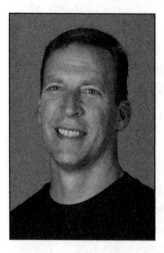

DAVID KIEFER

David Kiefer covered Jeremy Lin's Palo Alto High School teams as a sportswriter for the San Jose Mercury News. *Kiefer remembers profiling Lin as an underrated player that was poised to make an impact as a junior. Kiefer chronicled Palo Alto's 32-1 season in 2006 that was capped by a huge upset win in a state title game. He recalls his surprise that Lin didn't generate any recruiting attention, even among the local collegiate programs. Kiefer believed that Lin's abilities would translate to every level—but only if the guard was given a true opportunity. Kiefer, who lives in San Mateo, Calif., has written about high school sports for most of the past 30 years. He now works as an assistant media relations director in Stanford University's athletics department.*

As a sportswriter for the *San Jose Mercury News*, I covered a bunch of Jeremy Lin's games during his junior and senior years at Palo Alto High School. Paly invited me to their awards ceremony at the end of his senior year, and they had put together one of these books with the clips of all the newspaper articles. They gave one of those books to me, which was really nice. Looking back at that book, I realized what a huge part of that team Jeremy Lin was in every respect. For instance, Palo Alto had a lot of pretty good players—some good shooters and some other guys that really complemented each other, kind of the essence of what a team is all about— but everything went through Jeremy. When I look back on these clips, they describe how, if it was a close game, Jeremy Lin either had the big basket or the big assist or created the play that went to the big basket. Everything had his fingerprints on it. His numbers were good, but they weren't incredible. He averaged about 15 points and somewhere around four assists and six rebounds as a senior. But every time they needed something he made it happen. That was the most impressive thing.

Looking back at the state championship game in Jeremy's senior year, it's hard to imagine how big of an underdog Palo Alto was. Mater Dei's entire starting five was going to be going Division I and a number of players on their bench would eventually go to Division I, including the Wear brothers that are now at **UCLA***. Mater Dei was probably 8-10 deep in future Division I players. And if you look at Palo Alto and the players who went on to play beyond high school, it was just Jeremy Lin and Steve Brown, who played for Chico State. That was it— it was just those two guys taking on a team of possibly 10 future Division I players. For Palo Alto to win that game, it speaks to Jeremy Lin and his leadership, his talent and his ability to make people better. Mater Dei had a 7-foot-1 center in that game. Palo Alto's center was Kheaton Scott, and he was only 6-1. That was a huge illustration of what kind of a favorite Mater Dei was, just based on that alone. It ended up that Kheaton Scott won the opening tip and Palo Alto won the game. It was one of the huge upsets in state history.

Mater Dei was so deep and so talented. Peter Diepenbrock, who was the Palo Alto coach, told me after the game, 'If they just ran us up and down the court, we would have lost. We just didn't have the depth. We would have been dead tired, and they would have probably pulled away in the second half and run away from us.' Instead, Mater Dei decided to play them in a halfcourt game, probably thinking they would win because Palo Alto didn't have much size. So it was a slow-paced game and that totally played into Palo Alto's hands. Of course, Jeremy

*Legendary UCLA coach John Wooden was the first ever 3-time consensus All-American...as a player at Purdue.

Lin is so good at breaking down defenses, it only worked in Palo Alto's favor. Mater Dei may have been smug, thinking, 'We'll play whatever style we want and we'll kill these guys.' But it turned out that they paid for it, for their overconfidence.

Looking back, Jeremy Lin obviously had the leadership skills in high school. On the court, you saw a lot of the same things he's doing now. He was great at driving to the basket, a great passer, just a really good sense of what needs to be done. You could tell that all the Palo Alto guys had played together for years. I believe the big core of them had played together since they were fifth graders. That's what made them so good—they all knew what each other was doing and they all had skills that complemented each other. On the floor, Jeremy was able to put all that together. They all had these talents and skills and team ability, but he was the one that made it all work. This is a cliché, but he was the one who made the whole show possible.

> The ankle injury Jeremy suffered late in his junior year turned out to be a pretty significant moment in his life and career.

The ankle injury Jeremy suffered late in his junior year turned out to be a pretty significant moment in his life and career. The night before Palo Alto was supposed to play Archbishop Mitty High School in the Central Coast Section final, Jeremy went to the Y with his teammate Kheaton Scott. They were just going to shoot some baskets and stay loose; nothing more than that. Somehow they got goaded into joining a pickup game. Jeremy didn't want to do it, but somehow he got talked into it. So he said, 'OK, all I'm going to do is stay on the outside. I'm not going to go inside at all. I don't want to really be part of it all. I'm just going to help pass the ball, just stay out of everything.' And that's how he justified it. So people get competitive. Jeremy was sticking to his plan. There was a turnover and Jeremy was in the frontcourt. They threw him a long pass because he was open down the floor, staying away from everybody. He went up for a lay-up, and a guy came from behind and shoved him and he ended up landing awkwardly and broke his ankle. Jeremy ended up missing not only the Central Coast Section championship game, which they won, but also the Northern California playoffs.

What was interesting about the injury was that people were really down on Jeremy. They were saying, 'What's this guy thinking, playing a pickup game the night before the CCS championship?' He was characterized as a selfish guy and being stupid, which totally goes against what people see in him now. After that happened, people were talking about him behind his back. I decided to ask him what he thought. I was the only one to call him and actually ask him for his side of the story. He picked up the phone and he was like, 'Oh, I'm so glad somebody has finally asked for my side. This is what happened.' He felt like he was being persecuted in some way. He described how he didn't want to play in the pickup game and how he tried to stay out of it and how this guy pushed him from behind, the whole story. I just remember how he felt this sense of relief that he was finally able to get his side of the story out.

So Jeremy missed the rest of the playoffs. After Palo Alto lost in the Northern California finals to Oak Ridge of the Sacramento area, I remember seeing Jeremy in street clothes. He just looked really down, as if he felt responsible. Oak Ridge ended up going on to win the state championship. I think that was the moment that really changed Jeremy. He had that anger and all those feelings pent up, and he took it all out on preparing for the next season and correcting his mistakes. Palo Alto's state championship season was a result of that. I remember seeing an interview recently where he talked about his injury in high school and how that changed his whole outlook on basketball. They don't really talk about it much, but the whole idea of getting hurt before a championship game and the abuse he took and how he felt responsible...that was probably the key to making him the player he became.

Peter Diepenbrock told me that after Palo Alto won the state championship, somebody called or emailed him and told him something like, 'You've ruined this kid because you didn't get him a college scholarship. I watched this guy play in high school and I want to see him play in college and I'm never going to get that chance now because you didn't do your job of getting this guy a scholarship at a school.' And I remember Peter just saying, 'Geez, it's not my fault that nobody's interested in the guy.' But it was a sad feeling that people thought he was just going to drop off the face of the earth—not because he wasn't good enough, but because he just wouldn't get the opportunities. I always felt that he would be good wherever he went—even in the pros. When he started to really excel at Harvard, I was glad because I knew he could do it if he was given the chance, and he did eventually. The same thing with the pros, I just always felt that he could be just as successful if he was given the opportunity. It was just about whether someone would give him a real opportunity. That's why it's so gratifying to see him succeed.

> ...somebody called or emailed him and told him something like, 'You've ruined this kid because you didn't get him a college scholarship.

It was pretty clear that Jeremy was being overlooked in the college recruiting process when, as far as I could tell, he wasn't even getting looks from schools like Santa Clara or San Jose State, much less a Pac-10 school. I just wanted to pull then-Stanford coach Trent Johnson aside and say, 'Do you know what's happening across the street over here? Why don't you watch the guy play?' I mean, look at what Jeremy did with Palo Alto, just the fact alone that they went 32-1. To me, it's that coaches just are not doing their job. Maybe it was because

Jeremy Lin didn't fit in a certain mold or because he didn't go to the right camps or whatever. But it was pretty clear that everybody was missing the boat.

Jeremy was never the type of guy that would score 40 points a game. On the San Francisco Peninsula, top basketball prospects are few and far between coming out of high school. The ones that are really highly recruited are guys like a Drew Gordon at Archbishop Mitty, guys who would just fill up the stat sheet, get triple doubles or whatever, and be really imposing physically. So looking at Jeremy coming out of an area that's not known for having top recruits, he didn't have the specific physical traits that you could see as being a real highly recruitable guy. Yet Jeremy did everything he was supposed to and more, and his team won.

If you cover teams as a reporter enough at the high school level, you have your share of disappointments. There are always guys that you think can be real successful and they never really pan out how you hoped. Jeremy's the type of guy that you'd hope would make it, and he did.

During Jeremy's senior year at Palo Alto, there was another guy—Decensae White from **SERRA HIGH SCHOOL IN SAN MATEO***—who was probably regarded as the best player in the area at the time. I think Decensae had already gotten a scholarship offer from Texas Tech. Jeremy really didn't get the notice throughout the season. He got a lot of Player of the Year awards, but it was after he took the team to state. I wonder if Jeremy didn't win a state championship, if he might not have gotten any area Player of the Year awards. They probably would have gone to Decensae White. So even during Jeremy's rise to prominence on the high school level, he still wasn't regarded as 'the guy'—even though I'm sure he was the best player at the time. It's interesting—he was really overlooked

*SERRA HIGH SCHOOL is the alma mater of Tom Brady, Lynn Swann, and B*rry B*nds.

until Palo Alto started its playoff run. And then, people started to realize, 'Whoa.'

The first time I ever wrote about him for the *San Jose Mercury News* was his junior year. We were doing a high school basketball preview, and I was searching around for a player to do a short profile to go alongside our previews. I was targeting a player who people didn't really know about that might make an impact that year. Somehow I ended up with Jeremy. I don't know how I knew about him, but it's just funny because now people could look back and they'd say, 'Oh, that guy really knew what he was talking about.' But it's just funny how the guy that I ended up picking as the underrated guy who was poised to make an impact was Jeremy Lin.

At Stanford, where I now work, we've talked about Jeremy Lin in the past, and some of my colleagues said, 'Oh, he's going to be a bust. He's never going to make it in the NBA.' Or, 'Oh, he's just lucky he got signed by the Warriors. It was just a PR move. He'll be out of the league by next year.' I remember coming to Jeremy's defense and saying, 'You know what? Just you wait. If he's given a chance, he's going to be a really good player.' And they're like, 'Yeah, right.' And then Jeremy started having these great games this year, and I remember this one guy at work saying, 'All right, I'll give him credit. But he's not going to score 10 points against the **LAKERS***. If he scores 10 points, then I'll concede. But there's no way he's going to do it.' Sure enough, Jeremy scores 38, and so I sent the guy an email and I just wrote two words: 'I win.' And he sent one back, and it had one word: 'Clearly.' So I felt pretty good about that.

Looking at Jeremy in the NBA, I see the same player I saw years ago. I just see that he's stronger now. The biggest thing probably is that he's matured physically and he's really worked on

*Jerry Buss, owner of the Los Angeles **LAKERS**, once owned Market Square Arena in Indianapolis where the Pacers played for many years. Market Square Arena was the venue for Elvis Presley's last concert.

getting stronger. He is the same player now that he was back at Palo Alto—driving to the basket, dishing it off, creating opportunities, playing really good defense, being a leader, being a good shooter when he had to be. Who could've ever foreseen that Jeremy would become the sensation that he is? But anybody who's ever really seen him play knew that those skills and his ability could translate to whatever level he played—it was just whether he would get the chance. That was the big question. It wasn't that he couldn't do it; it was whether somebody would give him the chance to do it.

> **It wasn't that he couldn't do it; it was whether somebody would give him the chance to do it.**

In the Chinese league, we have two foreign imports on each team. They are very good players. This year they are NBA quality. We have J.R. Smith, Aaron Brooks, and Wilson Chandler. These guys are all NBA rotation players. The level of American players here is higher than the NBA D-League. There is probably not an abundance of talent among the Chinese players themselves but they are very competitive and some of them are very experienced basketball players.

Working with Yao Ming's team is refreshing. He's an owner who has an extremely sharp basketball mind. Actually, he's got as sharp a basketball mind—especially when it comes to defense—as you'll find anywhere. The other thing about him is that he is not a meddling owner. He lets you do your job and he supports you. He understands what the timetable needs to be. He's not impatient. He knows it's going to take time to build a successful player. He is very interested in developing Chinese players.

—**DAN PANAGGIO**, Head Coach of Yao Ming's Shanghai Sharks in the Chinese Basketball League

THE DOS AND DON'TS OF DEALIN' WITH JEREMY LIN: DO!

RAYMOND RIDDER

Raymond Ridder is the Golden State Warriors Vice President of Public Relations. He began his career as a public relations intern with the Los Angeles Lakers in 1989 and was promoted to assistant director of public relations in 1993. He is currently in his 14th season with the Warriors.

I was talking with Scott Howard-Cooper from NBA.com the other night and he was telling me that anything they can write about Jeremy Lin, the more the merrier. The number of hits that they are getting on NBA.com for anything related to Jeremy Lin is through the roof, more than anything they've ever had at least in the last few years. It is just absolutely incredible. If you look every night on NBA.com, whether the Knicks win or lose, I guarantee you that there's going to be a picture of him on the home page because he's generating so much traffic to that website. I'm sure it's the same way for ESPN.com, Yahoo and all of them.

The Knicks auctioned off his Lakers game jersey and got $42,000 for their foundation. That's unbelievable, absolutely unbelievable.

He's an unbelievable kid, one of the nicest, most-grounded kids I've met in my 20 years in this business. He's one of those kids that you root for. To be quite honest with you, former players that come through here, I very seldom text them after they leave here. When they come to town we'll say "hi" and exchange pleasantries. After his first game against the Nets when he had 25 points and seven assists I texted him and just said, "Hey, great job." He texted me right back the next day. My point being that I've probably done that twice in my 20 years with a former player, reaching out and congratulating him on a 20-point game or whatever. He's just one of those kids that you want to root for, so grounded, so down to earth, just a class, class act. His fam-

> We had more people show up for Jeremy Lin's media availability session than any press conference we had prior to 2006.

ily, everything about him is fantastic. I couldn't be happier for him, just a tremendous, tremendous kid.

The thing I remember most prominently about him was the week when we signed him in July, 2010. We didn't have a press conference, we had a media availability session here at our practice facility just to introduce him and make him available to our local media, the beat writers, the columnists, the TV people. We ended up having it in our players lounge downstairs and we just plopped him down in a chair in front of a banner, nothing set up where you have a podium and a dais. We had more people show up for Jeremy Lin's media availability session than any press conference we had prior to 2006, since Don Nelson's press conference when we intro-duced him as our new head coach. We had a bigger crowd for Jeremy's media availability session than for any press confer-ence or availability session over the previous four years. It was incredible, our entire players lounge was filled with TV cam-eras, columnists, beat writers, takeout writers. I equate that to him being a local kid who won a high school championship with Palo Alto at Arco Arena, a kid that went to Harvard after being completely overlooked by Stanford. The local kid makes good and now he's coming back to this area!

Just a couple of weeks ago we had a Chinese New Year event at one of our games and I did some demographic research to find out how many Asian-Americans and Chinese-Americans live in the area. There are 500,000 Chinese-Americans in the Bay Area which is number one in the United States. In fact, three of the top four cities in terms of population for Chinese-Americans are in the Bay Area. San Francisco is number one, Oakland is number two and San Jose is number four. So, you put that all together, a local kid that's Asian-American, went to a local high school and won a state championship. All of that added to his notoriety in the Bay Area in terms of why there was so much attention on him early on. Everything fell together in place and that's why we had such a large turnout for a simple media availability. That's the one thing I remember more than anything was just the amount of people that showed up the day we kind of introduced him to the local media.

We have the *Tsingtao Daily* and the *World Journal*, those are a couple of Chinese newspapers in the Bay Area, and we have a couple of Chinese and Asian-American TV stations. One thing we did a good job here dating back to when Yao Ming was in the league was forming a relationship with these outlets. They would come out once or twice a year when Yao Ming and the Rockets were in town. They would only come out on those specific nights. In terms of a typical press conference they would not come out if we signed a free agent or we made a trade. That was pretty much the only press conference when the Asian media came out to my recollection, but then they started to attend more games. They pretty much had to come when Yao came to town but now, early on during the pre-season and the first few games of the regular season, they started requesting credentials every night. I would say that probably about a third of the media for that press availability in July of 2010 were from the Asian-Chinese local media. We even had people come out on a national basis. We had a day or two advanced notice and I remember specifically that we had a crew from Washington and another crew from New York that flew out just for that media availability session.

I worked really closely last year with his agent, Roger Montgomery. We made a concerted effort last year to keep the media at an arm's length. We turned down 80 percent of the requests we got for him. The first three or four months from the time we signed him until two months into the season I had more requests for him than for any player on our roster, and that would include Steph Curry and Monta Ellis. Be it **USA TODAY*** or one of our beat writers, the amount of requests we got for him were overwhelming. We decided early on, who knows, is this kid going to play a lot? Is he going to go to the D-League? Is he going to play 20 minutes a night? So we took the approach that we wanted to keep the media pretty much at an arm's length. He could talk after practice to our local people but in terms of setting up features with national magazines, which we were getting from all over the place, we decided we wanted to basically not put too much pressure on the kid. Looking back on the season it all turned out well. He still got a fair amount of publicity but on the other hand he wasn't overwhelmed with requests and could focus on the basketball part, which was the most important thing for him last year.

What goes along with that is the reaction he got the first few games, dating back to our first pre-season game here and even in the first regular-season games. The second he stood up off the bench to check into a game the crowd would just go ballistic, they would just erupt. Half the crowd would stand up. In all of my years in the league, dating back to Magic coming back after getting the HIV virus and the reception he got when he checked into the game, I've never seen a guy checking into a game in the middle of the first quarter or, in the other case, at

*Minnesota Twins catcher Joe Mauer is the only athlete to be selected as **USA TODAY**'s High School Player of the Year in two sports (football and baseball).

the end of the fourth quarter in garbage time, to have a crowd give that kind of reaction to a player simply when he's standing up to walk to the scorer's table. That's another reason we kept the media at arm's length, to see the scrutiny, the attention and the love affair our fans had for him was just incredible for a guy who was just trying to make it in the NBA. He wasn't a superstar, the kid was just trying to find his way. That reaction simmered down once we got past the first couple of months of the regular season. He went to the D-League a few times and after that he'd still get a reaction when he checked into a game but, in terms of the overwhelming response when half the arena would stand up when he checked in, that dissipated as the season went on. It was just incredible the way the Bay Area embraced him.

> We played in Boston last year and during an off day he went back to Harvard to get his diploma.

We played in Boston last year and during an off day he went back to Harvard to get his diploma. We set up for a local TV crew to tag along with him. I can honestly say in all of my years in the league I never scheduled a crew to follow one of our players to Harvard to pick up his degree. He didn't have a chance with summer league and all of that to walk on graduation day at Harvard so he actually had to go back during our season to get his diploma, which was a neat thing.

I would reach out to Jeremy on several occasions when he went to the D-League three times. I tried to give him a phone call to make sure he was hanging in there. He's one of the hardest-working kids in all of the years since I've been in the league. Typically, he was the first one to practice and the last one to leave.

Media interest from Taiwan and China wasn't overwhelming. Everything was funneled through NBA International Public

Relations so I would say that at the outset we had more than we typically had, but it wasn't anything where we were overwhelmed. The way we worked it out with NBA International PR was only a selected number of international media could come per game. We had two seats or three seats per game for international media. One thing that contributed to that was that they all realized pretty quickly that he wasn't going to play a ton. Once we got through the pre-season and the first four or five regular-season games they knew it was pretty much going to be a developmental year for him and his minutes were probably going to be somewhat limited. That contributed to the fact of having a smaller number of media from that standpoint.

We kept him at arm's length from the media but he was very good, very accommodating. As you can see now on appearances, he's really big on his faith and religion . In terms of him spending the time I would ask him to do he was completely fine with it. He did a good job and always said the right thing. I look at him now and some of the things that impress me more than anything is how he's always crediting his teammates, and that's what he did when he was here. It's not about Jeremy Lin, it's about his teammates that helped him win the game. He's always done a really good job of understanding and trying to deflect the attention from him to credit other people.

When he first got here we got criticized a little bit, not a ton but a little bit. People thought it was a way to sell tickets, a PR thing to bring Jeremy on board. To have him playing with us in the Bay Area, a local kid, trying to sell some tickets. That had very, very little to do with it. Our people knew that potentially he had the chance to be a solid NBA player at some point down the road. We did get criticized a little early on from people that thought it was more of a publicity stunt signing him than somebody we thought had a chance to be a good basketball player, which is exactly what we thought.

Jeremy's had a close relationship with our owner, Joe Lacob, for quite some time. He played AAU basketball with his son, Kirk, who also works for us as Director of Basketball Operations. Joe and Kirk are from the Palo Alto area pretty close to where Jeremy grew up. They watched him all throughout his high school years and that's one of the reasons Jeremy ended up here. Our owner knew a little bit about him and thought he had a chance to be an NBA player at some point in time.

We did a little more with Jeremy in the Asian community. We do a certain number of events every year in the Asian community so when we did those we targeted him to be part of those events. Players are required to do a couple of community events per year so we just tried to strategically align him with the ones we did with the Asian community, even though they were scheduled before he was here. We did a little more than we normally would have but during the NBA season he couldn't do all of the requests. We got so many from the Asian community for him to read books to kids in schools or to go make an appearance somewhere. We had to reach a happy medium there where he did some of those, but the other ones we had to turn down. We tried strategically to fit it to where he would be the one to make an appearance whenever we went into the Asian community. In the past we sent any random player but this time we wanted to align him with that specific demographic and he was great about that.

We also have basketball camps every summer and that first summer he got here in 2010 we had a camp over in Palo Alto for a group of about 100 junior high school and high school kids, where he spoke to the kids. He was more than willing to do all the of the extracurricular things you might want a player to do. He was happy to do that kind of stuff, very accommodating. We would send out an advisory just saying that a player is going to be speaking to a group of kids at a basketball camp and typically you'd get maybe one media outlet to show up. The first we did in Palo Alto with Jeremy, which was after his initial press conference, we had four or five local media outlets that went to go cover it, just because, again, it was Jeremy Lin in the Palo Alto area where he went to high school. It might give you an idea of the attention that was bestowed upon him. We would get more reaction sending him somewhere than one of our veteran players who had been on our team previously.

I don't think there was a specific foundation or anything that he worked with when he was here, any type of special group. Whatever we aligned him with is what he did. His first year he was pretty much focused on just playing basketball. Keep in mind he was gone from here for at least half of the season when he was in Reno with our D-League team. He only played in 20-some games for us. There was no special community outreach group that he was actively involved with. He got involved with whatever direction we pointed him in.

We didn't want to release the kid. Our back-court was our strength with Monta Ellis, Steph Curry and some of the other players we have, the wing players. We've struggled recently at the "five" position so we wanted to make an offer to DeAndre Jordan, who was a restricted free agent. In order to make the biggest offer we possibly could it necessitated us to release Jeremy. The Clippers ended up matching the offer so we ended up not getting him. Had we not had to make that offer or didn't want to make that offer he more than likely would still be on our team. We need to upgrade our frontcourt and that's what we're trying to do. Mark Jackson never really got a chance to see him play. It was the first day of training camp when we actually had to waive him and we had just started practice when he was pulled off the practice court. We had to waive him on the day we made the offer to DeAndre Jordan. It was just circumstance. Because of the lockout everything with the free agents was so truncated. Typically all of your free-agent stuff is done before you get started with

> We didn't want to release the kid.

training camp but this year you were working on your roster a few days after training camp started.

He played for the Mavericks summer league team in the summer of 2010 in Las Vegas. There was all of that hype about how well he played against John Wall. The Mavericks ended up not signing him and that's when we came up and signed him. After we let him go then the Rockets picked him up for a few days and then they let him go and he ended up in **NEW YORK***. It turned out to be the perfect storm, everything aligned for him and it could not happen to a better kid.

He's a kid that's just gotten better. He wasn't this player two years ago or 16 months ago or probably even six months ago. He's getting an opportunity and when you have confidence, confidence is a great thing. When you're playing 40 minutes a night and you have the keys to the car he's taking full advantage of the situation.

It's an unbelievable story. You probably couldn't write a **MOVIE SCRIPT*** any better than the way this story has turned out for him. His numbers are going to come down, they pretty much have to. With the New York media, at some point if he runs into a slump or what-not and the expectations are just so high now, they all might jump on him.

It couldn't happen to a better kid, all of the attention he's getting now is just great for him. He deserves everything good that comes to him. Just a great, great kid.

*Thomas Edison sold the concrete to the **NEW YORK** Yankees that was used to build Yankee Stadium. Edison owned the huge Portland Cement Company...Edison's middle name was Alva, named after the father of onetime Cleveland Indians owner, Alva Bradley.

*In the "Jackie Robinson Story", Dick Williams (later a Hall of Fame Manager) was an extra. In one scene Williams is pitching for Jersey City when Robinson homers for Montreal...When Robinson nears second base on his home run trot, the second baseman is Dick Williams.

Chapter Five

JEREMYPALOOZA

So Say You One,
So Say You All

ZEKE FROM CABIN CREEK

JERRY WEST

Jerry West scored 25,192 points during a 14-year NBA career, all with the Los Angeles Lakers. He was inducted into the Naismith Memorial Basketball Hall of Fame in 1980 and has been further honored as the player depicted in silhouette on the NBA logo. He had an All-America career at West Virginia and was a member of the gold-medal-winning USA basketball team at the 1960 Summer Olympics in Rome. He has followed his playing career with a successful career as an executive and is regarded as one of the most highly-respected judges of basketball talent. West served as an executive with the Lakers from 1979 until 2000, a period in which the team won six NBA championships, and later spent five seasons as the President of Basketball Operations with the Memphis Grizzlies. He currently is a member of the Golden State Warriors Executive Board.

When you see Ivy League kids play they tend to play a little differently. They're often not as skilled as major college players and rely more on team play. They play very effective basketball because they really play together. Sometime you have to look at players differently. Harvard did play some big schools and he acquitted himself very well.

I didn't watch that much of the NBA last year. I knew that Joe Lacob, the Warriors owner, and his son, Kirk, had a big connection with him and signed him as an unrestricted free agent. They saw something there.

This story is not about the Warriors and the Rockets letting Jeremy go. It's more about his ability to persevere and it's really one of the better feel-good stories in the NBA in a long time.

He looks like he belongs. He's very clever and he's a unique player because he keeps working on his game. Give Mike D'Antoni credit for putting him out there and revitalizing the Knicks, hopefully his success will continue under Mike Woodson.

Once he figures out the people that he's playing against a little better you won't see as many turnovers from him. He's very clever with the ball and goes by people you don't think he'll be able to go by. I don't think his numbers, his points and assists, will stay as high but one number that will come down are his turnovers, by knowing his teammates and having a better understanding of his opponents and what defenses are doing to him.

Will he have a long career? Why not? A player's career is based on his ability to improve every year. He needs tons of experience.

People are enthralled by great stories and this is a great Cinderella story. It really is a story more like Cinderella.

This kid is going to have a career, he's going to be a good player. Experience will make him better.

The Warriors owner wanted to re-sign him but I do know the reason they let him go. They signed DeAndre Jordan to an offer sheet and Houston claimed Jeremy. The owners really wanted to re-sign him. I don't look at that as something to be critical of, just think of it as one of the great stories we've seen in the NBA. His Asian-American ancestry also makes it a big story.

He was at the press conference along with a couple of other players when the Warriors announced I was joining their organization. He's a nice kid and I'm delighted for him personally. What you see with him is what you get, there are no hidden agendas with him.

He wants to be a basketball player and you can't hide his intensity.

WASHINGTON: FIRST IN WAR, FIRST IN PEACE, LAST IN THE NATIONAL LEAGUE

BRUCE TINSLEY

Bruce Tinsley is a popular American cartoonist best known for his long running "Mallard Fillmore" series. Mallard Fillmore, *which has been written and illustrated by Tinsley since 1994, features a green duck who works as a conservative reporter at a Washington, D.C. television station. Of the many characters in the strip, the one perhaps most relevant to Jeremy Lin is Rush Quat, the son of Dave Quat, who is Fillmore's Vietnamese best friend in the series. Rush Quat is a fourth grader who hopes to one day become a basketball player.*

My strip started about 18 years ago when I was an editorial cartoonist. The strip started as and still is a commentary strip that comments on political, social and cultural issues. The Jeremy Lin thing was just perfect, it fell right in line with the kind of thing that I usually do in my strip. Ever since the strip began, I have had an eight-year old boy in there who has dreamed of being the first Asian-American player in the NBA. He just lives for basketball and he talks about it all the time, so it just fit right in.

It's always hard, because I have a two week lead time, so I find myself watching the news a lot. Knowing that the Jeremy Lin series was coming up, I'm thinking, 'I hope they win tonight, I hope he scores 28 points et cetera. You never know how long something like that is going to last.

I try to have ongoing characters with their own stories and their own personalities, but then I use them to comment on stuff. When I had this character who has been eight years old for 18 years, and he's a Vietnamese-American who always plays basketball, and then along came Jeremy Lin. He's from Harvard...I don't know if they give athletic scholarships now, I know they never used to...but he's from Harvard and he's the first Asian-American in the NBA, and he's a star and there's all this hype, so it jived perfectly with what I had been doing. My strip is a conservative strip, politically. I was brought up in an era when we were taught that the ideal thing was a colorblind society, you know. Everybody had equal opportunity. From my liberal college professors, and from watching TV, you hear that in certain fields, if there aren't the same amount of African-American neurosurgeons in society or the same amount of female physicists, well it's because of discrimination. It's got to be discrimination, the government needs to step in and do something about that. Well, here I've got this kid who looks at the NBA, and there's very few Asians in the first place, and no Asian-Americans. You look at the Olympics, and there's great athletes in China. So, I pretty much use it as a commentary in that, well, if you look at society and if you look at any profession. These NBA players are making a ton of money and they don't look like the rest of society. Asians now take up about five percent of American society, and with my really bad public school math, I figured out if they were really represented in the NBA proportional to the representation in society, you figure there would be 24 or

> ...but he's from Harvard and he's the first Asian-American in the NBA, and he's a star and there's all this hype, so it jived perfectly with what I had been doing.

25 of them, at least. Not Yao Ming and Asians from other Asian countries, but Asian-Americans who were born in this country. I've always used that to poke at people who say if there's any disparity at all, it's because of discrimination. Right now it's tougher for Asians and Asian-Americans to get into most elite universities than it is Caucasians, Hispanics, Blacks and everybody. A lot of these kids have parents who were boat people. They couldn't speak English, were dirt poor but they had a strong work ethic, working two and three jobs.

The next thing you know, they're valedictorians of their class and they're going on to bigger and better things. It sticks it to the old myth that you have to be rich and white to make it in America. These Asians come on, and they're not getting any breaks. They're working hard, and their parents care about whether they're in school and what they're studying.

I lived in Washington D.C. for awhile, and there was this diner I used to eat in all the time. I don't even think it's there anymore, but it was a Greek diner that was completely run by Koreans. But that was at the time when we were getting big influx of Vietnamese boat people, not right when they first started coming in, but when their kids were starting to grow up. I was seeing how these kids were achieving. I thought I'm going to have a character that runs a diner. I want to have his kid doing something different from the stereotype of every Asian kid, like he's great in math and science and so on.

I love basketball, I grew up in Kentucky and was a big UK fan all my life. I thought that I love basketball, so I'll have him be this kid who loves to play basketball. We need role models in our society, and this was right during the Tiger Woods phenomenon. Everybody was saying, 'Oh, this is wonderful, an African-American role model for young black kids who want to play golf.' And I'm thinking what about putting in a young Asian kid who wants to play basketball. Where are the role models if that's what we need is role models? It just went from my love of basketball. I'm 53, and I when I hear people talk about stickball, baseball, all kinds of sports they played when they were kids, I do not where that stuff was when I was a kid. Everybody where I was from, growing up in Kentucky, played basketball. Of course, being a Kentucky fan, I don't have much to root for all football season, so it was basketball for me. I had Rush being a big basketball fan, that's where that came from.

I do occasionally incorporate sports into the strip. In fact, I do it pretty often. Usually, every year around college bowl season, I have a couple strips about the BCS. I had one a few years ago where they finally came up with a match-up for the championship game that fans would like: It would be pitting the BCS Committee against a pack of rabid polar bears. That's one fans would like to see. I did some stuff with the Tim Tebow mania, when he was getting ragged on and got a lot of criticism. Then overnight people stopped criticizing him and started praising the same guy.

I did something about the Detroit Lions and them tradition-ally playing in the Thanksgiving Day game. I really like to watch the NCAA Tournament, so I wish college football would go to some kind of playoff system, even if it were a just a cou-ple of games, so I comment about that every year. To me, the NFL has gotten more and more boring, and I feel the same way about the NBA. They just play so many games. Maybe it's growing up in Kentucky, but I just can't see **BASEBALL*** any-more. I grew up as a **CINCINNATI REDS*** fan, and I knew like every player on "The Big Red Machine" and could name their

*Charles Schultz drew almost 18,000 Peanuts strips and almost 2,000 dealt with **BASEBALL**.

*In 1998 the **CINCINNATI REDS** started an outfield trio of Chris Stynes, Dimitri Young, and Mike Frank. You might know them better as Young, Frank, and Stynes. (The author couldn't resist. He'll show himself to the principal's office now.)

stats and everything. They stayed there forever, and you felt like it was a family thing. But now I'm convinced that baseball is more a game that people watch because it's a loyalty and a love of the atmosphere of the game rather than any particular excitement. Seeing Albert Pujols moving now, I don't know how people get excited anymore about baseball. To me, I can flip on a football game, and even if I don't particularly like either team, particularly with college football, I'm drawn into the game. The other thing I did most recently was a series on soccer being sort of a game that Americans think they're supposed to like. I hear it every time, that Americans just can't appreciate the nuances of soccer. I did this one strip where, in America, three-year old kids play soccer. Three-year old kids also eat paste. If they came up with a league where people ate paste, Americans would rather watch that than soccer.

> I did one thing where it was just making fun of the way everybody, particularly copy editors, just try to make up words with Lin in them, like "Linspiration" and "Linsanity" and all that.

With Jeremy, I did one thing where it was just making fun of the way everybody, particularly copy editors, just try to make up words with Lin in them, like "Linspiration" and "Linsanity" and all that. It got really tiresome after about the third day. One of them deals with that, and it's a guy at a restaurant proposing to his girlfriend and trying to incorporate Lin into every word in the sentence. She's just hoping it's going to be over soon. There's another one talking about where we just need 24 more Asian-American NBA players to be representative of the population. Several stories have come out recently about how Asian-Americans don't like checking the "Asian" box when they're applying to go to colleges and universities because it's become a disadvantage. Admissions committees, at least if you look at the statistics, expect higher SAT scores and higher grade point averages from Asians. In one of the strips, Rush, the little boy, was reading all these stories about Jeremy Lin. He was essentially saying that everybody's talking about him and that it was probably harder for him to get into Harvard than the NBA. There was one where Rush is upset. He's upset because he likes Jeremy Lin, but he's not the first Asian-American to play now. He wishes Jeremy Lin played for the Washington Wizards since he lives in D.C. He says it's my fault for putting him in a comic strip because he's been eight years old for the past 18 years. But he says that if you do the math and look at Jeremy Lin's real age, that he was probably Jeremy Lin's real inspiration for his career because he's actually older than Jeremy Lin.

I'm not as sure of the media reaction, because I usually look for this stuff on the internet and have been busy. But I can tell you I've been getting tons of e-mail from fans about the whole Jeremy Lin thing. The difference between that and most of my e-mail is that everybody likes it. Usually, I get lots and lots of hate mail, which I thrive on. I get critical mail from people calling me names and wanting to do terrible things with kitchen utensils. But this Jeremy Lin thing, everybody loves it, so it's like I don't know how to react. Usually, I get not as much hate mail as good mail, but close to it, so I feel like...man, am I not doing my job here? It didn't make anyone mad yet? There's been some coverage in the media as well, they mentioned it in *The New York Post*. They mentioned that Jeremy Lin couldn't even escape being in the comics, and there were posters now and memorabilia, basically that is everywhere now. It was as far as he could get from what you could usually expect somebody like that to get.

YEAH, THAT'S THE TICKET

JOELLEN FERRER

Joellen Ferrer has been with Stub-Hub! for the past six years, and currently serves as their Manager of Public Relations. She is the ticket company's most visible spokesperson, often traveling to various venues all while managing a popular blog and Twitter account.

As soon as Linsanity started to take off, we saw overall page views of people looking at the site and searches go up about ten times. This was both for home games and for road games, we started to see interest at that 10x level. As far as people actually **BUYING TICKETS***, we started to see an increase of about 5-7x, just depending on which game it was. That being said, prices didn't rise. We saw added activity, we saw a lot more people buying tickets, but we didn't see prices rise until after the buzzer beater on Valentine's Day in Toronto. As soon as that happened, we then began to see prices rise by about double. The one thing that I could liken it to, is the trends that we see when there are major trades...such as Carmelo going to the Knicks or LeBron going to Miami or even CP3 going to the Clippers at the start of the season. You see similar things where you'll see a boost in traffic or you'll see a boost in ticket sales, but what's interesting is that with those type of moves, we've seen an immediate price hike. It was incredibly interesting to see that prices didn't rise immediately for Linsanity. My thought process on that was that was

---

*The gate for an average NBA game is one million dollars. However, the Knicks and the Lakers gross $1.5 million per game in **TICKET SALES**.

that it was more the curiosity factor, that Jeremy wasn't quite the proven high-profile player. He still isn't compared to some of our top dogs, and that's why we didn't see the immediate price reaction. But as soon as that exciting game happened, it really turned things around, and we have not seen a drop in prices. It's gone up about 2x, and despite the losses there, prices have still remained pretty high and fans are continuing to buy more and more Knicks tickets.

The other person that comes to mind that made this kind of impact is Brett Favre. We immediately saw movement like this when he would go to the next team. When he retired and came back and went to the Jets and then to Minnesota, it was similar. Obviously Tiger Woods as well when he jumped back into the scene a couple years back, that's where we started to see some of these immediate trends. But to be completely honest, I've never seen anything quite in the same respect. At the end of the day, a lot of fans root for the underdog and a lot of fans look for that good story, and this is so unlike anything that we've seen. It's crossed more than just the sports headlines and it's entered into the pop culture realm. Just to give you some perspective on how far people are coming to watch some of these games, when they were in Miami (in mid-February) we saw fans as far away as China, **JAPAN***, the U.K., Argentina...it became one of these events where people weren't just coming from your local Florida market or just New York or just the United States. We definitely saw that folks were crossing borders to be in Miami to be at this game.

You know, his background adds an additional wrinkle. I don't think that it plays a huge, huge factor into it. It makes it that much more compelling of a story and obviously, it's brought

---

*The Yomiuri Giants are sometimes called "The New York Yankees of **JAPAN**." They have won the most pennants and have the deepest fan base in Yakyu (Japanese Baseball)....The Nippon Ham Fighters give free tickets to foreigners on "Yankees Day."

in fans from your Asian countries. But, I don't think that's a huge focus or a main driver.

Even at the start of the season, the Knicks alongside the Clippers were our two top selling ticket teams as far as actual transactions are concerned. A lot of it also is just due to the big markets, it's not like the apples to apples comparison if we were looking at Bucks tickets or Kings tickets or what have you. It continues to be the top draw as far as all NBA tickets are concerned. The other top teams, and this is on a year-to-year basis, we see in terms of ticket sales are the Lakers, the Bulls, the Celtics. Your larger-market teams that play well. Given this, we've certainly seen a big explosion in interest, and it's just because people want to be there and people want to experience Linsanity in person. Whether it's at home or on the road, we've seen increased activity.

> Even at the start of the season, the Knicks alongside the Clippers were our two top selling ticket teams

More people are buying the "get-ins". There's a fair amount of people buying the premium seats but the majority of our buyers are leaning towards either the "get-in" or your "so-so" seats that aren't terrible, but they're not great either. Maybe your lower corners or upper, maybe a little closer to center, but not quite right at center court. But we are seeing several courtside tickets being purchased and there are some premium seats are being traded on the site but it's not the majority.

It's difficult to compare them to other teams in the city. With baseball, you've got the sheer number of games that will trump things when it comes to buying tickets because they have the 81 home games compared to 41 for the NBA. I'd say that an interesting comparison would be the Nets versus the Knicks. All throughout the season, we've seen Nets tickets for less than five dollars. We've even seen a good number of instances where Nets tickets are a penny. You definitely see the difference in demand when you've got a Knicks game and a Nets game going on at the same time. It was sometime in mid-February when they were both playing at the same time. We had tickets going for $100 for the Knicks and then some for a dollar to see the Nets. It's very much a night and day differential for the demands to see both teams.

One thing I've been kicking around, and I'd love for somebody to be able to do this...we always see that people look at the prices like the stock market in that they go up and they go down, and it would be pretty cool for somebody to see that maybe his stock is a little lower than a couple weeks ago and they bought tickets for a few future games and bank on the fact that he'll most likely have another good run and see if you can "play the market" and buy tickets and then flip them and try to make a profit and potentially pay your way into the playoffs like that. We see a lot of people do this with their season tickets. They don't want to give up the seats and they know they want to go to a few games so they cherry pick what they want to go to and end up selling the rest. In theory, it helps them break even and if there's a postseason, it helps them off-set that initial investment.

> We had tickets going for $100 for the Knicks and then some for a dollar to see the Nets.

Our corporate office is in San Francisco. Many of us in the office are Warriors fans. It's a little disappointing because they let Jeremy go. But at the same time too, it's exciting because it's piqued the interest of the so-so NBA fan. People have really been trying to follow it, and it's hard not to get excited over something like this. Ticket sales aside, at the end of the day, it's a good story. We continue to see that people are itching to go to any of his games.

SOMETIMES GOD JUST HANDS YOU ONE

STEPHEN CHEN

Stephen Chen is Jeremy Lin's pastor at Redeemer Bible Fellowship, the English ministry of Chinese Church in Christ in Mountain View, Calif. When they first met more than 10 years ago, Chen was Lin's youth counselor. The two built their friendship on a mutually beneficial arrangement—Lin taught Chen how to play basketball, and Chen taught his young pupil the Bible.

The first time I met Jeremy Lin was when he was 13. I was a youth counselor at our church, Redeemer Bible Fellowship. On one of our church-cleaning days, Jeremy, who was this athletic boy, was throwing a ball around as everybody was working to tidy things up. He was rambunctious—full of energy. I remember taking him aside and saying, 'Hey, we're trying to clean up the church and you're making a mess of it.' That was our first encounter, so we didn't really get off on the best footing. But we became fast friends after that.

When I first became Jeremy's youth counselor, he was definitely shorter than me, and I'm 5-foot-8. Even at that age, I remember him saying, 'I'm going to be 6 feet tall and I'm going to play in the NBA. I'm going to dunk.' Looking at him, you wouldn't think that he would. So I asked, 'How are you going to do that?' And he said, 'Well, I'm going to drink a lot of milk. I'm going to practice hard. And I'm going to take a lot of calcium pills and try to get taller.' And sure enough, he shot up and he's over 6 feet now and he's dunking and he's in the NBA.

Jeremy was always really into basketball. I'd never played any basketball before, so the two of us struck up a deal. I would teach him the Bible and he would teach me basketball. So I'd go out to play basketball with him and his brother Josh, who was also in the youth group. Jeremy taught me how to make a lay-up and he taught me how to shoot. Sometimes on Friday nights after church, we would go out and we would play basketball until 1 or 2 in the morning. We would play against a lot of Stanford students, and I would be on a team with him and Josh. Jeremy wasn't afraid to give me the ball. Even though I had never played, he always wanted to get me involved. He wasn't afraid of losing. He just enjoyed the game a lot.

Jeremy always set his goal on living out an active faith—to honor Jesus Christ with undivided love and devotion. He has continued to seek to do that on the basketball court. Throughout his high school years, Jeremy was a part of our youth leadership team. He was a natural leader, a natural servant to the people of the church. When he was at Harvard, he would come back and be a youth counselor and he would be involved in our summer camp. Then last year, when he was playing for the Golden State Warriors, he would sometimes lead our men's group ministry.

> Jeremy always set his goal on living out an active faith—to honor Jesus Christ with undivided love and devotion.

Jeremy's faith has had a very big impact on who he is, especially because he understands that his identity is in Christ. He understands that he is a basketball player, that he was a student at Harvard, and that he's also Chinese-American. But first and foremost, he understands who he is as a Christian and that that's what makes him who he is. Jeremy is always eager to learn more and more about God. He wants to read scriptures more and continue to grow in his love and affection for his Lord and Savior.

In terms of how his faith has been helpful, I think that Jeremy doesn't believe in any type of prosperity gospel. He believes that God is gracious in providing all good things. So even in the midst of difficulties and uncertainties, Jeremy focuses on what is true and what is certain—that God is unwavering and faithful and working all things for the good of those who love him and are called according to his good purpose. These are the things that Jeremy latches onto. He trusts in God for all things. And he knows that whether he finds great success in his basketball or not, what's most important at the end of the day is not the basketball game itself, it's having a relationship with **JESUS***.

Our church family at Redeemer Bible Fellowship is very, very happy to see Jeremy's success this year. Our church has always been very involved with basketball. We've had a tradition for as long as I can remember of playing Sunday evening basketball. So we rejoice over his success on the basketball court. For us, at church at least, everyone is a Knicks fan. No matter what allegiance we may have had in the past, we're all Knicks fans now. And we continue to pray for Jeremy and to encourage him in the faith.

Some members of our congregation have become interested in basketball for the first time. And this isn't just in our church. I would say that after hearing Jeremy's story, more and more people are interested in the sport. His success has generated a lot of excitement amongst the Asian-American Christian community. While his impact is difficult to quantify, his story has certainly provided many opportunities for Asian-American Christians to discuss their faith. In terms of that effect, he keeps making an impact.

*Graffiti seen in a Nebraska truck stop, 1973:

(Written on wall)	The answer is **JESUS**.
(Written below)	What is the question?
(Written below)	The question is: What is the name of Felipe Alou's brother?

Now, with Jeremy on the road so much, we know that it's hard for him to really have a church community. We do our best to pray for him as a church leadership. We know we're kind of his anchor point, so we'll text or call and check in with one another regularly. He's part of our church family. He loves us and we love him, and obviously he's still a part of a lot of the things that we do here. He's a son of the church, so we just enjoy our times together. He still comes out to open gym at our church in the summertime. We just simply give him a handicap and tell him, 'No dunking.' He's allowed to play 'D' but we limit him to outside shots.

For me, it's exciting to see Jeremy's long-time dream come to fruition, knowing that these things can be ephemeral and that they can vanish in an instant as well. It's been a joy to see him excel in the things that God has given him to do. I'm just very happy for Jeremy, and very thankful to God for giving him something so wonderful. Getting a shot in the NBA and becoming a star were gifts from God, so hopefully he can continue to use those gifts to honor his God.

> It's exciting to see Jeremy's dream come to fruition, knowing that these things can be ephemeral and… can vanish in an instant as well.

When the crowd at Madison Square Garden chants your name it's a feeling like no other. Not only in the arena but out on the streets when people start cheering your name, showing you respect, telling you "good game." But Jeremy is a little different because of the minutes that he plays ands the things that he brings to the table as opposed to me. I was mostly a backup to Patrick Ewing, He's a starter, he comes in and plays starter minutes and he was the glue that came in and put us together.
—**HERB WILLIAMS**, Knicks Assistant Coach, one of the most popular Knicks players ever

HERE'S WHAT LOVE'S GOT TO DO WITH IT

PASTOR JOHN LOVE

Pastor John Love is in his 22nd season as the New York Knicks team chaplain. He also has worked with children for the last 28 years and currently does so through the Greater Grace World Outreach church in Baltimore, where he resides. He commutes to Knicks homes games.

When Jeremy first arrived here I went to him because a friend of mine, Bill Alexson, who was the Celtics chaplain for 20 years, he's from the Boston area and I'm from the Boston area, his brother told us about Jeremy Lin. He said that not only is he a great basketball player but that he has a very genuine, authentic kind of faith. He mentioned that to Bill and Bill, in turn, shared that with me. He said you should look for him when you get up there. But I didn't have to look for him, he was looking for me. He sought me out the first night, his first home game here. I introduced myself and as soon as I introduced myself he said "I'll be there." He hasn't missed a chapel since.

Jeremy and Landry Fields are the two guys who anchor our chapel program. They come very faithfully. Chapel starts an hour before tip-off. What's very unusual about this young man is that he's in there 20 minutes before the chapel starts. He's been doing that lately, perhaps, to give himself some quiet time just so that he can get his thoughts straight. Maybe it's a way where he doesn't have to answer all of the questions before game time. But he comes in there just to get himself prepared mentally and emotionally. After the Linsanity started it was a quiet place where he could go and he knew that no one would come in there after him. In fact, when I'm in there and he comes in, I leave. I want him to have that time, because if he's coming in there to retreat from all of the madness, great, I don't want to get in the way of that. Take the time that you need to prepare yourself and when we have to start, we start. Then we do the chapel service and it seems like that really helps, he really responds while he's in there and he receives something from what we share. He's ready to go after that.

We talk before we officially get started, then we open with a prayer, sometimes one of the players will lead us in a prayer. Then I'll take about 15 minutes and I'll share a Biblically-based message. Something that I always like to make sure that the principles are sound theologically and, even more than that, that there is a real practical edge to what I'm saying. Because if it's just theology then there is no way they can relate it to their practical lives, so I like to have something that has a practical edge that they can identify with.

Sometimes there is some interaction before and after the chapel and we talk about which authors he likes to read, what authors he focuses on and is reading right now. He's well-read. One of them is John Piper and we talked a little bit tonight about Max Lucado, a very popular author in Christian circles. These are the kind of books that he's reading. He seems like he reads a lot. I get the impression from him that he's got a real devotional make-up to his personality. He likes to get quiet, he likes time where he can think and meditate and that seems to be part of his game preparation as well.

He seems very, very quiet. I know that the word has been used and overused but his humility is

> His prayer, the prayer from his heart was "Lord, if you give me this opportunity, if I get to play basketball in the NBA, I'm going to make your name known…

genuine. Somebody once said that to be conscience of humility is its utter ruin. I don't think that he perceives himself that way. There is a story about a young boy in a class who was given a badge for being the most humble and when he started to tell everybody about it they took it away. You can be proud of that, I suppose, but that's not who he is. He's always deflecting all of the attention about himself to his teammates. He would like to get into a mindset that "this is not just about me," but that this is about a very good team here in New York that's been rebuilt. We're starting to put things together and maybe make a good run in the second half of the season.

I'm still trying to digest it. His prayer, the prayer from his heart was "Lord, if you give me this opportunity, if I get to play basketball in the NBA, I'm going to make your name known, I'm going to make people know about you." That was something he did, it might have been on a youtube video, but it was something that I had heard that he did, "God, if you give me the opportunity I will glorify your name." And I think that that's happened. He's a young man that when you talk to him, inevitably, he's going to talk about his faith. He's going to talk about his relationship with God and what it means to him and how he can use that platform, this platform, to impact other people's lives. It's almost like he's become a billboard for the glory of God, that's the way he kind of looks at it.

When I look at him I just wonder how he's done it. When you go from obscurity to this meteoric rise I can't even imagine what that's like. Everybody wants a piece of you and all of a sudden you're on the cover of **TIME MAGAZINE***. I'm still trying to digest it and fathom it and figure it all out and take it all in. I can't even imagine what he has to deal with.

---

*What former Major League manager was once **TIME MAGAZINE**'s Man of the Year? The Mouth of the South, Ted Turner. Turner managed one game for his Atlanta Braves before Commissioner Bowie Kuhn put a stop to it...Bowie Kuhn's high school basketball coach was Red Auerbach.

He seems to be dealing with it incredibly well. But, on the other hand, I've seen it take a toll on him in just a few short weeks. I've seen a young man come in that didn't look like he had the weight of the world on his shoulders to, next thing you know, looking like, "Wow, you look like you're taking a lot of burdens in here with you." Clearly it has impacted him and he would like to settle into more of a consistent role as a player that is on par with his fellow teammates, just making his contribution, doing what he does to help his team, so that all of the Linsanity will quiet down.

We've talked about dealing with all of the attention. I asked him how he's dealing with and he said "It's overwhelming, I'm not finding a lot of time to just settle down, relax, reflect. You can imagine all of the media requests, it was just out of control. But we talk about it. I asked him how he was holding up and he said "all right. God sustains me. But I wish it would decrease."

There is a passage in the Psalms, Psalm 46, verse 10, that says "Be still and know that I am God. Let the Lord be your confidence and don't cast that confidence away." We talked also about one message that really struck home to him. We talked about his value. Jeremy Lin's value in the eyes of God existed long before anybody knew about Jeremy Lin. Jeremy Lin was the object of God's love before anybody knew his name, before Linsanity began. And his value has not increased in the eyes of God because of his sensational play and the impact that he's made, it has always been the same. That appeared to mean a lot to him because sometimes our value is determined by our popularity, what people think about us, how much attention people pay to us, but I said not in the eyes of God. In the eyes of man, certainly, but not in the eyes of God. You have always been valuable, you have always been God's masterpiece. You can't become more valuable. I said to him that God thinks that you're worth the death of his son, that's how valuable you are. And it appeared that that really spoke to him because I heard him later that evening in a press conference talking about those principles. So I realized that it probably spoke to his heart.

I have never seen anything like this, never have, not in my life. And up here in New York we've seen some great moments, thrilling moments. That 1999 season when the eighth seed, the New York Knicks, beat Miami and went on to the NBA Finals, that was a great season. There was a lot of talk about faith and believing, we were having those prayer circles out in the middle of the floor at the end of every game. There's been some great times and there's been some tragic moments when players have lost their lives like Bobby Phills, when he played for the Charlotte Hornets. There have been memorable moments, both good and bad, but nothing quite like this. This has been quite a ride.

> **Jeremy Lin's value in the eyes of God existed long before anybody knew about Jeremy Lin.**

The day after I saw him play in New York, he called me around noon and I went over to his apartment to have lunch. I asked him, 'How does your body feel? What's hurting? Are you resting? What are you eating?' After we finished talking about that, he asked me about my family. He talked about how crazy everything is. Then he talked about how much he loves his team. His best friend on the Knicks is Landry Fields, so he told me about what a great guy Landry is. He was inviting some of his teammates—Tyson Chandler, Jared Jeffries and Fields—over to his apartment that night because the Knicks had the day off. He got a text and he started laughing. I said, 'What're you laughing at?' He said, 'I texted Landry and asked, 'Are you in or out? Are you coming over tonight or not?" And Landry texted back, 'I'm Lin.' Jeremy thought that was pretty funny. You can tell they all stick together. Jeremy was the same exact guy—really funny and fun to be with. You forget you're with someone who's so crazy popular just because he's so humble and down to earth.

—**E.J. COSTELLO**, Lin's personal trainer from Concord, CA

A GOOD LAWYER KNOWS THE LAW
A GREAT LAWYER KNOWS THE JUDGE

DAVID WEAVER

David Weaver, a Seattle-based attorney who specializes in construction litigation, has enjoyed living vicariously through Lin during the star guard's meteoric rise with the New York Knicks. That's because when Weaver looks at Lin, he sees a younger version of himself—up until Lin began to make his way in the NBA. Like Lin would 13 years later, Weaver led Palo Alto High School to a state championship and landed all-state honors as a senior. Like Lin, Weaver was bypassed in the college recruiting process by Stanford and other major Division I programs before finding his way to the Ivy League. Like Lin, Weaver played at Harvard (for his final two years) and then embarked on a professional career. Weaver, who played for two years in the Irish Basketball Association, has cast an admiring eye on Lin ever since he coached him as a Palo Alto High School assistant during Lin's superb freshman year. Weaver has been a sounding board for Lin and Lin's mother, Shirley, ever since. Weaver credits Lin for sparking the remarkable turnaround in Harvard's program.

I first became aware of Jeremy Lin more than 10 years ago when I was coaching a National Junior Basketball (NJB) team made up of eighth graders. One of my friends, a former teammate of mine at Palo Alto High School, was coaching a team of seventh graders that included Jeremy, and we arranged for our teams to play. My eighth-grade team had a number of players who went on to excel in high school, a bunch of all-league type players. And Jeremy's seventh grade team absolutely blew us away. It was unbelievable. It must've been a 30-point game. I remember telling my guys, 'Can you believe you just lost to a seventh-grade team like that!?' Looking back on it, they had a future NBA player who's now on his way to becoming an All-Star. But at the time, Jeremy was maybe 5-foot or 5-1. Anyway, I didn't take much away from it because I just thought my team had played badly.

> Jeremy's seventh grade team absolutely blew us away. It was unbelievable. It must've been a 30-point game.

I started to get to know Jeremy a little bit because he began to work with my mom, Patricia, when he was in eighth grade. My mom has an academic-enrichment business where she advises students who are intelligent and ambitious. She helps them take their writing skills to the next level, and she's also a counselor who advises on the college application process. Jeremy went to her through his senior year in high school, so my mom saw him grow up and develop as well.

During Jeremy's freshman year at Palo Alto High School, I was an assistant coach for the boys varsity basketball team. Jeremy was on the JV team all the way through the end of the league season. I'd always watch the JV games just to see how those guys were doing. In just about every single game, Jeremy had somewhere between 15 and 20 points in the first half, and his team would be up big. So I started getting there early just to make sure I wasn't missing anything he was doing. Jeremy was 5-3 and 120 pounds at that point. So seeing him taking bigger and stronger guys to school over and over and over again, it was just fun to watch. Of course, I had no idea that what's taking place now with Jeremy in the NBA could ever become a possibility. I thought I was looking at a guy who would be a good high school player, who was fun to watch.

At the end of his freshman season on JV, Jeremy came up to the varsity team, where I was coaching. To that point, our team had been a little bit better than average, but we'd still made the Central Coast Section playoffs. Jeremy and another freshman came up to the squad and immediately started playing. We ended up winning the CCS championship that year—only the third time that Palo Alto had ever done that—and I attribute it to them for sure. Jeremy's mere presence really made a big difference. I don't know if it was the confidence that he brought or the overall sense of team unity, but once he came up to the team, all of a sudden we started to play together as a unit. If you look at how we were before he was there and then afterwards, it was night and day. Watching the impact Jeremy made as a freshman, that was a point when I thought, 'Wow, this guy is really something special.'

Some of the things that really stood out to me were how refined his fundamentals were, even as a small freshman. His jab-stepping and pump-faking, his understanding of when to shoot and when to pass were really advanced. One play when he caught the ball at the wing sticks out. After Jeremy pump-faked a guy who was running at him, he took one dribble like he was going to go up and shoot. The defense recovered on him, which left one of our post guys wide open down low. So in the process of going up to shoot, Jeremy just redirected the ball down to the post man, who went up for a dunk. I'd been playing all my life, and I don't know if I would've made that play. It was just that kind of court sense that showed that Jeremy was wise beyond his years.

Another memory that stands out from that year was our first-round game in the Northern California playoffs, a game we ended up losing. We were playing against Sacramento High School, a long, athletic team packed with seniors. They were just pressing the heck out of our guards and making them look like they didn't really belong out there. But they weren't pressuring Jeremy. I remember thinking, 'This is strange. These guys are pressuring everybody else on our team. Why aren't they getting up on him?' But two or three plays later, somebody tried to do it, and Jeremy made a hard dribble left and brought the ball between his legs, leaving his defender 4 or 5 feet off of him. And I thought, 'OK, that's why they aren't pressuring him. If they do, he's going to go right around them.' It was one of those surprising moments because you wouldn't think he'd have that kind of quickness or ball-handling or that kind of understanding of what to do with the ball. That was a time when you realized, 'Hey, this guy may not look like much, but he's really got an elevated skill set.'

I didn't get to follow Jeremy's progress too closely the next couple years because I was in law school. But I remember during his junior year, Palo Alto made it to the Central Coast Section championship again. The night before the title game, Jeremy was playing basketball down at the YMCA and he broke his ankle. What really stuck out to me was that the night before the most important game of his career, he was playing basketball at the YMCA at 10 o'clock at night. That was a testament to how much he loved the game and how much he was interested in improving. The fact that he was playing in the CCS championship game the next day didn't dissuade him. He was just thinking, 'I want to go out and shoot.'

Jeremy's senior year, I started following the team pretty devotedly. When I was a senior at Palo Alto in 1993, we went 31-0 and won the state championship against a team that was supposed to be much better than we were. So I had an extra sense of excitement about the whole thing when Jeremy's team started making its great playoff run. Here we were, 13 years later, and the team was on track to do it again. I remember watching the state championship game against Mater Dei and thinking, 'Wow, it's going to be tough playing against a bunch of high school All-Americans, all of whom have full rides to big Division I schools. And here's our little group of guys led by our star who can't get a scholarship anywhere.' But sure enough, we surpassed everyone's expectations again. Jeremy made several key shots in that game, one of them being a prayer from about 28 feet as the shot clock ran down that banked in and put us up by five points with about a minute to go. That was kind of the moment where everyone in the crowd looked around and said, 'Wow, we're going to win this game! I can't believe this is happening!' It was just this euphoric feeling. We all had the realization at the same exact time—'We're going to do it. It's going to be a huge upset.' To this day, six years later, I remember it like it was yesterday.

> ...all of whom have full rides to big Division I schools. And here's our little group of guys led by our star who can't get a scholarship anywhere.

In the state championship, Jeremy didn't play one of his best games. He ended up with 17 points. But when it was crunch time, he completely took the game over. It was, 'I'm making decisions. I'm deciding when to shoot the ball or when to take it to the hoop. I'm taking it down the lane for a lay-in or I'm kicking it to someone who's open.' What stuck out to me the most there was his willingness to take over the game—to be *the guy* at the biggest moment of his entire life and the biggest moment of all his teammates' lives. I thought, 'Wow, this guy has a whole lot of courage and a whole lot of belief in himself.' Jeremy took every big shot down the stretch and I think he made three or four of them to either take the lead or keep Mater Dei at bay.

Jeremy and I had very similar experiences in terms of being recruited and having the Ivy League being the one spot that really wanted us. So we definitely had discussions about that. I knew Jeremy was really down about not being recruited even though he was an all-state guy. I remember talking with him right after his senior year and telling him, 'Hey, this doesn't mean this is the end for you at all. This is only the beginning. Let's just take this and use it as motivation. Let's have it be a chip on your shoulder because it's only going to help you excel.'

I spoke a lot with Jeremy's mom, who I got to know when she would bring Jeremy and his brother, Joseph, over to work with my mom on the academic advisement stuff. Jeremy's mom, Shirley, was very active in the recruiting process, and she was discouraged just like him. I remember telling her, 'I think this has a whole lot to do with the way he looks, with his race. College coaches are in love with big, tall, strong, athletic-looking people, and generally that's not an Asian-American. And because of that, he's being overlooked.'

UCLA was ultimately Jeremy's first choice. But Stanford was right across the street from our high school and they needed a point guard in the worst way at that point in time. Jeremy had just come off of winning a state championship and he was a first-team, all-state player. The fact that Stanford wasn't recruiting him ... it messed with his head a little bit. The coaches had made it seem like, 'Oh, we're going to have a place for you. We're going to have a scholarship for you.' And then in the end, they didn't. A push and pull took place where he was all excited and had his expectations set on getting a scholarship to Stanford, and then at the last second had that pulled away. It was very frustrating and almost a humiliating thing for him. Or if not humiliating, it was at a sobering experience.

> UCLA was ultimately Jeremy's first choice. But Stanford was right across the street from our high school...

When it was happening to me as a senior at Palo Alto, I wanted to go to Stanford, just like Jeremy did. Mike Montgomery was coaching at the time, and he said, 'We'd love to have you as a player. We think you could definitely help us. But it would be in a walk-on capacity. I don't think that's what you want to do, so I don't think this is the place for you.' I remember being heartbroken. And pretty much the exact same thing happened to Jeremy. So while I was trying to console him a little bit, my point was, 'Let this drive you. Use this to motivate you.'

Then Jeremy chose Harvard, which is where I played for my last two years in college. Of course I watched him pretty closely, and the two of us continued to see each other in passing quite a bit. When he was a sophomore at Harvard, I went out to visit as a part of an alumni weekend. After the alumni game, Jeremy and I had a 30-minute conversation, and what jumped out to me at that point in time was how big he had gotten. He went from being a real lanky 6-foot, 160-pound guy to a 6-3 or 6-4 guy with a huge chest and totally developed arms. He had turned into a man in those two years. I remember commenting on that and he said, 'Yeah, I've just been in the weight room, doing my thing.' Jeremy and my mom had also become friends, so he immediately asked me how she was doing and asked me to say hello to her.

The moment that stuck out to me in Jeremy's college career came when I sat and watched the Harvard practice after our chat that day. This was right after coach Tommy Amaker had arrived, and one of my concerns was that Amaker was not going to be aware of what Jeremy was capable of doing because Jeremy was former coach Frank Sullivan's recruit and not his. But after watching the first 45 minutes of that practice, I realized, 'OK, Jeremy's got no problem.' As a sophomore, he was the best player on the floor and you could tell that right away. It was his decision-making, his court sense, his presence out there and just his ability to get all of his teammates moving and working as a unit. That was something I'd never seen at Harvard. My senior year, we had the best record of any Harvard team since the 1940's, but one of my chief complaints coming out of there was it was not a team-oriented offense. It was more that we had two guys in the post that we'd just feed the ball to, and we had a point guard who'd dribble for 30 seconds. I was incredibly frustrated about that because I didn't think we were maximizing our team's talent. Immediately upon watching that practice with Jeremy, it was clear that things had completely changed at Harvard, and it was because of the way Jeremy was getting everybody involved. It was team-first basketball. It wasn't about him—it was about getting the ball moving and cutting and being in the right place at the right time. That was where I saw that there had been a fundamental change in the program.

Looking back, it's really apparent how driven Jeremy was during his time at Harvard. That wasn't necessarily something that came up in our conversations; it's more 20-20 hindsight and me connecting the dots after seeing what he went on to do. After Jeremy's sophomore year, he was invited to play with the Chinese National Team. During his junior year, he goes for 27 points against Boston College right after they had beaten the No. 1 team in the country. And then senior year, everything explodes and he has a feature article in *Sports Illustrated*.

My conversations with Jeremy from college on were more personal—How're you doing, how're things going, how's your family, how're you liking Harvard? He definitely seemed to be happy. He was in the right place and doing exactly what he was supposed to do. That was the feeling I gathered from talking to him and talking to his mom. I would have long conversations with her about what Jeremy was doing at Harvard. She'd always say how he was in the perfect place, exactly where God wanted him to be—because you know they're a very religious family. There was definitely a sense of contentment about where he was and what he doing.

I live in Seattle, and when Jeremy was a senior, Harvard came out to play **SEATTLE*** University. I got a chance to talk with him

---

*During the **SEATTLE** Mariners' first year in 1977, the distance to the fences was measured in fathoms. A fathom is 6 feet. For instance, whereas one park might have a sign that denotes 360 feet, the Kingdome sign would have the number 60...

for 15-20 minutes after the game. The funny thing to me was how he was mentioning how Key Arena has such better locker rooms than Harvard does. He was saying, 'This is what we need to have.' I'm thinking, 'It's funny that that's what's on your mind. You just scored 20 points against Seattle, you've got the national media following you, and your concern is about the state of the locker rooms.'

Over the course of the next three months and the Ivy League season, Jeremy and I would text about once a week about the upcoming games—what the team was thinking about when they were playing Princeton and Penn, and the big game coming up against Cornell. Late that year, I told him I wanted to play one-on-one against him to see who the true all-time Palo Alto basketball player was. Obviously, it was tongue in cheek because I was 35 years old and he was in his prime. He sent me something back, joking, 'Yeah, I'm afraid you're just going to back me down and post me up.' He did a good job of humoring this cynical old man who can't let go of his high school glory.

> Jeremy absolutely revolutionized the Harvard program and took it to a new height.

Jeremy absolutely revolutionized the Harvard program and took it to a new height. He and Tommy Amaker put that program on the map. I still keep in touch with a lot of my teammates from the 1997 year. Obviously, since Jeremy and I went to the same high school, I'd get a lot of people telling me how proud they were of what he was doing and how he'd given the program the respect we'd always wanted it to have. That's first and foremost. Harvard has had a lot of good players go through there, and no one was quite able to do the things that he was capable of doing. A lot of it had to do with the athletic director that is there now who really has a basketball-first focus, whereas when I went to Harvard, the basketball program was at the same level of priority as the women's squash team. The combination of Jeremy, Amaker and the basket-ball-focused athletic director played a huge part in pushing Harvard basketball over the top. If you get a future NBA player playing anywhere, you're going to do well, and it was just great to see what Jeremy did at Harvard. Those efforts culminated with Harvard's NCAA Tournament appearance this year. Jeremy had everything to do with that.

Jeremy's impact comes down to the fact that he has been a transcendent basketball talent. People still say, 'Oh, he's not the most athletic guy. He's not the best shooter.' But what Jeremy has is the ability to slow the game down, to see things as they're happening or even before they're happening. He's got that sixth sense that very few people have. He was able to bring that to the group at Harvard, and he's obviously been able to do that at the next level, too. The two players that come to mind when I think about him, just in terms of their ability to slow the game down, are Jason Kidd and Steve Nash. I'm going to stop short of putting Jeremy on their level. But in terms of how he moves with the ball, what he's saying and what he's thinking, it just reminds me of what I remember seeing with Jason Kidd at the high school and college level. And it's the same thing with Steve Nash.

After Jeremy graduated from Harvard, I heard a lot about how he was pursuing his NBA dream through conversations with Peter Diepenbrock, his coach at Palo Alto. Jeremy was telling Peter, 'I know I can do this. I know I can play at this level.' It was frustrating to Jeremy that the NBA teams were almost paying lip service to him. They all said, 'Hey, you're doing a good job. We think you can play at this level.' But at the same time, no one was really expressing a whole lot of interest. But then when he was on the Dallas Mavericks summer-league team, he did his thing against John Wall. And I remember telling coach Diepenbrock, 'When have you ever seen Jeremy fail? Every single time there's an obstacle in front of him, not only does he exceed expectations but he blows them out of the water.' Then Jeremy got signed by the Golden State Warriors, and Linsanity started in the Bay Area. That lasted all through the preseason and up until the time it became clear he wasn't going to play very much as a rookie.

I went to Jeremy's first preseason game that year. It was against the Clippers and I was sitting courtside with a couple of his teammates from high school and coach Diepenbrock. His mom and dad were nearby, and they'd made a bunch of Jeremy Lin shirts to wear. The crowd was chanting, 'We want Jeremy!' Then with about 4 minutes to play, he gets in the game and the entire place just explodes. Immediately, he gets a steal and goes down, gets an and-one and there was just pandemonium. I think Jeremy ended up with seven points, three steals and a couple of nice assists in 4 minutes of play. Watching that, I said, 'This guy not only belongs out there, he needs to be playing a lot of minutes.' He looked great. This was his first-ever pro game, and he goes out there and acts like he's a five-year veteran.

After the game, we all went back to talk with Jeremy. When I saw him, there was this moment of quiet euphoria, just, 'I cannot believe you're doing this.' There was definitely a lot of joy coming out of him at that time. He gave us a rundown of all the things he was going through at practice and how good his teammates were being to him. He'd just gotten a new car that day because his teammates had been ribbing him that he was driving a car they didn't believe was befitting of an NBA player. We went outside and Jeremy showed us his new Mercedes. He was like this wide-eyed kid. 'Look at all of this *stuff!* Look at all of these toys!' He was just someone who was really excited. He wasn't someone who was saying, 'This is something I deserve.' It was more, 'This is just really cool.'

During the course of Jeremy's first NBA season, his mom, Shirley, and I would email back and forth. She keeps in touch with a group of people via email. I would always give my two cents about, 'Just be patient. His time is coming. Tell him not to get too flustered by the fact that he's not playing even though he believes he should be in the game. Rely on your faith. He's gotten this far—there's no way that the story's ending now.' Those were the types of sentiments I would pass along to his mom, and she would say, 'Yeah, I'm going to tell Jeremy that.' Based on my memory, last year was a real trying time not just for him but for his family. His family, they live and die...they're so emotionally involved in what's taking place that I think it took its toll on them.

Then with the lockout, Jeremy's knee surgery and then him getting released by the Warriors on the first day of training camp this season, there was just a real, real down feeling. The emails I remember getting from his mom were just, 'Please keep him in your prayers.' And my responses were, 'This is all for a reason. Don't worry about it. His time is coming.' It's funny because I wrote that—'His time is coming'—in an email to his mom, and then two days later he explodes against the New Jersey Nets. Obviously I can't take credit for being a prophet or anything because 'His time is coming' could mean anything. But my feeling was, 'Be patient. This guy is meant to play basketball. It's going to happen.' Then Linsanity just went out of control and he became the biggest sports personality on earth for two or three weeks.

I've been a huge Linsanity convert. For the first two weeks when he was exploding like he was, I couldn't focus on anything. People at work had turned me into a little bit of a celebrity just because of my affiliation with him. I got the opportunity to go out to New York to watch him play against the Mavericks, and that was just an absolute blast. We had a big litigation meeting on the Saturday I left, but the partners at my firm were saying, 'Hey, you have to go. We don't want you to be here. We want you to go watch that basketball game.'

I've also been living vicariously through Jeremy a little bit because we had the exact same high school career—we both won a state championship in our senior year, we were both first-team all-state, and we both were county player of the year and league MVP—and then we both played basketball at Harvard. It was definitely a dream of mine to do exactly what he's doing. So to see him do it, I feel as though I'm living a little bit of my dream through him. But I feel nothing but pure joy for him. I don't think there's any envy or jealousy going on. It's much more, 'I'm so proud of you. I'm so proud of what you're doing. This is great for Palo Alto basketball. This is great for Harvard. This is great for you.' And really, it's something that's great for me.

> I've also been living vicariously through Jeremy a little bit because we had the exact same high school career.

Obviously, there's been a ton of talk in the Palo Alto and Harvard basketball communities about what Jeremy's done. You should look at my entire inbox of emails in Yahoo! and Hotmail. For about a three-week period of time, that was all the conversation. It ended up being a little mini-reunion for all the Palo Alto guys from our state championship team in 1993 because everybody was so excited about the whole thing that they wanted to get back in touch so they could talk about it.

One of the Harvard conversations was pretty funny. Back when Jeremy was a sophomore at Harvard, I sent out an email where I told some of my old teammates, 'Hey, you guys have got to keep an eye on this guy.' I'd send out pretty frequent emails hyping up his stats. I'd always end it with something like, 'That's Palo Alto basketball!' After a while, my teammates were thinking, 'OK, we've heard enough.' One of my friends went back and found that email chain and sent it to a group of us a couple weeks ago and said, 'Well, you were the first person to call this out.' There's been a lot of conversation that after all the hype I gave him, he's gone above and beyond that.

There's also been a lot of talk about Knicks games in general. My childhood friends and I all grew up diehard Warriors fans, but we've all turned into Knicks fans all of a sudden. Now they tell me The Old Pro, a sports bar in downtown Palo Alto, is standing room only to watch the New York games. One of my friends was texting me to say, 'We can't get a seat at this place because everybody's here watching Jeremy play. Every single screen is on the Knicks game.'

> ...when Jeremy was a sophomore at Harvard, I sent out an email where I told some of my old teammates, 'Hey, you guys have got to keep an eye on this guy.'

Just watching Jeremy's games this year, one of the things that stood out the most was that he was in complete control of the team, especially before Carmelo Anthony came back from his injury. In the first two or three weeks, what I saw was a guy who not only was playing with the joy of a high school player but a guy who had brought that joy to his teammates. And Jeremy had brought that to basketball. He brought that team-first aspect that he has taken everywhere he's gone. Now we're talking at the NBA level—a star-focused system where certain people are entitled to shots and certain people demand their touches. And here we have Jeremy, who is getting everybody involved. Everybody's trying to make the smart pass instead of the big shot. That's what he was getting everyone doing in high school, that's what he was doing in college, and that's what's been interesting to me in watching him at the pro level. He's turned a me-first star system into a team-first system. It's been a joy to watch.

On a more modest level, Jeremy's overall presence and his humbleness in the locker room are infectious. You see it with guys like Tim Tebow of the Jets, where he's able to take over a locker room and people want to be more like him. They want to be a little bit more selfless. You can't really express how much of an effect that has on a team's morale and on team chemistry.

Every year for the past six or seven years, I've seen Jeremy once or twice and I've been able to get a gauge of how he's been doing and what's taking place. But I haven't gotten to speak with him since his pro career has taken off. I missed my chance to do that when I went to see him play in New York. When his old teammates and those close to the situation went out for the Mavericks game, Jeremy organized a lunch for us the next day. But because of my work obligations, I felt I like could only stay for the Sunday game and that I needed to be back on the day he was having the lunch. I wrote an email to his mom expressing my disappointment in not being able to just touch base and see Jeremy now. That would've been my chance to catch up and just see how he's doing personally, and I was really disappointed at not being able to get that experience this time after what has taken place. I've got his phone number and I'm friends with him on Facebook, but I don't want to reach out to him just because I know there are a ton of people who're doing that. It's one of those things where when I get a chance to see him, we'll have a good discussion. But I don't want to be one of those people who are constantly biding for his time.

Personally, it's almost like Jeremy is living out my childhood dream. I don't want to sound too pathetic because I'm pretty happy with where I am in my life. But our basketball career paths had mirrored each other's through college at least. The best way I could sum it up is they diverged when I was playing in the Irish Basketball League and Jeremy was lighting up the Lakers for 38 points on national TV. He's doing something I had always wanted to do and probably did not have the talent to do. But he is making it happen and he is doing it in big-time fashion.

> Personally, it's almost like Jeremy is living out my childhood dream.

To see him develop at every stage of his career—from a small, little guy who you'd think might get bullied in the schoolyard; to someone who guided his high school team to a state championship; to someone who revolutionized his college basketball program; to someone who is now a big-time sports personality and living out his dream on the biggest media stage on the world—it is very fulfilling to see it happen. So for me, I almost get choked up thinking about it because I know how much the game means to him and I know how much he has put into this. Just seeing him succeeding the way he is, I know it's a dream come true for him. It's a dream come true for all those who have been emotionally tied to his career, including me.

Now that Linsanity has died down and things are a little bit normalized, my overall feeling is, 'Just wait. There's more. There's way more to come with this guy.' We're just seeing the beginning of it right now. The sky's the limit. We're looking at someone who can bring the game back to what it is in its truest form—and that's a team game where it's all about winning.

... MEANWHILE, IN **N.Y.** HARBOR...

OTHER BOOKS BY RICH WOLFE

For Yankee Fans Only—Volume I
For Yankee Fans Only—Volume II
For Mets Fans Only
Ron Santo: A Perfect 10
I Remember Harry Caray
Da Coach (Mike Ditka)
Tim Russert, We Heartily Knew Ye
I Love It, I Love It, I Love It (with Jim Zabel, Iowa announcer)
Oh, What a Knight (Bob Knight)
There's No Expiration Date on Dreams (Tom Brady)
He Graduated Life with Honors and No Regrets (Pat Tillman)
Take This Job and Love It (Jon Gruden)
Remembering Harry Kalas
Been There, Shoulda Done That (John Daly)
And the Last Shall Be First (Kurt Warner)
Remembering Jack Buck
Sports Fans Who Made Headlines
Fandemonium
Remembering Dale Earnhardt
I Saw It On the Radio (Vin Scully)
The Real McCoy (Al McCoy, Phoenix Suns announcer)

For Bronco Fans Only
For Browns Fans Only
For Buckeye Fans Only
For Cardinals Fans Only
For Clemson Fans Only
For Cubs Fans Only
For Cubs Fans Only—Volume II
For Georgia Bulldog Fans Only
For Hawkeye Fans Only
For Kansas City Chiefs Fans Only
For K-State Fans Only
For KU Fans Only (Kansas)

For Notre Dame Fans Only—
   The New Saturday Bible
For Michigan Fans Only
For Milwaukee Braves Fans Only
For Mizzou Fans Only
For Nebraska Fans Only
For Oklahoma Fans Only
For Packers Fans Only
For Phillies Fans Only
For Red Sox Fans Only
For South Carolina Fans Only

All books are the same size, format and price.
Questions or to order? Contact the author directly at 602-738-5889.